REFORM or REVOLUTION?

A Diary of Reform in England, 1830 – 2

For our children

Paul and Susan
Lucy and James

REFORM or REVOLUTION?

A Diary of Reform in England, 1830–2

E.A. SMITH

ALAN SUTTON

First published in the United Kingdom in 1992 by
Alan Sutton Publishing Limited
Phoenix Mill · Far Thrupp · Stroud · Gloucestershire

First published in the United States of America in 1992 by
Alan Sutton Publishing Inc · Wolfeboro Falls · NH · 03896–0848

British Library Cataloguing in Publication Data

Smith, E.A.
Reform or Revolution? Diary of Reform in England, 1830–32
I. Title
942.07
ISBN 0 7509 0187 X

Library of Congress Cataloging in Publication Data applied for

Cover illustration: New Reform Coach *by John Doyle, 17 June 1832.*

Typeset in 10/11 Plantin.
Typesetting and origination by
Alan Sutton Publishing Limited.
Printed in Great Britain by
The Bath Press, Bath, Avon.

Contents

List of Plates

Acknowledgements

The idea for this book came from my wife. I am grateful to her also for her encouragement and criticism while it was in progress, and for her approval of the result.

My thanks are due to the following owners of copyright material for permission to include extracts in this work: Cambridge University Press for *The Letters of T.B. Macaulay*, ed. T. Pinney, vol. I, 1974; Constable & Co. for *An Eton Boy, 1820–1830*, ed. C.M. Gaskell, 1939; The Macmillan Press Ltd for *The Journal of Mrs Arbuthnot 1820–1832*, ed. F. Bamford & the Duke of Wellington, vol. II, 1950, and for *Wellington and his Friends*, ed. Duke of Wellington, 1965; John Murray (Publishers) Ltd for *Three Howard Sisters*, Lady Leconfield and J. Gore, 1955; Routledge for *The Holland House Diaries, 1831–1840*, ed. A.D. Kriegel, 1977; Oxford University Press for The Pilgrim Edition of *The Letters of Charles Dickens*, vol. I, ed. M. House and G. Storey, 1965.

Introduction

The Reform Act of 1832, christened 'Great' by historians, was a landmark in the constitutional and political history of the United Kingdom. It has sometimes been regarded in popular history as the first step towards modern democracy and as marking the end of the 'old corruption' of eighteenth-century aristocratic domination of the political system. This is because the Act swept away most of the numerous 'close' or 'pocket' boroughs by which members of the aristocracy, owners of property, and the Treasury imposed members of parliament on the country without any vestige of free popular election. It redistributed seats to newer and larger centres of population and enfranchised at least the middle classes of society. This was seen as the beginning of an inevitable progress towards the modern system of universal suffrage and popular democracy. This was not only the view of later commentators: it was also the fear of those contemporaries of the Reform Bill who dreaded just that future and who consequently opposed the passing of the Bill with vehemence. It was also the vision of the future which many so-called Radicals and members of the still unenfranchised working classes dreamt of and which induced them to give it widespread and enthusiastic support by street demonstrations and riots. These events in turn confirmed the fears of the propertied minority and intensified their opposition to what they saw as a coming revolution which would destroy their property and privileges. Both were mistaken: popular democracy was no part of the scheme which the framers of the Bill, Lord Grey and the Whig Ministry of 1830, had in mind. Their aim was simply to conciliate opposition to the old regime by timely but moderate concessions and to leave the essential structure of the social and political system unchanged. Whether they were right or not, they were certainly not social or political revolutionaries. All the same, the dramatic events of 1830–2 engendered tensions throughout society which made it seem to many that the country was facing an unprecedented crisis and that the outcome was impossible to predict. This book brings to life the hopes, fears, forebodings and terrors of people who lived through the crisis and who expressed these sentiments in their private letters, journals and diaries, so providing for a later generation vivid personal accounts of how it felt to witness what seemed to be the end of one age and the beginning of another.

CHAPTER ONE

Dramatis Personae

The leading figures in the struggle for reform were: the king, William IV, who came to the throne in June 1830 on the death of his reactionary brother, George IV; the Duke of Wellington, the hero of Waterloo and now prime minister of a government which was broadly 'Tory' in politics; Charles, 2nd Earl Grey, leader of the opposing Whig party, who had been an advocate of cautious and moderate reform for forty years and, having spent almost all his political life in fruitless and frustrating opposition, was shortly to become prime minister of a government pledged to a reform bill; John Charles, Viscount Althorp, elder son of Earl Spencer, who was to serve in Grey's administration as Leader of the House of Commons; and Sir Robert Peel, Wellington's colleague and leader of the moderate Tories in the House of Commons. The characters of these individuals are described by several of our contemporary witnesses of their activities.

KING WILLIAM IV

Charles Greville's[1] Journal of the Reigns of King George IV and King William IV

London, 16 July 1830
. . . Never was elevation like that of King William IV. His life has been hitherto passed in obscurity and neglect, in miserable poverty, surrounded by a numerous progeny of bastards, without consideration or friends, and he was ridiculous from his grotesque ways and little meddling curiosity. Nobody ever invited him into their house, or thought it necessary to honour him with any mark of attention or respect; and so he went on for above forty years, till Canning brought him into notice by making him Lord High Admiral at the time of his grand Ministerial schism. In that post he distinguished himself by making absurd speeches, by a morbid official activity, and by a general wildness which was thought to indicate incipient insanity, till shortly after Canning's death and the Duke [of Wellington]'s accession, as is well known, the latter dismissed him. He then dropped back into obscurity, but had become by this time somewhat more of a personage than he was before. His brief administration of the navy, the death of the Duke of York, which made him heir to the throne, his increased wealth and regular habits, had procured him more consideration, though not a great deal. Such was his position when George IV broke all at once, and after three months of expectation William finds himself King.

18 July

The new King began very well. Everybody expected he would keep the Ministers in office, but he threw himself into the arms of the Duke of Wellington with the strongest expressions of confidence and esteem. He proposed to all the Household as well as to the members of Government to keep their places, which they all did except Lord Conyngham and the Duke of Montrose. He soon after, however, dismissed most of the equerries, that he might fill their places with the members of his own family. Of course such a King wanted not due praise, and plenty of anecdotes were raked up of his former generosities and kindnesses. His first speech to the Council was well enough given, but his burlesque character began even then to show itself. Nobody expected from him much real grief, but he does not seem to know how to act it consistently; he spoke of his brother with all the semblance of feeling, and in a tone of voice properly softened and subdued, but just afterwards, when they gave him the pen to sign the declaration, he said in his usual tone, 'This is a damned bad pen you have given me.' My worthy colleague Mr James Buller began to swear Privy Councillors in the name of 'King George IV – William, I mean,' to the great diversion of the Council.

A few days after my return I was sworn in, all the Ministers and some others being present. His Majesty presided very decently, and looked like a respectable old admiral. The Duke [of Wellington] told me he was delighted with him – 'If I had been able to deal with my late master as I do with my present, I should have got on much better' – that he was so reasonable and tractable, and that he had done more business with him in ten minutes than with the other in as many days. . . .

He began immediately to do good-natured things, to provide for old friends and professional adherents. . . . There never was anything like the enthusiasm with which he was greeted by all ranks; though he has trotted about both town and country for sixty-four years, and nobody ever turned round to look at him, he cannot stir now without a mob, patrician as well as plebeian, at his heels. All the Park congregated round the gate to see him drive into town the day before yesterday. But in the midst of all this success and good conduct certain indications of strangeness and oddness peep out which are not a little alarming, and he promises to realise the fears of his Ministers that he will do and say too much, though they flatter themselves that they have muzzled him in his approaching progress by reminding him that his words will be taken as his Ministers', and he must, therefore, be chary of them.

At the late King's funeral he behaved with great indecency. That ceremony was very well managed, and a fine sight, the military part particularly, and the Guards were magnificent. The attendance was not very numerous, and when they had all got together in St. George's Hall a gayer company I never beheld; with the exception of Mount Charles, who was deeply affected, they were all as merry as grigs. The King was chief mourner, and, to my astonishment, as he entered the chapel directly behind the body, in a situation in which he should have been apparently, if not really, absorbed in the melancholy duty he was performing, he darted up to Strathaven, who was ranged on one side below the Dean's stall, shook him heartily by the hand, and then went on nodding to the right and left. He had previously gone as chief mourner to sit for an hour at the head of the body as it lay in state, and he walked in procession with his household to the apartment. . . . The morning after the funeral, having slept at Frogmore, he went all over the Castle, into every room in the house, which he had never seen before except when he came there as a guest; after which he received an address from the ecclesiastical bodies of Windsor and Eton, and returned an answer quite unpremeditated which they told me was excellent. . . .

The King's good-nature, simplicity, and affability to all about him are certainly very striking, and in his elevation he does not forget any of his old friends and companions. He was in no hurry to take upon himself the dignity of King, nor to throw off the habits and manners of a country gentleman. When Lord Chesterfield went to Bushy to kiss his hand, and be presented to the Queen, he found Sir John and Lady Gore there lunching, and when they went away the King called for their carriage, handed Lady Gore into it, and stood at the door to see them off. When Lord Howe came over from Twickenham to see him, he said the Queen was going out driving, and should 'drop him' at his own house. The Queen, they say, is by no means delighted at her elevation. She likes quiet and retirement and Bushy (of which the King has made her Ranger), and does not want to be a Queen. However, 'l'appetit viendra en mangeant.' He says he does not want luxury and magnificence, has slept in a cot, and he has dismissed the King's cooks, 'renversé la marmite.' He keeps the stud (which is to be diminished) because he thinks he ought to support the turf. He has made Mount Charles a Lord of the Bedchamber, and given the Robes to Sir C. Pole, an admiral. Altogether he seems a kind-hearted, well-meaning, not stupid, burlesque, bustling old fellow, and if he doesn't go mad may make a very decent King, but he exhibits oddities.

Greville writes at the time of the king's death in 1837

King William IV, if he had been born in a private station, would have passed unobserved through life like millions of other men, looked upon as possessing a good-natured and affectionate disposition, but without either elevation of mind or brightness of intellect. During many years of his life the Duke of Clarence was an obscure individual, without consideration, moving in a limited circle, and altogether forgotten by the great world. He resided at Bushy with Mrs Jordan, and brought up his numerous children with very tender affection: with them, and for them, he seemed entirely to live. The cause of his separation from Mrs Jordan has not been explained, but it probably arose from his desire to better his condition by a good marriage, and he wanted to marry Miss Wykeham, a half-crazy woman of large fortune, on whom he afterwards conferred a peerage. George IV, I believe, put a spoke in the wheel, fortunately for the Duke as well as for the country. The death of the Princess Charlotte opened to him a new prospect, and the lack of royal progeny made his marriage as desirable an event to the public as it was convenient to himself. The subsequent death of the Duke of York, which made him heir to the throne, at once exalted him into a personage of political importance. . . .

His exaltation (for the moment) completely turned his head, but as his situation got familiar to him he became more composed and rational, if not more dignified in his behaviour. The moral and intellectual qualities of the King, however insignificant in themselves, now became, from their unavoidable influence, an object of great interest and importance, and in the early part of his reign he acquired no small share of popularity. People liked a King whose habits presented such a striking contrast to those of his predecessor. His attention to business, his frank and good-humoured familiarity, and his general hospitality, were advantageously compared with the luxurious and selfish indolence and habits of seclusion in the society of dull and grasping favourites which characterised the former reign.

The King seemed to be more occupied with the pleasing novelty of his situation, providing for his children, and actively discharging the duties of his high function, than in giving effect to any political opinions: and he took a correct view of his constitutional obligations, for although he continued his confidence to the Duke of Wellington unabated to the last, he transferred it as entirely to Lord Grey when the Whigs came in. He went on with his second Ministry as cordially as he had done with his first, nor does it appear that he took fright at their extensive plans of reform when they were first promulgated. He was probably bit by the popularity which the Reform Bill procured him, and it was not until he had gone too far to recede with safety that he was roused from his state of measureless content and unthinking security. The roar of the mighty conflict which the Reform Bill brought on filled him with dismay, and very soon with detestation of the principles of which he had unwittingly permitted himself to be the professor and the promoter; and as these feelings and apprehensions were continually stimulated by almost all the members of his family, legitimate and illegitimate, they led him into those unavailing struggles which embroiled him with his Ministers, rendered him obnoxious to the Liberal party, compromised the dignity of the Crown, and the tranquillity of the country, and grievously embittered the latter years of his life. But although King William was sometimes weak, sometimes obstinate, and miserably deficient in penetration and judgement, he was manly, sincere, honest, and straightforward. . . . Of political dexterity and artifice he was altogether incapable, and although, if he had been false, able, and artful, he might have caused more perplexity to his Whig Government and have played a better party game, it is perhaps fortunate for the country, and certainly happy for his own reputation, that his virtues thus predominated over his talents. The most remarkable foible of the late King was his passion for speechifying, and I have recorded some of his curious exhibitions in this way. He had considerable facility in expressing himself, but what he said was generally useless or improper.

He never received the homage of a Bishop without giving him a lecture; and the custom he introduced of giving toasts and making speeches at all his dinners was more suitable to a tavern than to a palace. He was totally deficient in dignity or refinement, and neither his elevation to the throne nor his association with people of the most distinguished manners could give him any tincture of the one or the other. Though a good-natured and amiable man, he was passionate and hasty, and thus he was led into those bickerings and quarrels with the Duchess of Kent and with his own children, which were a perpetual source of discomfort or disgrace to him, and all of which might have been avoided by a more consistent course of firmness and temper on his part. His sons generally behaved to him with great insolence and ingratitude, except Adolphus. Of the daughters I know nothing.

THE DUKE OF WELLINGTON

Arthur Wellesley, 1st Duke of Wellington (1769–1852), was Prime Minister from 1828 to 1830.

James Grant[2] on the Duke of Wellington

I now come to speak of the most distinguished man of the present day, either in this or in any other country. I allude to the Duke of WEL-LINGTON. It will at once be understood, that in characterising his Grace as the most distinguished man of the present day, I speak of him in his capacity of a general, and not in that of a statesman. In this latter respect, however, I am disposed to assign him a much higher rank than he is generally allowed to fill by those who entertain political principles opposite to his. If on some great occasions he has failed in his calculation of the probable effects of circumstances, and the probable course of events, it is not to be disputed by his most implacable foes that he has been, in cases of unusual difficulty, successful in others. The mere fact of his carrying on the government of the country during the eventful period which inter-vened between the resignation of Lord Goderich and the dissolution of his own administration, is of itself unanswerable proof, – known as it is by everyone that that government was almost entirely under his own individual guidance, – that his mental resources must be very far from those of a commonplace character. . . .

Not only did the noble Duke conduct his government safely through the storms and tempests of the period referred to, but at the very moment he made his ill-judged declaration against all reform, it seemed to be resting more securely than ever. That declaration was not only the most foolish that he ever made – . . . it was decidedly the most imprudent that ever proceeded from the lips of a Minister of the Crown. It could not fail to prove, in the then existing circumstances of the country, the destruction of the government. . . .

But that the Duke of Wellington, notwithstanding defects in his character which prevent his being a statesman of the first class, is more than respectable in that capacity, must be abundantly clear to every mind not blinded by prejudice. . . . Though mistaking the signs of the times, and ignorant of the state and force of public opinion in other instances, he clearly saw those signs, and correctly estimated the force of that opinion, as regarded the Test and Corporation Acts, and the disabilities under which the Roman Catholics then laboured. . . .

Perhaps no man of the present day possesses greater moral courage than the Duke of Wellington. It is that peculiar description of moral courage, too, which teaches him to disregard alike the opinions of both friends and foes. Let him be but convinced that a certain measure has become indispensable to the peace or welfare of the country, and to the carrying of that measure he will lend all his energies in utter disregard alike of the smiles and frowns of others. . . . He appears as indifferent to popularity as any public man I know of the present day. . . .

One of the greatest defects in the character of the Duke as a statesman is, his neither anticipating public opinion, nor keeping abreast with it. He generally resists it until it has acquired an overwhelming power. Had he, when in office, only granted a moderate measure of reform, the nation would have been satisfied at least for a time, and he might still have been Prime Minister of the country. But by his refusal to yield one iota to the public demand, that demand became more extensive in its scope, and louder in its tone, until it could no longer be resisted with safety to the public peace. – He refuses the little which could be gratefully received as an act of grace, and then finds himself in the end compelled to make a much larger concession, for which he does not even receive the thanks of his countrymen.

His general information is neither varied nor profound; but he very seldom commits blunders in his speeches. . . . His mind is acute, and his understanding vigorous. . . . He is always clear; you can never mistake the position he labours to establish. . . .

Were his diction and manner good, the noble Duke would rank high as a speaker, but both are bad. His style is rough and disjointed – sometimes positively incorrect: it is always, however, nervous and expressive. His manner of speaking is much worse than his diction. He has a bad screeching sort of voice, aggravated by an awkward mode of mouthing the words. His enunciation is so bad, owing in some measure to the loss of several of his teeth, that often, when at the full stretch of his voice, you do not know what particular words he is using. At other times, and this too while his gesture is vehement, he speaks in so low and peculiar a sort of tone, that you lose, perhaps, whole sentences together.

The Duke feels strongly on political questions, and there is always great energy in his manner when expressing his sentiments. He generally makes a liberal use of his arms, especially the right one, when on his legs, and moves his body about for the purpose of enabling him to look his own friends, in different parts of the House, in the face. In his more vehement moods, he frequently falls into what, in parliamentary language, is called the habit of expectoration. . . .

Notwithstanding his having attained the advanced age of sixty-seven, he is full of spirits, and apparently in excellent health. The conformation of his face is, by portraits, or otherwise, so familiar to every one, that it is unnecessary to describe it. I may simply mention that his hair is of a greyish colour and that his complexion is pale and wan. His eye is quick and piercing, and his whole countenance is highly indicative of energy and determination. In height, he is rather above the middle size. His form, for one of his years, is slender, and remarkably erect. In his clothes he appears to evince a partiality to a blue coat, and light vest and trousers. They are seldom well made, but hang rather loosely on him.

Benjamin Haydon[3] on Wellington

Sunday – I found the Duke on the leads. After breakfast, Mr Arbuthnot told me to go to the village church and ask for the Duke's pew. I walked, and was shown into a large pew near the pulpit.

A few moments after the service had begun, the Duke and Mr Arbuthnot came up – no pomp, no servants in livery with a pile of books. The Duke came into the presence of his Maker without cant, without affectation – a simple human being.

From the bare wainscot, the absence of curtains, the dirty green footstools, and common chairs, I feared I was in the wrong pew, and very quietly sat myself down in the Duke's place. Mr Arbuthnot squeezed my arm before it was too late, and I crossed in an instant. The Duke pulled out his Prayer Book, and followed the clergyman in the simplest way. I got deeply affected. Here was the greatest hero in the world, who had conquered the greatest genius, prostrating his heart and being before his God in his venerable age, and praying for His mercy. However high his destiny above my own, here we were at least equal before our Creator. Here we were stripped of extrinsic distinctions; and I looked at this wonderful man with an interest and feeling that touched my imagination beyond belief. The silence and embosomed solitude of the village church, the simplicity of its architecture, rather deepened than decreased the depth of my sensibilities. At the name of Jesus Christ the Duke bowed his silvery hairs like the humblest labourer, and yet not more than others, but to the same degree. He seemed to wish for no distinction. At the epistle he stood upright, like a soldier, and when the blessing was pronounced, he buried his head in one hand and uttered his prayer as if it came from his heart in humbleness.

Arthur Wellesley in the village church of Walmer this day was more interesting to me than at the last charge of the Guards at Waterloo, or in all the glory and paraphernalia of his entry into Paris. I would not have missed seeing him, for this will be the germ of some interesting work of art – perhaps his youth, his manhood, and his age in a series.

The Duke after dinner retired, and we all followed him. He then took the *Spectator* and, placing a candle on each side of his venerable head, read it through. I watched him the whole time. . . .

I looked up and studied the venerable white head that God still protected. There he was, contented, happy, aged, but vigorous, enjoying his leisure in dignity; God knows as he deserves. After reading till his eyes were tired, he put down the paper, and said, 'There are a great many curious things in it, I assure you.' He then yawned, as he always did before retiring, and said, 'I'll give you an early sitting to-morrow, at nine.' I wished His Grace a good night, and went to bed. At half-past five I was up, set my palette, got all ready, and went to work to get the head in from the drawing. By nine the door opened, and in he walked, looking extremely worn – his skin drawn tight over his face; his eye was watery and aged; his head nodded a little. I put the chair; he mumbled 'I'd as soon stand.' I thought, 'You will get tired,' but I said nothing; down he sat – how altered from the fresh old man after Saturday's hunting. It affected me. He looked like an aged eagle beginning to totter from his perch. He took out his watch three times, and at ten up he got, and said, 'It's ten.' I opened the door, and he went out. He had been impatient all the time. At breakfast he brightened at the sight of the children, and after distributing toast and tea to them, I got him on art. He talked of a picture of 'Copenhagen' by Ward, which the Duke of Northumberland bought, and which he wanted, and suddenly looking up at me, said, 'D'ye want another sitting?' I replied, 'If you please, Your Grace.' 'Very well; after hunting, I'll come'. . . . At lunch I was called in. . . . Lady Burghersh came in also, and again he was fresher . . . It is evident, at times, he is beginning to sink, though the sea air at Walmer keeps him up, and he is better than he was.

Lady Burghersh kept him talking, but the expression I had already hit was much finer than the present, and I resolved not to endanger what I had secured. I therefore corrected the figure and shoulders, and told Lady Burghersh I had done. 'He has done,' she said, 'and it's very fine.' 'Is it though?' said the Duke; 'I'm very glad.' 'And now,' said she, 'you must stand.' So up he got, and I sketched two views of his back, his hands, legs, etc. etc. I did him so instantaneously that his eagle eyes looked me right through several times, when he thought I was not looking. As it was a point of honour with him not to see any sketch connected with my picture, he never glanced that way. He looked at the designs for the House of Lords on the chimney-piece, but said nothing. He then retired, and appeared gay and better. He had put on a fine dashing waistcoat for the Russian ambassador. . . .

At night, as I took leave of the Duke, he said, 'I hope you are satisfied. Good-bye.' I heard him go to bed after me, laughing, and he roared out to Arbuthnot, 'Good-night.' I then heard him slam the door of his room, No. 11, next to mine, No. 10, but on the opposite side, and a little farther on. I soon fell asleep. . . .

It is curious to have known thus the two great heads of the two great parties, the Duke and Lord Grey. I prefer the Duke infinitely. He is more manly, has no vanity, is not deluded by any flattery or humbug, and is, in every way, much as I admire Lord Grey, a grander character, though Lord Grey is a fine, amiable, venerable, vain man.

CHARLES, EARL GREY

Charles Grey, 2nd Earl Grey (1764–1845), was Prime Minister from 1830 to 1834.

James Grant's character of Lord Grey

The name of Earl GREY is one which . . . is, without question, destined to be better known by posterity than of any other statesman of the present day. The zeal and energy with which, in early life, . . . he espoused those liberal principles of Reform which he afterwards not only lived to see triumphant, but whose triumph was chiefly brought about by his own instrumentality – brought his name familiarly before the public upwards of forty years ago. . . . But it is the circumstance of his having been the author of that great measure, and the Minister under whose auspices it was triumphantly carried through both Houses of Parliament, in defiance of a most decided and powerful opposition, that gives him that commanding station which he now occupies in the eyes of the country, and which his memory will inevitably occupy in the eyes of future ages. . . .

Earl Grey was a man of sound judgment, and always acted with great deliberation. . . . His high family connections, his great talents, his unimpeachable integrity, his stainless consistency of public conduct, and his known determination and energy of purpose, all concur to invest him with an importance, and give him a weight of character such as no man of the present day possesses. Neither Lord Melbourne nor any other man but Lord Grey, could have carried the Reform Bill. . . .

Earl Grey was dignified in his manner as well as in his mind. This was apparent the moment you saw him. No one ever yet glanced his eye at the noble Earl without being that instant struck with the dignity of his appearance. There was dignity in his looks and in every movement he made. It was still more visible when he rose to speak. Apart from the exalted station he filled in the councils of the King, and the large space he filled in the public eye . . . there was something in his aspect and demeanour the moment he began to speak which could not fail to attract all eyes towards him, and command the deepest attention.

With the dignified expression of his countenance, there was blended a deep-seated habitual gravity, and a profoundly thoughtful air. . . . When he began his speech he usually did so in so low a tone as to be hardly audible twelve or fourteen yards distant. His utterance in the outset was slow, and his manner partook a good deal of the gravity of his appearance. As he advanced, his voice gradually rose in the distinctness of its tones, till he became perfectly audible in all parts of the House. . . . His voice was soft and pleasant, and his articulation clear. He could moderate his voice at pleasure, and generally did so with great judgment and effect. He was not a showy speaker: there was nothing of a clap-trap character in his oratory; but he was always graceful and correct as well as dignified. The tones of his voice often indicated strong feeling and considerable animation; his action hardly ever. He seldom made any use of his arms when speaking. His usual practice was to join his hands, and then allow them to repose on his person for eight or ten minutes. He would then separate them, and after suffering them to hang loose by his side, would put both to his back, where he would again join them, and continue in that attitude for [an]other eight or ten minutes. . . . When speaking with unwonted warmth or energy, he seldom stood many seconds on the same spot, or presented to the House the same attitude. He would first advance two or three steps towards the centre of the House, and then retrace them. At one time he turned his face in the direction of the Lord Chancellor on the Woolsack immediately before the throne; at another you saw his back to the Woolsack, and his face towards the bar. When addressing their Lordships, he never looked any of them in the face: his eyes were usually fixed on the floor, or on some of the benches, a few feet from where he stood. . . .

To say that Earl Grey was altogether indifferent towards the approbation of his fellow men, would be to say of him what could not, with truth, be said of any man who has the ordinary feelings of human nature in his bosom. But I believe there are few men who would be more ready to sacrifice their popularity to their principles, when the necessity arose, than the noble Earl at all times was. Grateful as the approbation of his fellow-subjects must have been to his mind . . . he never allowed the acquisition or forfeiture of that approbation to weigh a feather in the scale when framing his measures. . . .

Perhaps few Ministers have ever had to carry on the government of any country amidst such formidable difficulties as those with which the noble Earl had to contend. He was placed betwixt two great parties – the one great in underhand influence, and the other great both in numbers and moral power. I refer to the Court party on the one hand, and to the people on the other. The views and interests of these were wide as the poles asunder. The one pulled one way, the other another. . . . Both, however, laboured in vain. . . .

I am inclined to think that his temper was easily irritated; and I have on two or three occasions seen it burst through all the restraints he had imposed upon it. . . .

Lord Grey has a great deal of the aristocrat about him. He is proud of his title; he rejoices in the long line of an illustrious ancestry. He appreciates learning and talent; but the nobility of nature could never in his eyes atone for the want of nobility of name. I question whether the most unintellectual nobleman in the realm was not a far greater man, in his estimation, than Sir Walter Scott. In his manners there was a good deal of this aristocratic feeling visible. Most persons who have had occasion to meet with him, have observed a certain distancy and reservedness about him. It was the same feeling that made him openly avow, in his place in

Parliament, that if a conflict should happen to take place between his order and the people, he would stand or fall by his order; in other words, he would sacrifice the interests of the whole nation to the preservation of a mere artificial distinction to about four hundred individuals moving in the same rank of society as himself. . . .

Lord Grey is somewhat above the middle size, and of slender form for one of his advanced age. . . . His countenance, as I have already intimated, indicates deep thought, mingled with an expression of melancholy. His eyes are small, but beam with intelligence. In the latter respect they harmonize with his finely developed ample forehead. His features are small and regular, and the wrinkles the finger of time has left on his face are neither so numerous or deep as might be expected in one who has not only seen so many years pass over his head, but of whose protracted existence so large a part has been occupied with matters of the deepest importance. . . . His complexion presents a mixture of ruddiness and paleness. What the original colour of his hair may have been, I know not; now it is a light grey, made so by the number of years which have stolen over his head. . . .

Benjamin Haydon on Lord Grey, 1834

When Lord Grey, during his badgering in the Lords, whilst the Reform Bill was passing, used to come to me, he looked like, what he was, an aged and veteran noble, collecting his energies to defy the devil; but there was an air of breeding and aristocracy in him which interested me. Napoleon . . . had not the least look of mercy, breeding, or high-mindedness. . . .

January 11th, 1834. Lord Grey sat [for his portrait] very pleasantly indeed, and I made, in my own opinion, and that of Lord Lansdowne, a successful drawing. Sir W. Gordon came in, and suggested one or two things of great use. He said the basis of Lord Grey's character was excessive amiability, and it was this which attached others to him. . . . Velasquez would have gone 500 miles for such a brow and nostril as Lord Grey's; and to suit the weakness of modern effeminacy I will not emasculate the one, or dress the other. . . .

February 16th. . . . Lord Grey . . . looked capitally well; and I could not help thinking, as I looked at him, what a very interesting head he had got – peaceable, delicate, and touching in expression. . . .

August 16th 1834. I awoke early. As I lay musing I thought, 'Lord Grey leaves Downing Street today. It is my duty to go, and take a last look.' Lord Grey was at breakfast with Lady Georgina and some one else. Lord Grey shook my hand heartily. I was affected, and as I shook his I thanked him for all his goodness to me. . . . I never saw him looking better, fresher, or stronger – no longer that horrid, gasping anxiety. I took my leave, and wished him health and happiness. Lord Grey was receiving my adieu as an official thing, but the moment my voice gave evidence of my sensibility, I shall never forget the look of his keen eye, as he examined my face. I am sure it must have convinced him of my sincere feelings. I

shall never see him again there as First Lord. Hail and farewell! He has
done little for art. . . .

Lord Hatherton[4] on Grey

Lord Grey's decease has long been expected – he was 82 – the uncompro-
mising friend of Fox in the height of revolutionary madness in France, and
of jacobinical sympathy here – he gradually mellowed down into Conservative Whiggism, as years and experience advanced: and died as much a
Conservative as Peel himself – and I believe strictly approving all he has
recently done. After he quitted the Government, he gradually dropped all
intimacy with the political associates of his Administration. Lord John
Russell he declined even to acknowledge, if he met him, for some reason I
never understood – of Lord Spencer [the former Lord Althorp], Lord
Palmerston, Lord Melbourne, he saw nothing. In short he seemed to
resent the conduct of all those who assisted Melbourne in reconstructing a
Liberal Government. To me individually nothing could surpass the
kindness of his conduct. While I was in his Government he was open,
candid, and most friendly – and I felt for him the warmest attachment –
Indeed that feeling towards him seemed universal on the part of all the
Members of his Administration. After Lord Grey's retirement in 1834, in
consequence of Lord Spencer's resignation, which he rendered very
absurdly I thought in consequence of the publicity given to his opinion on
the project of renewing the old [Irish] Coercion Bill in my affair with
O'Connell, I expected a change of feeling towards me on the part of Lord
Grey – but he behaved to me in the most forgiving and the noblest manner
– and though I observed that some time afterwards he addressed me as
'My Dear Sir', and not as 'My Dear Littleton', I never met him, that he
was not personally kind and courteous to me – and for two or three years,
when I always called on him on his arrival in Town, he always returned my
visit.
    He was considered by his friends throughout his life to be liable to be
influenced very much by pique and jealousy – and personal feeling – I fear
that his belief that Brougham was plotting against him, had much to do
with his resignation. . . . And yet no idea could be more unfounded – as
will be seen by my faithful Memoir of the proceedings that led to Lord
Grey's retirement.
    Lord Grey's mien and carriage was aristocratic and lofty in the extreme;
But still his Address – which could be most repulsive – was in its general
character most winning and attractive. His style of speaking partook of his
nature – It was a fine thing to see him with his erect stature and graceful
figure – and bald elevated forehead – on the floor of the H. of Lords,
delivering one of his great orations, which were always vigorously
conceived, lucidly arranged, and given in fine classical language – in
measured and stately phraseology. He was generally in evening dress – black
pantaloons (tight) and a white waistcoat, with Blue Ribbon and Garter.
    He was greatly beloved by his family and Domestics.

LORD ALTHORP

John Charles Spencer (1782–1845), Viscount Althorp, 3rd Earl Spencer (1834), a lifelong admirer of C.J. Fox and a renowned sportsman, became Leader of the House of Commons at Grey's insistence in 1830. His attempted resignation in 1834 led directly to Grey's own retirement.

T.B. Macaulay[5] to his sister Hannah, 29 August 1831

. . . We talked about timidity in speaking. Lord Althorp said that he had only just got over his apprehensions. 'I was as much afraid', he said, 'last year as when I first came into parliament. But now I am forced to speak so often that I am quite hardened. Last Thursday I was up forty times.' I was not much surprised at this in Lord Althorp – as he is certainly one of the most modest men in existence. . . .

My opinion of Lord Althorp is extremely high. In fact his character is the only stay of the ministry. I doubt whether any person has ever lived in England who, with no eloquence, no brilliant talents, no profound information, – with nothing in short but plain good sense and an excellent heart, possessed as much influence both in and out of Parliament. His temper is an absolute miracle. He has been worse used than any minister ever was in debate; and he has never said one thing inconsistent, I do not say with gentlemanlike courtesy, but with real benevolence. His candour is absolutely a vice in debate. He is perpetually shewing excuses and ways of escape to his adversaries which they would never find of themselves. Lord North perhaps was his equal in suavity and good nature. But Lord North was not a man of strict principles. His administration was not only an administration hostile to liberty; but it was supported by vile and corrupt means – by direct bribery, I fear, in many cases. Lord Althorp has the temper of Lord North with the principles of Romilly. If he had the oratorical powers of either of those men, he might do anything. But his understanding, though just, is slow; and his elocution painfully defective. It is however only justice to him to say that he has done more service to the Reform Bill even as a debater than all the other ministers together, Stanley excepted. Graham is either afraid or idle. Grant and Palmerston are idle, and, I suspect, not very hearty. Lord John Russell gives all that he has – to wit two mites which make a farthing. I must in fairness say, however, that Lord John made a better speech on Saturday than any that I have heard from him for a long time.

We are going – by *we* I mean the Members of Parliament who are for reform – as soon as the Bill is through the Commons, to give a grand dinner to Lord Althorp and Lord John Russell as a mark of our respect. Some people wished to have the other Cabinet Ministers included. But Grant and Palmerston are not in sufficiently high esteem among the Whigs to be honoured with such a compliment. Here we [are to] hold our festivities – whether at the Albion or the City of London Tavern, or whether we shall go to Greenwich to eat whitebait is undecided. . . .

Sarah, Lady Lyttelton[6] to Earl Spencer, London, 15 October 1831

Yesterday I went to see poor dear Althorp at his dinner, and so hurried and uneasy a meal I never saw. I was some time waiting in his private room, and stood looking through his poor little myrtle garden on the window at the parade, where there were people running and shouting and meeting – signs of the awful times – and I could fancy myself admitted to the Captain's cabin on the eve of a hurricane. He looked fagged and ill, just out of a long Cabinet sitting, and before he had eaten one cutlet arrived the Governor of the Bank, . . . I felt quite oppressed with the air of Downing Street, and envying for Althorp every dandy and lounger I met afterwards with no responsibility on his mind.

E.J. Littleton's[7] diary, 8 March 1832

A great meeting of the English members supporting Government was held by invitation from Lord Althorp in the dining room at the Foreign Office this morning at 12. About 200 attended. The Irish members had been there yesterday. The object was to beg support for the Government plan with respect to the gradual extinction of tithes in Ireland. The Irish members, especially the Catholics, were many of them disposed to be refractory, and nothing but a sacrifice of opinion on minute points of difference on the part of the English members would keep the helm of the vessel straight amidst the conflict of interests and opinions. Althorp opened the business. Surely never was there such a figure for an orator – especially to my eye – who had there seen on similar occasions Castlereagh, with his elegant and well-dressed figure and high bred carriage, and Canning, with his air of quickness and intelligence greater than ever distinguished man. There stood Althorp at the top of the room, with his stout, honest face, and farmer-like figure, habited in ill-made black clothes, his trousers rucked up in a heap round his legs, one coat flap turned round, and exposing his posterior, and the pocket of the other crammed full of papers – his hat held awkwardly in one hand and his large snuff box in the other, with which he kept playing the Devil's tattoo on his thigh – while he briefly and bluntly told his plain, unsophisticated tale with his usual correct feeling and stout sense, and was warmly responded to by the whole party. . . .

William Howitt[8] on Lord Althorp

On the formation of Earl Grey's Government in 1830, Lord Althorp was appointed to the office of Chancellor of the Exchequer; and this he retained through all the trials and difficulties of that government, and amidst a conflict of opinions not to be paralleled in the recent annals of parliament, until his accession to the peerage in 1834 – an elevation which involved the downfall of the administration of which he was the leader in the House of Commons.

During this reign of four years as leader of the Lower House, his Lordship's authority and influence were unbounded. No minister perhaps ever possessed more individual power in that assembly than he had. His Lordship was never an orator, yet who spoke so irresistibly as he did? Who that happened to be in the House can ever forget the reiterated acclamations which responded to his Lordship's spontaneous appeal to the representatives of the people in a moment of temporary embarrassment to the ministry. 'Has the House confidence in me?' was the demand; and all idea of dissent, all sense of difficulty, all conflicting sentiment, was instantly drowned in the tumultuous expression of one absorbing, and as it seemed, universal feeling – a feeling of personal attachment to the noble Lord representing the government, and of confidence in that government upon his account. Mr Pitt bullied the House, and frightened it; 'he was lord paramount, and would have his own way, simply because he chose it.' This was not Lord Althorp's plan, and yet his influence was scarcely less complete. Whatever was done amiss, Lord Althorp, either by his candid confession of a blunder, or his good humoured mode of justifying it, contrived to make all well again, or to reconcile the House to what was not well. Whatever was, was right, during his Lordship's reign as ministerial leader. Dissensions in the cabinet, and opposition at court, frequently forced him into the backward road, instead of the advancing one – still Lord Althorp was sure of a majority to follow him. The cabinet might adopt the very course which Reformers in the House, and the represented out of doors, least expected and desired them to take – still among those cabinet ministers there was a Lord Althorp, and in him the House had faith. His Lordship might, from his view of the ultimate prosperity of the reform-cause as depending on the ministerial existence of those who had for so many years supported it, depart from the line he had taken when in opposition, and break the promises he had formerly given; still his Lordship was understood to mean only, that he postponed the perform-ance of his engagement, that the fulfilment of his promise would come in due season, and in him, meantime, the House had faith! The preservation of the cabinet, – the Grey cabinet first, the Melbourne cabinet afterwards, – seemed to depend from night to night solely upon the strength of the personal respect in which the ministerial leader was held; solely on the popularity of Lord Althorp, the indulgence with which his mistakes, as a finance-minister, were entertained, and the confidence which was reposed in the excellence of his intentions. He was, in all cases, in all perplexities, in all emergencies, 'the minister who meant well;' and, assuredly, the world has never had a more striking example of the vast value which is attached to a reputation for good intentions. Nor did the existence of a liberal government merely *seem* to depend solely upon him. He *was* its sole dependence. The King had understood from his prime minister that it was impossible to carry on the government without Lord Althorp as leader in the Commons; and the prime minister understood from the King, not long after, that he was by no means to be allowed to make the experiment, as the Royal mind had come to the same conclusion. Accordingly, Lord Althorp simply became Lord Spencer – he was merely transferred from one house to another – he only shifted his seat in the cabinet, without retiring from office; and the apparently unimportant movement was fatal to the ministry. It was his Lordship's personal qualities, operating upon the minds of the Commons, that secured at that time official power to his party. Those qualities had obtained for him the distinguishing epithet of 'honest Lord Althorp'. They especially fitted him for such a post *at such a time*; and these weighed powerfully and effectually against all objections that might be raised against him on the score of unfitness in a financial point of view, for the office which he held. Those who denied to his Lordship the possession of 'the high qualifications necessary to constitute a statesman or a finance-minister,' were nevertheless constrained to add, '*excepting* the moral qualities of honesty, good temper, and singleness of purpose!' The exceptions, it will be admitted, are important; and let Earl Spencer's history be written as it may, if these qualities are by common consent accorded to him, he has little occasion to 'break his heart' (as Sir William Molesworth says) about the refusal to assign to him the rest, even though that refusal be unanimous.

There appears to be little doubt that it was the consciousness which his political friends had of his possession of these qualities for command in the Commons – their estimation of his general character, the placidity of his temper, and conciliatory disposition – their sense of the influence which his station gave him, and of the popularity he derived from a long advocacy of liberal measures, that prevailed upon the noble Lord to accept the office of 'leader,' rather than any personal ambition of his own. This was felt long before he ceased to hold the office of Chancellor of the Exchequer. It was known as well out of the House as in it that his Lordship retained office purely out of consideration for his colleagues and their cause, and against his own inclination. The termination of his official career was, accordingly, tantamount to the termination of his political life. It was the end of his sacrifices. Since that period, he has scarcely taken part at all in the political struggle which has been so fiercely carried on; devoting himself to agricultural and farming pursuits, to obtaining prizes for achievements in improving the breed of cattle, and to the maintenance of the character of a 'fine old English *country* gentleman.'. . .

SIR ROBERT PEEL

Peel (1788–1850) was Home Secretary in Wellington's administration, 1828–30, and led the Tory opposition to the Reform Bill in the House of Commons. He was Prime Minister from 1834 to 1835, and from 1841 to 1846.

Mrs Arbuthnot's[9] Journal, *8 June 1831*

As to Peel, he appears to hate every body & every body hates him, but he shewed consummate ability & powers of speaking of the highest order during the late short session; & it is not possible for any one to lead except him, but he is cross grained, timid, afraid of committing himself, afraid of having followers & a party for fear they shd be a clog upon him in any future arrangements; not that he has any projects of joining the enemy but, if called on to form a Govt, he wd like to be in a position to choose who he pleased without any one having claims on him. If any of the young men are anxious to speak, he throws cold water on it because speaking well wd give claims; & yet, while he was in office, he never ceased to complain of getting no support. He is supercilious, haughty & arrogant & a most bitter & determined hater. He has been down as his place in Staffordshire almost ever since the dissolution, & has scarcely had any communication with any one. He is, however, firm & determined against reform &, being a very honest man, we must hope he will so manage as to make our party as formidable as good management certainly can make it. . . .

Horace Twiss's[10] opinion of Peel

He was the best man of business and the best debater in England – but always thinking of his reputation and his outward character – content to 'dwell in decencies' – never decided and courageous – thinking more of getting well through a business into which he had been led by circumstance, than bold and decided in his pursuit and assertion of great principles and worthy objects. With great occasional *show* of affability and condescension (which is always offensive when seen through, especially in a 'new man'), he was in reality selfish, cold, and unconciliatory – and therefore never had, and never would have a personal following.' He 'doubted whether his conduct on the catholic question, and on that of Reform would not throw him out of office for some years, and whether the new men coming on in office, and acquiring official habits and information would not keep him out afterwards.' This appeared to me a just criticism on his character and position.

Charles Greville on Peel, February 1833

. . . Under that placid exterior he conceals, I believe, a boundless ambition, and hatred and jealousy lurk under his professions of esteem and political attachment. His is one of those contradictory characters, containing in it so much of mixed good and evil, that it is difficult to strike an accurate balance between the two, and the acts of his political life are of a corresponding description, of questionable utility and merit, though always marked by great ability. It is very sure that he has been the instrument of great good, or of enormous evil, and apparently more of the latter. He came into life the child and champion of a political system which has been for a long time crumbling to pieces; and if the perils which are produced by its fall are great, they are mainly attributable to the manner in which it was upheld by Peel, and to his want of sagacity, in a wrong estimate of his means of defence and of the force of the antagonist power with which he had to contend. The leading principles of his political conduct have been constantly erroneous, and his dexterity and ability in supporting them have only made the consequences of his errors more extensively pernicious. If we look back through the long course of Peel's life, and enquire what have been the great political measures with which his name is particularly connected, we shall find, first, the return to cash payments, which almost everybody now agrees was a fatal mistake, though it would not be fair to visit him with extraordinary censure for a measure which was sanctioned by almost all the great financial authorities; secondly, opposition to Reform in Parliament and to religious emancipation of every kind, the maintenance of the exclusive system, and support, untouched and uncorrected, of the Church, both English and Irish. His resistance to alterations on these heads was conducted with great ability, and for a long time with success; but he was endeavouring to uphold a system which was no longer supportable, and having imbibed in his career much of the liberal spirit of the age, he found himself in a state of no small perplexity between his old connexions and his more enlarged propensities. Still he was chained down by the former, and consequently being beaten from all his positions, he was continually obliged to give way, but never did so till rather too late for his own credit, and much too late for the interest at stake. Notwithstanding, therefore, the reputation he has acquired, the hold he has had of office, and is probably destined to have again, his political life has been a considerable failure, though not such an one as to render it more probable than not that his future life will be a failure too. He has hitherto been encumbered with embarrassing questions and an unmanageable party. Time has disposed of the first, and he is divorced from the last; if his great experience and talents have a fair field to act upon, he may yet, in spite of his selfish and unamiable character, be a distinguished and successful minister.

Greville after Peel's death in 1850

. . . The sympathy, the feeling, and the regret which have been displayed on every side and in all quarters, are to the last degree striking. Every imaginable honour has been lavished on his memory. The Sovereign, both Houses of Parliament, the press and the people, from the highest to the lowest, have all joined in acts of homage to his character, and in magnifying the loss which the nation has sustained. When we remember that Peel was an object of bitter hatred to one great party, that he was never liked by the other party, and that he had no popular and ingratiating qualities, and very few intimate friends, it is surprising to see the warm and universal feeling which his death has elicited. It is a prodigious testimony to the greatness of his capacity, to the profound conviction of his public usefulness and importance, and of the purity of the motives by which his public conduct has been guided. . . . My acquaintance with Peel was slight and superficial. I never associated with him, and never was in his house except on two or three occasions at rare intervals. He scarcely lived at all in society; he was reserved but cordial in his manner, had few intimate friends, and it may be doubted whether there was any one person, except his wife, to whom he was in the habit of disclosing his thoughts, feelings, and intentions with entire frankness and freedom. In his private relations he was not merely irreproachable, but good, kind, and amiable. The remarkable decorum of his life, the domestic harmony and happiness he enjoyed, and the simplicity of his habits and demeanour, contributed largely without doubt to the estimation in which he was held. He was easy of access, courteous and patient, and those who approached him generally left him gratified by his affability and edified and astonished at the extensive and accurate knowledge, as well as the sound practical sense and judgement, which he displayed on all subjects. It was by the continual exhibition of these qualities that he gained such a mastery over the public mind, and such prodigious influence in the House of Commons; but it is only now manifested to the world how great his influence was by the effect which his death has produced, and by the universal sentiment that the country has to deplore an irreparable loss. . . .

It is difficult to discern any proofs of sound judgement and foresight in Peel's conduct in regard to Parliamentary Reform. If he had adopted the same course as Huskisson on the East Retford question, and manifested a disposition to concede some moderate and reasonable reforms as fit occasions presented themselves, it is by no means improbable that the country might have been satisfied; but . . . Peel evidently made an incorrect estimate of the state of the public mind upon the question of Parliamentary Reform. He could not indeed foresee the French Revolution [of 1830] or its contagious effects here; but unless the country had been already combustible, it would not have been so inflamed as it was; and if he had been aware of its temper and disposition, he never would have opposed the general sentiment so pertinaciously as he did. I think, therefore, that his course in respect to Reform exhibits a deficiency in sagacity and foresight, and must be accounted one of the blemishes of his political career. . . .

Lord Hatherton on Peel

Hatherton writes at the time of Peel's death in 1850.

. . . He always seemed to me the most fautless of Ministers. He was not in any degree a man of genius. He had nothing of Canning or Burke about him, for if he had generosity or elevation of aim, it was always 'reflechi', but he gave a passionate observation to events and considered profoundly their causes, never acting on any question or treating any matters till he thoroughly understood them. . . . The steadiness of his application and his facility of research, acquired from habit and good memory, were quite wonderful; he always appeared to me to do everything with great ease. He seemed to me not to have a particle of vanity or of undue ambition about him, but a constant love of truth and desire to give it the victory. Naturally he did not appear to me good-tempered, but his temperament was not hasty, and his feelings were held under wonderful control. His prominent fault was a too great reserve and a cold repulsiveness of manner, resulting partly from physical constitution, partly from a just mistrust of the hastier judgments of other men, and partly from a natural or acquired habit of self reliance. His friends, and even his most intimate colleagues, all complained that they could never learn his mind; yet at table or in the society of those he liked, or in a country ride or walk, he seemed unreserved and cordial, and at such times the good sense of his remarks and the liveliness of his anecdotes were very charming. His oratory was always above the level of ordinary speakers, and his command of language always prompt and adequate to the occasion, but it never rose quite to the height of the first speakers. He frequently carried the House away with him, but it was by his greater knowledge of his subject, and his superior power in handling facts, and by the moral character of his sentiments. His pace of delivery also was very agreeable. For every-day purposes there was no one at all equal to him of his time. Probably it is not saying too much that, taking into account his vast information about all the affairs of this country, in every department, and all his moral and physical qualities, the country never before had witnessed a man so made for the times in which he lived. . . . Peel's great misfortune was to have been introduced into political life under the auspices of his father, and Mr. Perceval. He was thus engaged in all the strife of Catholic Emancipation and reforms of various sorts – on the wrong side. His good sense enabled him gradually to throw off the thraldom of early connection, and when he became his own master, to disavow the false principles he had been made to defend. He thus appeared to forfeit consistency and character, though every man in his situation did the same thing. I too, and hundreds like me, born and bred and sent into public life under the same influences, like him rejected them as we advanced in years, but we could do it unobserved and earlier than he could, for we had no engagements, and to us our constituents freely granted forgiveness of errors of opinion and the privilege to grow wiser with events. But classes and party attempted to hold him rigidly to the execution of their work, and on his refusal, attempted to brand him with infamy. No Minister in the history of the world ever before made such sacrifices to a sense of duty. I can find no words to express my sense of the purity and greatness of his conduct. With posterity he will be the greatest Minister this country has produced. Not the least part of his fame will be in the Christian and manly temper in which he withstood his assailants.

Notes

1. Charles Greville (1794–1865) was Clerk to the Privy Council at this time. His journals are full of gossip and information about politics and politicians. Here he gives his first impressions of William at his accession in June 1830.
2. Grant was a parliamentary reporter during this period.

3. Haydon (1786–1846), the painter, visited Wellington at Walmer Castle in 1839 to do sketches for the duke's portrait.
4. E.J. Littleton (1791–1863), 1st Lord Hatherton (1835), was Chief Secretary for Ireland in Grey's Ministry. A misunderstanding between him and Daniel O'Connell led to his and Grey's resignations in 1834. He writes in his diary in 1845, about the time of Grey's death.
5. Thomas Babington Macaulay (1800–59), politician, journalist and historian, was a Whig-Liberal Member of Parliament during the Reform Bill period.
6. Sarah Spencer (1787–1870) was the elder daughter of the 2nd Earl Spencer and Lord Althorp's sister. In 1813 she married William Henry Lyttelton, who became Lord Lyttelton in 1828.
7. For E.J. Littleton see Lord Hatherton, above.
8. William Howitt's character sketches of *Eminent Living Political Reformers* was published in 1840.
9. Harriet, wife of Charles Arbuthnot MP, was the daughter of Henry Fane MP, second son of the 8th Earl of Westmorland. She and her husband were intimate friends of the Duke of Wellington and she was his closest confidante. She died of cholera in 1834 at the age of forty. Her dislike of Peel may have arisen from her awareness of Peel's (erroneous) belief that she had been the duke's mistress.
10. From E.J. Littleton's diary, 20 November 1831. Twiss was Under-Secretary of State for War and the Colonies in Wellington's administration, 1828–30.

CHAPTER TWO

The Fall of Wellington, November 1830

The Duke of Wellington became Prime Minister in 1828. The Duke saw himself as the servant of king and country rather than as a party leader, but his Ministry was mainly Tory, though of a moderate and pragmatic kind. This attitude was particularly associated with Robert Peel, Home Secretary and Leader of the Commons, whose reforms of the criminal law were an important element in the evolution of 'Liberal Toryism' in the 1820s.

The main opposition group consisted of the Whigs, led by Charles, 2nd Earl Grey. Grey had been committed to parliamentary reform since 1792, but he was a cautious and moderate reformer, as suspicious of radicalism as of Toryism. He differed most from Wellington on foreign policy and thought him too friendly towards the absolutist monarchies of Europe, particularly that of Charles X, the last of the Bourbon monarchs in France, and his Minister Polignac. Many Whigs thought that Wellington's military career disposed him to authoritarian methods and feared that his style of government might lead Britain in that direction.

The King, George IV, did little to reassure them. He had become Prince Regent in 1810, when he was already notorious for his selfish and spendthrift character, and when he became king in 1820 he continued to scandalize his subjects by his attempt to divorce his wife Caroline on the grounds of her immorality. In his younger days George had been introduced to all the dissipations of the age by Charles James Fox, who was also the close friend of the young Charles Grey, but Grey and the Prince were never really friends: in particular the Prince resented Grey's courtship of Georgiana, the Duchess of Devonshire, who bore a daughter by him in 1792. After Fox's death in 1806 Grey and the Prince drew further apart and Grey's opposition to the divorce in 1820 hardened the split. When Wellington formed his cabinet, the King told him, 'He could have any Whig he liked – except Lord Grey'. Grey's exclusion meant that his party remained aloof, and Wellington was forced to rely on the support of the Ultra Tories on the right.

That support melted in 1829, when the threat of revolution in Ireland convinced Wellington and Peel that they must give Catholic Emancipation, to allow Roman Catholics to sit in Parliament and to qualify for most government offices. In this they had Whig support, but they were opposed by the 'Ultras', who were never to forgive Peel for abandoning the 'Protestant cause' which he had championed in earlier days when he was nicknamed 'Orange Peel'. This split in Wellington's following had ominous consequences in 1830.

In the summer of that year the political situation suddenly changed. There were four reasons. Firstly, King George IV died at the end of June. The new monarch, William IV, was George's brother and though he was not liberal by inclination, he was not prejudiced like his predecessor against Grey. If Grey was to become acceptable to the crown, Wellington would be less secure.

Secondly, the death of the king meant that there had to be a general election. The results were not dramatic and there was little change in the political balance in the Commons. During the elections, however, news arrived of a revolution in Paris. Events in France again awakened enthusiasm in England: the middle classes in particular were now likely to influence Parliament in favour of liberal measures. Unless Wellington could respond, his public support would begin to melt.

Thirdly, the summer and autumn of 1830 were times of distress and disturbance among the people, particularly in the rural counties of south and eastern England. The economy was depressed, and the invention of the threshing machine threatened to reduce the opportunities for employment of the agricultural labourers, particularly in the coming winter. This was the more serious because they were being pauperized by the effects of the poor law, which, by allowing the parish to supplement agricultural wages from the poor rate funds, encouraged farmers to pay low wages, so forcing the labourers 'on to the parish' even when they had work. In 1830 their protests turned to violence and a wave of riots, rick-burnings, and machine-breaking spread across the south-eastern counties. Though the 'last labourers' revolt' had little political content, its coincidence with the revival of the cry for reform in the towns and from the middle classes made it seem that the country was on the brink of revolution – a revolution Wellington's government was too weak to put down. Those who would have tolerated the duke longer now looked to a reinforcement of his government: but Grey saw his opportunity to replace it by his own and moved into outright opposition. He was no longer a political outcast, convinced that at the age of sixty-six his political career was over: he was an alternative prime minister, waiting in the wings.

When the new Parliament assembled at the beginning of November, crisis was in the air. It was at this moment that, by an almost inconceivable error of judgment, Wellington chose to reply to Grey's first speech in the new session, which declared that reform was the only way to satisfy the country, with a declaration that not only was reform inappropriate, and that he had no intention of proposing it, but that the existing constitution was so perfect that he could not imagine any possible alternative that would be an improvement. The speech created a sensation. Within a fortnight the government was defeated in the Commons on the new monarch's civil list – tantamount to a vote of no confidence – and Grey was sent for by William IV to form a new government and to introduce a Reform Bill. The reform crisis was about to begin.

The Duke of Rutland[1] to Lady Shelley, 31 October

It is my firm belief that we are nearer to a tremendous explosion than we have ever been. It is hard to say how the poison has been so deeply and widely circulated in the minds of the people. Some friends of mine ascribe it to the schoolmasters! . . .

What say you to a recent meeting held at Leicester, when one of the speakers predicted that, ere long, not a vestige of Nobility would be left in England; to which the whole meeting responded: 'The sooner it is done away with, the better!'. . . .

Mrs Arbuthnot's Journal

Nov. 4th. – Parliament was opened by the King on the 2d. He was very well received by the people who, however, were very disorderly, hooted and hissed the Duke wherever they could see him, called out 'No police,' 'No Polignac'! (wise creatures) and, in various parts of the town, attacked the police most furiously. In general, however, they did not appear very much out of humour, and it was only the very lowest class of blackguards that were at all active. Since that, everything has been perfectly tranquil and, tho' some affect to be frightened and to give that fright as a reason for advocating Parliamentary Reform, I don't believe there will be any disturbance. The wretched state to which Belgium is reduced by their desire for *reform* is a pretty good lesson for sober & reflecting people such as we are. . . .

People complain that the Duke did harm by declaring publicly he wd not lend himself to any reform, & that he thought, in its *results*, no form of representation could be better than ours. This odious *reform* question seems as much a stumbling block as the Catholic question was. . . . The Duke and Peel are quite determined to resist, the Duke from honestly and conscientiously thinking that strengthening the democratic part of the H. of Commons at the expense of the aristocratic is most pernicious and dangerous, Peel from feeling that *he* would be thought shabby if he lent himself again to a measure he had hitherto opposed. . . .

7th. – We are in a great fuss about the dinner which the City of London give to the King on the 9th. We hear the radicals are determined to make a riot, and the Lord Mayor has written to the Duke to say he cannot answer for his safety unless he comes with an escort, he gets quantities of letters every day telling him he will be murdered, the King is very much frightened, the Queen cries half the day with fright at the idea of going; altogether, we are in a nice predicament. And all *about nothing*, for it is quite preposterous to imagine that the idle vagabonds who compose the mob of London care a pin about Parliamentary Reform. What they want is plunder; those who have nothing want the property of those who have something, & the stupid Liberals in the House of Commons fancy they can reform just as much as satisfies them & no more, & even in that they are all divided. . . .

The Duke is greatly affected by all this state of affairs. He feels that beginning reform is beginning revolution, that therefore he must endeavour to stem the tide as long as possible, and that all he has to do is to see *when & how* it will be best for the country that he shd resign. He thinks he cannot till he is beat in the H. of Commons. He talked about this with me yesterday and I told him that, in my opinion, if he really & honestly believed that the reformers obtaining power wd lead to revolution, he was bound in honour as an honest man to resist that to the last & to keep his place as long as he cd possibly be supported. He seemed to agree in that and I hope he will do it. We hear the Opposition are calculating confidently upon coming in, but that the most sober among them are somewhat alarmed at the difficulties they will have to contend with, at the violence of party in England and the disturbed and wretched state of France & the Netherlands, all which will be aggravated by the overturn of the Duke. . . .

10th. – The Guildhall dinner was given up in consequence of the threatening aspect of the mob, and the Lord Mayor coming to Sir Robt Peel to say that he cd not answer for the maintenance of the peace of the City. The pickpockets and thieves of London are so exasperated against the new Police that they had determined to have a *row*. It is supposed they intended to disable the horses in the carriages and then attack the persons inside and take their chance of plunder and murder. The Duke of Wellington is their great object of hatred just now. They affect to want *reform* & to hoot and pelt him because he is against it!! & there are really sensible men who will tell you that reform is therefore necessary, & that the Govt must go out because the Duke is opposed to it! However, if they like reform they can have it, but they can't have it & the Duke, and they must choose between the two. I don't believe we shall be beat.

We have taken great precautions against the mobs. Troops and artillery have been brought to London, the guards doubled, the police all on the alert & the consequence has been that, whenever the mobs have assembled, they have been routed & severely beat by the police who are exasperated against them to the highest degree. It is a great scandal, but Hunt & Cobbett have opened a meeting house they call the Rotunda near Blackfriars Bridge, and there they assemble & harangue crowds of the lower orders in the most seditious manner, and from that place they issue in large bodies & come & alarm the peaceable people in the West End of the town. I can't understand why it is allowed. However, I hope the mob will soon be tired of getting nothing but blows from the police.

Nothing can behave more amiably than the King. He is very much annoyed & out of spirits, very sorry no connection cd be formed with Palmerston but determined to support the Ministers, & frightened to death for fear any thing shd happen to the Duke. He and the Queen had determined, if the dinner had taken place at Guildhall, to have brought the Duke back in their carriage to prevent his being exposed to any danger from the populace. . . .

J.C. Hobhouse's[2] Recollections

The Duke of Wellington made a speech in the Lords, and declared against Reform. I hear he was hissed, and hurt by a stone. The King was applauded. . . .

November 4. – . . . I heard this evening that a very unpleasant feeling was rising among the working classes, and that the shopkeepers in the Metropolis were so much alarmed that they talked of arming themselves. The Duke of Wellington was not one of the alarmists; on the contrary, he told Lord Tweeddale that everything would end peaceably, and he might go to Scotland if he chose. Lord Tweeddale told this to me; but said, 'Notwithstanding the Duke's opinion, I shall stay here. I am afraid of some catastrophe.'

I heard everywhere that a great change had taken place in public opinion since the meeting of Parliament. The Duke was scarcely safe in the streets, and the King's popularity was evidently on the wane. . . .

November 6. – I walked about with Cornwall, son of the Bishop of Hereford, a Ministerial MP. He told me the Government were taking extraordinary measures to provide against the threatened commotions of the next week. Some of the treasure had been removed from the Bank, and

several regiments ordered up to London. Many special constables had also
been sworn in. . . .

People seem to think that Ministers will be turned out on the Reform
question. Lord Stafford and Lord Talbot have declared for Reform. The
potentates begin to tremble for their acres.

Greville's Journal

8 November

. . . Parliament met, and a great clamour was raised against the King's
Speech, without much reason; but it was immediately evident that the
Government was in a very tottering condition, and the first night of this
session the Duke of Wellington made a violent and uncalled-for declaration against Reform, which has without doubt sealed his fate. Never was
there an act of more egregious folly, or one so universally condemned by
friends and foes. The Chancellor said to Lady Lyndhurst after the first
night's debate in the House of Lords, 'You have often asked me why the
Duke did not take in Lord Grey; read these two speeches (Lord Grey's
and the Duke's), and then you will see why. Do you think he would like to
have a colleague under him, who should get up and make such a speech
after such another as his?'

The effect produced by this declaration exceeds anything I ever saw,
and it has at once destroyed what little popularity the Duke had left, and
lowered him in public estimation so much that when he does go out of
office, as most assuredly he must, he will leave it without any of the
dignity and credit which might have accompanied his retirement. The
sensation produced in the country has not yet been ascertained, but it is
sure to be immense. I came to town last night, and found the town ringing
with his imprudence and everybody expecting that a few days would
produce his resignation.

The King's visit to the City was regarded with great apprehension, as it
was suspected that attempts would be made to produce riot and confusion
at night, and consequently all the troops that could be mustered were
prepared, together with thousands of special constables, new police,
volunteers, sailors, and marines; but last night a Cabinet Council was
held, when it was definitively arranged to put it off altogether, and this
morning the announcement has appeared in the newspapers. Every sort of
ridicule and abuse was heaped upon the Government, the Lord Mayor,
and all who had any share in putting off the King's visit to the City; very
droll caricatures were circulated. . . .

In Downing Street we met George Dawson, who told us the funds had
fallen three per cent., and that the panic was tremendous, so much so that
they were not without alarm lest there should be a run on the Bank for
gold. Later in the day, however, the funds improved. In the House of
Lords I heard the Duke's explanation of putting off the dinner in the City.
On the whole they seem to have done well to put it off, but the case did not
sound a strong one; it rested on a letter from the Lord Mayor telling the

Duke an attempt would be made on his life. Still it is a hundred to one that there would have been riot, and possibly all its worst evils and crimes. The King is said to be very low, hating Reform, desirous of supporting the Duke, but feeling that he can do nothing. However, in the House of Lords last night the speakers vied with each other in praising his Majesty and extolling his popularity. Lady Jersey told me that the Duke had said to her 'Lord, I shall not go out; you will see we shall go on very well.'

November 10th. – It was expected last night that there would be a great riot, and preparations were made to meet it. Troops were called up to London, and a large body of civil power put in motion. People had come in from the country in the morning, and everything indicated a disturbance. After dinner I walked out to see how things were going on. There was little mob in the west end of the town, and in New Street, Spring Gardens, a large body of the new police was drawn up in three divisions, ready to be employed if wanted. The Duke of Wellington expected Apsley House to be attacked, and made preparations accordingly. . . .

The Duke of Wellington to the Rt. Hon. Maurice Fitzgerald,[3] 6 November

My Dear Sir,

I have received your letter and the enclosure, and I am obliged to you for the friendly motive in writing it, and for the frankness with which it is written.

I have not leisure to discuss Parliamentary Reform either in writing or in conversation. I confess that I doubt that it will be carried in Parliament.

If it should be carried it must occasion a total change in the whole system of that society called the British Empire; and I don't see how I could be a party to such changes, entertaining the opinions that I do.

To tell you the truth I must add that I feel no strength excepting my character for plain manly dealing. I could not pretend that I wished sincerely well to the measures, which I should become not merely a party but the principal in recommending.

I shall sincerely lament if I should be mistaken, and that Parliament should adopt the new course proposed. I foresee nothing but a series of misfortunes for the country in all its interests, and even affecting its safety. I cannot be a party in inflicting those misfortunes.
Believe me, &c.,
Wellington

Memorandum[4] – Measures to be taken to put an end to the seditious meetings at the Rotunda, etc.

9 November
It appears to me that we ought to consider without loss of time respecting these meetings at the Rotunda in Blackfriars-road.
1.   Whether they can be prevented.

2. Whether they can be dispersed.
3. The measures to be adopted respecting them.

The two first are legal questions. From what I saw and knew last night it appears to me to be impossible that such meetings, rendering necessary the assemblage of hundreds of police officers and the putting the garrison under arms, should be legal. If however these meetings can neither be prevented nor dispersed, we cannot continue our proceedings as last night. The police as well as the military will be worn out by bodily fatigue and reduced in spirit.

A police cannot act in large bodies upon the defensive. That which must be done is to observe what is passing at the Rotunda, with very few people.

To take the necessary measures regarding property and persons likely to be the objects of attack, and to have police and military ready to be turned out at a short notice to act with efficiency under the direction of the magistrates in case a serious attack should be made upon any person, house, or place.

If two armies were *en presence* the proper mode of proceeding would be to prevent the enemy from crossing the river. But, as we saw last night, this object cannot be attained in this case. The police may watch the meeting during the night. It may disperse on the spot of meeting in such manner as to deceive the police; but at the same time meet again, or proceed in separate parties to do a great deal of mischief, possibly without being interrupted; while our police and military will have been fatigued by fruitlessly watching the bridges or other points all night.

The measure to be adopted appears then to be to secure such houses and other places as are liable to be attacked, to have the Guards on duty, particularly the Horse Guards, much on the alert ready to turn out.

To have an inlying picquet in each of the barracks ready to turn out at a moment's notice.

That the great body of the police should be likewise ready to turn out, and their officers ready at Colonel Rowan's to direct them to any point at which their services might be required.

During this state of alarm two or three of the most active and intelligent magistrates should sleep every night at the Home Office.
Wellington

Memorandum – Precautions to be taken to defend Apsley House in case of attack

9 November
In all probability the windows on the park front of Apsley House will be broken between sunset and the hour at which the park gates are shut.

It is desirable that the window-shutters of the gallery should be shut as well as those of the rooms below.

It is possible that at a later hour the house will be attacked.

As soon as there is the appearance of a mob collecting there somebody should say that preparations are made for the defence of the house, and that the mob had better go somewhere else.

The following preparations must be made.

The gates into the stable and the yard to be well locked and secured.

A man with arms to be stationed at the window of the Duchess's passage, at each of the two windows of what is called the red drawing-room, at each of the two windows of the bed-room over that drawing-room, all looking towards the right-hand gate.

A man with arms at each of the windows of the inner hall, and of John's room, and at the left-hand window of the Piccadilly drawing-room; and in Lord Douro's sitting-room, looking towards the left-hand gate.

A man with arms to be in the Duchess's bath-room above stairs: and in the coachman's-room in case an attempt should be made to break into the stable-yard.

In case there should be any persons in the park the remainder must be placed in the Duchess's rooms below stairs; in the Duke's room, particularly his bed-room; and in the window of the staircase over his room.

Nobody must fire unless the gates should be broken open, or any person should enter the garden over the rails, or by pulling down the rails.

In that case every effort must be made to prevent the approach to or the entry of the house.

Wellington

Princess Lieven[5] to her brother Alexander, 6 November

. . . I have just seen the Duke of Wellington – in the midst of the worries of his position, which I have explained – in spite of his evident disfavour with all classes, for he has suddenly become extremely unpopular even in the City, where his last speech brought about an alarming fall in the Funds; although he is followed in the streets, hooted, and almost attacked by the mob – in the midst of all this he maintains an impassive demeanour, is wholly undisturbed, even gay and cheerful. This is to me unintelligible. The Chancellor told me in confidence that they could not possibly go on any longer, that their position is too humiliating, and, in a word, that the outcry against them is from all quarters. You see now, dear Alexander, the difficulty in which we are placed between on one side a Government well disposed towards our interests and our political principles, but incapable, absolutely *incapable*, of acting on these principles, and on the other an Opposition which any day may become the Government, enouncing and supporting in Parliament doctrines which are altogether unsuitable to us. In the worst case, however – that is, should Wellington be upset and his place occupied by the Whigs – I should hope that once in power they would amend their ways considerably. . . .

9 November

We too, in England, dear Alexander, are just on the brink of a revolution.

For the last two days, agitation reigns in London. It began to show itself on the day of the opening of Parliament. The Duke of Wellington's peremptory declaration against any sort of reform has dissatisfied the upper classes, aroused fear in the middle class, and exasperated the populace. Disturbances have taken place and troops have been brought up to London. In view, moreover, of the threatening attitude assumed by the Government, it was asserted that the occasion of the King and Queen's visit to the City tonight was to be taken to make a popular demonstration, of which the object was to assassinate the Duke of Wellington and to create confusion and provoke disorder. Ministers, having been informed of these intentions, persuaded their Majesties to give up their visit to the City, thereby causing general consternation and nervous anxiety. All yesterday was passed in comings and goings, and the public of all classes never for an instant doubted that the Ministry would be dismissed forthwith, on the ground that the King could not submit to be made the victim of the Duke of Wellington's unpopularity. Matters have turned out quite otherwise. I dined last night with the King and all his Ministers. He treated them with greater cordiality and attention than ever. The Duke, for his part, told me that he was quite right in his course, that as for the disorders of the mob he knew how to repress them, and that as for reform it was with it as it had been with the Catholic Question, that it could not be passed without him, and that he would have none of it, therefore it would not pass at all. I have never seen anyone take a firmer and more confident attitude than the Duke. Meanwhile it is generally believed that there will be riots; but precautions have been taken, and 10,000 troops, who can be relied on, are quartered in London. Moreover, the London parishes have spontaneously offered to provide their own special constables and to answer for the peace of their respective divisions. Permission has been accorded to them, but no arms are to be issued to them.

This is the exact state of things at the moment of my writing to you.

I will not venture upon any prophecy. The Opposition is already shouting victory and allotting posts; not a soul doubts for a moment of a change of Ministry, except perhaps myself. I still believe the Duke to be very strong, although one cannot hide from oneself that his declaration has caused him the loss of numerous adherents. . . .

Lady Carlisle to her daughter, Caroline Lascelles[6]

Grosvenor Place, November 16, 1830. . . . Government beat by 29! George brought the news to us as we were sitting a quiet little party at Mr. Grenville's. Soon after Sir Watkin [Williams Wynn] tumbled in, so inarticulate that I was glad we had some other means of information. We went to my sister's and found her at tea with Lord Granville – as excited as you may suppose. He went away soon to a little *soirée* at Mde de Dino's, where he expected to find Ly Jersey, etc. Georgiana and Blanche were dining at Lansdowne House, where Mr Ellis arrived with the news, quite tipsy with joy. . . . At Mde de Dino's someone heard Talleyrand asking the Chancellor if the question on which they had been defeated was one of much consequence – and he answered '*C'est une affaire bien grave.*'

Georgiana Ellis to Caroline Lascelles

Spring Gardens. November 18, 1830. . . . . The most exciting moment was on the Monday evening, when Mr Ellis came to Lansdowne House with the news of the complete defeat of the Ministers. The next day at about 2 o'clock one heard of their having sent in their resignations. The certainty of the fact was not as pleasant as the anticipation and, whether from its never being (in my opinion) agreeable to have one's own friends in, or from its being the most dreadful day that ever was known, one certainly felt rather flat. . . . George came later; he had not heard decidedly of Lord Grey being sent for, and we did not know it till we went to Ly Granville's in the evening. There it was known that he had received *carte blanche* to do what he pleased. . . . There are different stories as to the intention of the Ministers about going out, but it almost appears as if they intended going out on the Civil List rather than on Reform, which was much better for both parties. Some say that the Duke of W. when he heard of it asked why Peel had not spoke, and said he must have lost his head. He had a dinner that day, and when he heard the division, he desired that the women might not be told. Ly Jersey, who was there, went to Mde de Dino's without knowing it, and they say was very near crying when she heard it; Ld Jersey on the contrary was in great spirits. Ly Lyndhurst was going about saying how delighted she was at their being turned out!. . . .

Le Marchant's[7] diary, November 1830

The division on the Civil List on the night of the 15th November decided the fate of the Ministry. They were the only persons taken by surprise. Peel had been told in the morning that if he divided he would be left in a minority, and showed some want of humour at the mere mention of such a thing – he thought it absolutely impossible. The Duke was in the same error. He gave a large dinner party. At 10 o'clock he said to Lord Worcester, 'It is time for you to go to the House; there will be a division. When it is over come back and tell us the news.' Lord Worcester accordingly got into his cabriolet and departed. As he was driving down St. James Street a friend called out to him, 'You are too late, the division has taken place.' 'Well, what are the numbers?' '233 to 204.' Lord W. waited not for more and in a few minutes he was at the Duke's again, with the information that Ministers were in a majority of 29. 'What, no *more*! said the Duke. 'I don't understand it. There must be some mistake.' The mistake, such as it was, was soon cleared up. Mr William Holmes in a few minutes was announced in the other room. The Duke began by complaining of the smallness of the majority. Mr Holmes was thunderstruck, but his Grace was soon undeceived and then returned to his guests. It is said that Mrs Arbuthnot was the only one to whom he communicated the intelligence. The rest went away believing the accuracy of Lord Worcester's report. Lady Jersey went to Prince Lieven's, where she rated some inoffensive member very roundly for presuming to state that the majority was against Ministers instead of for them. When the truth was demonstrated to her she burst into tears.

The report is that the Duke has felt it severely not only because he loves power but because he conceives himself to have been deceived by his Party. He imputes their defection to his retrenchments of patronage, and accuses them of having themselves created the tempest that drove him from the helm. It certainly seems doubtful whether the usual adherents of the Administration gave very explicit notice before of their intentions. The fact is that neither Peel nor the Duke are men of social habits. Indeed they even associate very little with each other, and keeping themselves also aloof from the subordinate members of their Government, they knew very little of what was going on. The Government too had been for a long time only supported by the division among its opponents, and . . . there is no instance on record of the long duration of a Government on such support. On the first favourable opportunity their opponents coalesce and overwhelm them.

Mrs Arbuthnot's Journal, *20–3 November*

20th. – At length we have broke down! On Monday last, the 15th, on the debate whether the Civil List shd be referred to a Committee or not, a question of no sort of consequence, the ultra-Tories united with the Whigs & Hume, & we were beat by 29.

I was dining at the Duke of Wellington's with the Prince of Orange and a large party when the Duke got a note telling him what had happened, & that Peel, Goulburn & Mr Arbuthnot were come up to talk to him. He whispered to me before he went down what had happened, & went away, saying nothing to anyone else. I stayed till they were all gone & then went down stairs and heard *all about it*. I never saw a man so delighted as Peel. He said, when the Opposition cheered at the division that he did not join in it but that it was with difficulty he refrained, he was so delighted at having so good an opportunity for resigning.

It was agreed the Duke shd go the next morning to the King and tell him that, having had this proof of the want of confidence of the H. of Commons in the Govt, they must resign. He accordingly did this. The King was excessively distressed, asked him whether it was really inevitable, whether no junction cd be formed, no strength gained, said that he had unbounded confidence in the Duke & that, if there was anything he cd do to prevent this misfortune, he was willing to do it & wd stand by him to the last. He cried & was in the greatest possible agitation. The Duke told him it was impossible; that, for his (the King's) own sake, he had better try another arrangement. He expressed unbounded gratitude for the King's kindness & deepest regret at being unable to continue to serve him.

The King saw Peel and, finding the resignation must be accepted, he acquiesced & sent for Lord Grey.

I hardly know how to state what was the effect produced. The radicals had laboured to make the Duke odious because he wd not consent to Parliamentary Reform, and the situation of the Government had long been so unpleasant that the catastrophe excited little surprise. The persons most grieved were the foreign ministers, who dread any appearance of revolution in this country; but altogether, and for a variety of reasons, every one felt a break-up was scarcely to be regretted. Almost without exception the members of the Govt were delighted, feeling that their situation had been irksome beyond endurance and, when such a feeling does exist, a govt *cannot* go on.

I am vexed to death, but solely because I cannot bear the Duke shd be defeated, and defeated by a faction who have vowed vengeance against him on account of the Catholic Relief Bill. At a time, too, when by his good management he had guided us thro' the difficulties of the French revolution in peace & in an honorable way. During the three years of his Govt he has relieved the Catholics and the Dissenters, he has cut down the estimates *many millions*, he has put every possible office down as they became vacant, he has taken off above three million of taxes, he, in conjunction with Peel, has improved the police, simplified the laws; in short, in three years he has introduced great & substantial reforms &, because he will not play tricks with the Constitution & give more power to the democrats than they ought to have, he is hooted & abused & driven from the helm. I am more vexed and annoyed than I can say. I think he is *very much* annoyed too, tho' he will not own it.

Peel is *delighted*, entirely without the slightest feeling of regret & looking forward to heading a most powerful Opposition with unmixed pleasure. Many of those who voted against us now pretend to be very sorry & to say they wd not have done it if they had thought it wd produce such a result, which is all nonsense & only provokes me the more. If they did not want the Govt to go out, why did they vote against us?

23d. – The new Govt are formed & received the seals yesterday. The Duke went & took leave of the King & Queen. The former was (the Duke told me) very much agitated & affected & told the Duke he cd not express how grieved and distressed he was; that, on coming to the Crown, he had reposed entire confidence in him, & that every thing that had passed since had only more & more proved to him how deserving the Duke was of such confidence, & that it was with the utmost pain & sorrow that he parted from him. . . .

Greville's Journal, *16 November*

The Duke of Wellington's Administration is at an end. If he has not already resigned, he probably will do so in the course of the day. Everybody was so intent on the Reform question that the Civil List was not thought of, and consequently the defeat of Government last night was unexpected. Although numbers of members were shut out there was a great attendance, and a majority of twenty-nine. Of those who were shut out, almost all declare that they meant to have voted in the majority.

I went to Mrs Taylor's at night and found Ferguson, Denman, and Taylor, who had just brought the news. The exultation of the Opposition was immense. Word was sent down their line not to cheer, but they were not to be restrained, and Sefton's yell was heard triumphant in the din. The Tories voted with them. There had been a meeting at Knatchbull's in the morning, when they decided to go against Government. Worcester had dined at Apsley House, and returned with the news, but merely said that they had had a bad division – twenty-nine. Everybody thought he meant a majority *for* Government, and the Duke, who already knew what had happened, made a sign to him to say nothing. Worcester knew nothing himself, having arrived after the division; they told him the numbers, and he came away fancying they were for Government. So off the company went to Madame de Dino, where they heard the truth. Great was the consternation and long were the faces, but the outs affected to be merry and the ins were serious. Talleyrand fired off a courier to Paris forthwith. . . .

Benjamin Haydon's Autobiography, *18/22 November*

Wellington is out! Thus ends that immortal Tory ministry, whose energy and true English feeling carried them through the most tremendous contest that ever nation was engaged in. The military vigour, the despotic feeling engendered by twenty-five years of furious war, rendered them unfit, perhaps, to guide the domestic policy of the country, and though the Whigs would have sacrificed the honour and grandeur of Old England, for the sake of advancing the abstract principles of the French Revolution, and consequently were very unfit for the war with Napoleon, now that the danger is over, they are perhaps more adapted to carry the country through its present crisis. God grant they may. . . . If they rise in proportion to the tide, they will prove a blessing to the world. I dread their inexperience in office.

Mrs Arbuthnot's Journal

23 November
. . . I confess I am vexed & mortified beyond expression, solely on the Duke's account. I sometimes think it is most unfortunate but it is quite true that, excepting my husband & his children, I have no feeling of warm interest for any human being but the Duke. There is something about him that fascinates me to a degree that is silly, but which I cannot resist. He is so amiable, so kind hearted with a great appearance of roughness, & so frank that I always feel I wd die for him & tho' he does not say it & bears

his loss of office with great philosophy, still I am sure he must feel it & it makes me miserable to think he shd have anything to vex him. I certainly think he was wrong in being persuaded we did not want more speaking talent in the House of Commons; it is that which has broke us down; but still, he had a very difficult game to play with Peel, who always made the most of every difficulty & invariably rejected every proposal for a remedy & never made any himself. Putting aside the vexation of having been beat, he will be more at ease and happy, I hope, now it is over &, if he ever returns to office, it will be under better auspices.

29th. – I shall write very seldom now, I dare say, in my book for, except the Duke, none of the public men interest me; and I don't feel now the excitement I did during Canning's Govt.

I earnestly hope this Govt will not last and I don't expect it, for they are a most heterogeneous mass of persons taken from all parties and have made some most extraordinary appointments. Ld Grey has given *good* places to his son, his three sons-in-law, three brothers-in-law, besides nephews; has made two merchants, one Secy to the Treasury & the other Vice-President of the Board of Trade, and the same Gazette, which announced their appointments, notified the dissolution of their part-nerships with houses in the City. This is all *quite new*. No merchants were ever before put into financial situations, & certainly the Duke of Wel-lington did not crowd the offices with his sons & nephews. We hear they mean to reduce salaries greatly. If they do, none but men of large fortune can serve the public, or the offices will fall into the hands of a lower class of persons, who will sell the patronage. It is impossible, as the salaries now are, for a person in office to save one farthing; and I dare say, if all the late officials were put upon their oaths, it wd be found that not three of them wd be one shilling richer for their public services, & many of them very seriously poorer. I hope Sir Rt Peel will oppose the reduction in the House of Commons. . . .

He [Arbuthnot] had a long audience with the King when he gave up the seals. The King seemed very uneasy & unhappy about the new Govt, abused Brougham & said he has positively determined he wd not go to dine in the City. It was clear from what he said that his new Govt had tried to make him go.

The Times,[8] 22 November

There has not been, within our memory, a resignation of an entire Cabinet, upon which public opinion may be said to have borne so directly and so powerfully, as that of the Duke of Wellington and his colleagues. It must, nevertheless, be acknowledged, that in no instance was a change effected in public opinion so absolute, so obvious, and so *sudden*, as that which His Grace experienced within a single fortnight, which he had the misfortune to produce by his own words, and to disregard utterly until it struck and overwhelmed him.

So long as the Duke of Wellington moved in harmony with the predominating spirit of the nation, he was the most popular of all public servants. Notwithstanding the murmurs of a bigoted and narrow-minded faction, he lost nothing in the eyes of the country generally by his Catholic bill or Dissenters' bill, while the earnest he had afforded of his desire to retrench, even before his humane and considerate abolition of the beer-tax, and the credit he thus obtained as an economist, down almost to the eve of the late meeting of Parliament, were such, that not more than six weeks ago he never showed himself to the people without being loudly cheered.

The revulsion, as we have said, was not capricious on the part of the people of England. The Minister, instead of the national colours under which he had served since his accession to office, seemed all at once to hoist an unconstitutional ensign, to desert with it to the headquarters of the rotten borough system, and to aggravate this unhappy dereliction, by an attempt, after the fashion of former times, to fix upon the neck of the country a pledge of supporting a large amount of civil list, inaccessible to any effort at alleviation or revision, during the whole reign of his present Majesty.

The Duke, then, has fallen – for a fall it is: there is no evidence (though suspicion there may be) that his Grace would ever have resigned, if in his power to avoid it.

What, then, is the lesson to be drawn from this downfall of a man, celebrated, esteemed, admired, until very lately endeared to his country-men, and, in spite of every failure, immortal in the records of England and of Europe? The lesson is an important one for those who succeed in office the baffled Administration of the Duke of Wellington.

The exigency to which the new Ministry owe their admission to power, is not one produced by Court intrigue, or by mere party triumph: it is founded on that opinion which caused the overthrow of a Government hostile to reform, not enough zealous for retrenchment, and supposed to be, though perhaps unjustly, not quite impartial as between the interests of freedom, and prerogative in the concern of foreign nations.

By the tide of opinion, then, floated into office, it is upon it they must continue to buoy themselves, or they will inevitably perish. . . .

Notes

1. John Henry Manners, 5th Duke of Rutland (1778–1857), a member of the Tory party, writes to Frances, wife of Sir John Shelley. She was a close friend of the Duke of Wellington.
2. John Cam Hobhouse (1786–1869), Baron Broughton (1851), Radical, then Whig MP for Westminster between 1820 and 1833, was a friend of Byron and a critic of Lord Grey. His *Recollections of a Long Life* were published in 1865.
3. Maurice Fitzgerald (1774–1849), Knight of Kerry, was an MP and friend of Wellington. He lost his seat for County Kerry after the Reform Act.
4. From the Duke of Wellington's papers.
5. Dorothea Christopherovna Benckendorf, Princess Lieven (1785–1857), wife of the

Russian ambassador to London, was an intimate friend of many leading politicians, including Grey and Wellington, and a close observer of the political and social scene.

6. Caroline, Harriet and Georgiana Howard were the three daughters of the 6th Earl of Carlisle. Caroline married W.S.S. Lascelles, younger son of the 2nd Earl of Harewood, in 1823, Harriet married Earl Gower, later the 2nd Duke of Sutherland, in the same year, and Georgiana married George Welbore Agar Ellis, later Lord Dover, in 1822.

7. Sir Denis Le Marchant (1795–1874) was a Liberal MP. His *Memoir of John Charles Viscount Althorp, 3rd Earl Spencer* was published in 1876.

8. *The Times* was edited during this period by Thomas Barnes (1785–1841), under whom it was a fervent, but occasionally critical, supporter of the Reform Ministry.

CHAPTER THREE

Winter of Discontent, November–December 1830

The 'labourers' revolt' swept across southern England in the last months of 1830. For the third year in succession crop failures and high food prices added to the misery of a rural population beset by low wages, pauperization at the hands of the poor law authorities, and squalid living conditions. Protests began in Kent in September and by the middle of November, as Grey's administration was taking office, disturbances were spreading through Sussex, Hampshire, Berkshire, and Wiltshire. Groups of unemployed labourers attacked threshing machines which deprived them of winter employment, and their anger spilled over into demonstrations against farmers, landlords, the clergy and the local authority of the propertied classes in general. The 'rioters' were hardly conscious of political issues and their protests were much more to do with their individual and family hardships than with political reform, but the upper classes took alarm at what seemed a breakdown of law and order in the countryside, where landlords and the clergy had always been able to control the 'lower orders' and had expected their unquestioning deference. When even the unusually submissive peasantry of Dorset and other south-western counties gathered in mobs to protest and to threaten their betters, it seemed as though the secure, ordered world in which the wealthy lived was coming to an end. Leading noblemen like the Duke of Richmond at Goodwood, and Wellington himself in Hampshire, hurried to their estates to lead attempts to restore order, troops were called out, and special commissions were sent out from London to try those captured and accused of incendiarism, riot, and destruction of property. Melbourne, Grey's Home Secretary, with the full support of the Cabinet, acted ruthlessly to restore authority, not only because they were themselves men of substantial wealth and property, but also to show the country that liberal reform did not imply the tolerance of anarchy and insubordination. Nearly 1,000 persons were tried by the special commissions, and others by the ordinary courts: over 450 were sentenced to transportation to Australia and 200 received sentence of death, though in the end only three were hanged.

The revolution expected by alarmists like Mrs Arbuthnot never materialized, but as the following extracts show, for a short time the state of the rural counties gave cause for alarm as families barricaded themselves in their country houses and sat up through the night awaiting attacks which hardly ever came. London now had its new metropolitan police, set up by Peel in 1829, but in the country law and order was in the hands of amateur magistrates, parish constables, and the men of property themselves. The fabric of rural society was still fragile enough to give way if the conventions of deference broke down and it was this fear that made the winter in which the country waited to hear what Grey's reform government would do a time of apprehension for the future of society as the men and women of the time knew it.

The Gentleman's Magazine

November

In our last we mentioned the riotous proceedings of the peasantry in the county of Kent, which had been attended by incendiary acts. Since when, we lament to say, this diabolical spirit has spread through several counties. Not only Kent, but Sussex, Suffolk, Surrey, Hants, Wilts, Berks, Bucks, Hunts, &c. are the extensive theatre of arson and disorder. Accounts of fires have been received from Beccles, Newton, Pulborough, Albury, Wavington, Gosport, Norwich, Arundel, Caterham, Windsor, Dorking, Minster, Marlow, High Wycombe, Battle, and Rye. Much property has been destroyed, more is threatened, and the agitation and alarm consequent on these fearful proceedings are most calamitous. The fire instrument, it appears, is of a slowly explosive character, and being deposited beneath the stack, after a certain period it ignites and explodes. Immense rewards are offered, and every exertion used, for the discovery of the miscreants. But a mystery surrounds the fire raiser which it seems impossible to penetrate. The conduct of the peasantry is remarkable, even if acquitted of the capital charge. Their first object appears to be the destruction of machinery, an object they have systematically pursued and effected. Their next object is to muster men. This they do openly, by forcing the farm labourers to join them: we mean, that a few of the more determined insist on the company of others, and their demands increase with their numbers. They aim first at the incumbent of the parish, who is forced to promise a reduction of his tithes. In the case of the Rev. Mr Kirby, of Mayfield, Sussex, the tithes were brought down from 1,400l. to 400l. and the remaining sum divided among the farmers for the payment of the labourer. They then visit the holder of lay tithes, with whom they deal less mercifully. With overseers, tithe-gatherers, and land bailiffs, they have recourse to the still more summary process of 'carting', the procession being generally formed of twelve men to 500 women and children. From the farmers they demand 2s. 6d. per day in summer, and 2s. in winter, as their wages for work, and constant employment. They go from farm to farm, accept what is offered in the shape of drink, victuals, or money, and generally conduct themselves with firmness and moderation. A farmer in Sussex refused to sign the contract for an advance of wages, when a rope was brought out, and he was assured that he must accept either the one or the other. The different parishes communicate by beacon fires, and there seems a regular though secret head throughout the country. Threatening letters, signed 'Swing', do not always precede the conflagrations. Machinery is almost wholly discontinued, and tithes generally lowered, but there is little return to peace and regularity. Dragoons are stationed in different parts of the country, who have interfered with good effect in meetings where tumult was threatened. Nightly patrols are established, and a day-watch set, but still no discovery has been made of the incendiaries, no stop put to the dangerous musters of men. A most respectable meeting of the men of Kent was held at Canterbury on the 6th, when it was resolved that the persons present would co-operate with the magistrates, landholders, and tenantry, in resisting outrages, alleviating distress, and restoring the independence of the peasantry.

A royal proclamation, dated Nov. 23, offers to informers a reward of 50l. for every person convicted as authors or perpetrators of the outrages, and 500l. for the conviction of an incendiary. The counties of Wilts, Kent, Sussex, Surrey, Hants, and Berks, are alone mentioned; but the mischief is spreading, particularly in Huntingdon and Cambridge shires.

December
We feel great satisfaction in stating that the late diabolical acts of the midnight incendiaries, and the riotous proceedings of agricultural labourers have in some degree subsided, though many lawless acts of violence have been perpetrated in Hants, Berks, Wilts, &c. At Pit-house, the seat of John Benett, Esq., MP for Wilts, a desperate affray took place. On hearing that a mob (about 500) was approaching his house, he went out on horseback to remonstrate with them, when they began to pelt him with flint-stones and brickbats; just at this moment the Hindon troop, under the command of Capt. Wyndham, came up, and saved Mr Benett, who was very much wounded on the head, as well as Capt. Wyndham. The cavalry attempted to charge upon them, but the mob rushed into the plantations which surround the house, where they continued pelting the cavalry, who at last effected the charge, when several were wounded, and some mortally; one man was shot dead on the spot. A great number were taken prisoners, twenty-five of whom were brought to Fisherton gaol the same night.

The promptitude and energy of the local authorities, in addition to the conciliatory spirit manifested by the resident gentry and clergy in ameliorating the wretched condition of the generality of labourers, have materially conduced to allay the disturbances; though it must be admitted, that the same hostility to tithes, high rents, and machinery, continues unabated.

On Dec. 8th, a circular was addressed by the Home Secretary to the magistracy of the various counties, dictating a discontinuance of all yielding to threat or intimidation, either as respects the recommendation of an uniform rate of wages or the non-employment of the thrashing-machines, which, it is justly observed, are as much under the protection of the law as any other machinery. . . .

Several Special Commissions have been issued by Government, for the purpose of trying the individuals who have been arrested for incendiary acts and the destruction of thrashing machines, in the different southern counties. The Special Sessions of East Kent, held at Canterbury, concluded on the 26th Nov., when the following sentences were passed on the machine breakers:- Tho. Read, 25, for breaking a machine on the premises of Sarah Matson, at Wingham, to be transported for life; John Stannard, 26; W. Siddons *alias* William Davison, 25; Thos. Strood, 19; H. Andrews, do; and H. Halkes, 22; several of whom had been convicted on two or three indictments, for machine-breaking, were each sentenced to transportation for seven years. Several others were sentenced to various terms of imprisonment from twelve months to one, according to the nature or degree of their offences. . . .

We have received accounts of various fires in different parts of the country, which have doubtless been caused by incendiaries. The extensive conflagration which took place at the village of Coton, near Cambridge, is thus described in a communication from a resident member of the University, who was on the spot at the time. 'We had all separated to our rooms, after chapel, without the slightest anticipation of any alarm, when suddenly there was raised in the quadrangle a shout of fire. I ran out, and beheld the whole western sky clothed in the most awful glare. Our back gates were instantly thrown open, and a general rush took place in the direction of the light. In a lane at the back of the colleges, the different streams from all the colleges mingled, when a most extraordinary scene of confusion ensued. After traversing ploughed fields, hedges, and ditches, lighted by the increasing conflagration, we reached the spot, and found nearly 600 persons already arrived, and the gownsmen working like horses. There were then burning 25 ricks of corn, hay, and clover, with barns and outhouses of different descriptions, connected with the largest farm in the neighbourhood. The stable, by the exertions of the University students, (who worked the engines, climbed the roof with their gowns, and poured buckets of water, handed to them from below, on the embers, as they fell on the thatch), was saved, and by that means the dwelling-house also, which was completely *surrounded with fire*. Some of the gownsmen stood up to their waists in water, filling the buckets, others entirely pulled down an outbuilding, which it was thought might endanger the house. Some continued to work during the whole night. This terrible event produced of course a great state of excitement in the place, increased by some letters, threatening an attack on the University, on the following market day. No sooner was this report promulgated, than every man began to provide himself with arms; 1500 bludgeons were sold in two days. There was not a pistol to be had in the town, and all the conversation was about companies and captains, and every other hostile preparation. Besides this, 1000 special constables were sworn in from the townspeople. The day, however, went off without disturbance.'

Charles Greville's Journal, *21 November*

. . . The new Government will find plenty to occupy their most serious thoughts and employ their best talents. The state of the country is dreadful; every post brings fresh accounts of conflagrations, destruction of machinery, association of labourers, and compulsory rise of wages. Cobbett and Carlile write and harangue to inflame the minds of the people, who are already set in motion and excited by all the events which have happened abroad. Distress is certainly not the cause of these commotions, for the people have patiently supported far greater privations than they had been exposed to before these riots, and the country was generally in an improving state.

The Duke of Richmond went down to Sussex and had a battle with a mob of 200 labourers, whom he beat with fifty of his own farmers and tenants, harangued them, and sent them away in good humour. He is, however, very popular. In Hants the disturbances have been dreadful. There was an assemblage of 1,000 or 1,500 men, a part of whom went towards Baring's house (the Grange) after destroying threshing machines and other agricultural implements; they were met by Bingham Baring, who attempted to address them, when a fellow (who had been employed at a guinea a week by his father up to four days before) knocked him down with an iron bar and nearly killed him. They have no troops in that part of the country, and there is a depot of arms at Winchester. . . .

Mrs Arbuthnot's[1] Journal, 29 November

. . . The country is in a terrible state, thanks to all the people who have been lauding the French revolution up to the skies and dinning in the ears of the people that, if they choose to rise, nothing can resist them. The consequence has been that all over the country the peasantry, who in many parts do really suffer under great privations, have been worked upon by incendiaries & agitators & have burnt rickyards & broke machines to a great extent; in many parts there have been violent conflicts between the mob & the constables &, wherever they have been stoutly resisted, they have shewn great cowardice, & nothing is necessary but promptitude & energy in the magistrates to put an end to it. The Duke went down into Hampshire the day after he quitted the office & had a meeting at Winchester; they have taken above 200 prisoners & a special commission is going down to try them. In Kent some of the rioters have been transported, & I hope these measures will put a stop to the outrages.

We have been threatened with having a mob coming to break our machine, & Mr Arbuthnot went off yesterday with Chas, two servants, four soldiers & arms & ammunition in abundance & if he arrives in time, will, I have no doubt, effectually defend his property. Our own labourers & our part of the country are perfectly satisfied & it is quite intolerable that vagabonds are to come from a distance (the mob we were threatened with came from Huntingdonshire) to burn & destroy all they approach. Our things were safe yesterday & I hope he will therefore be in time. . . .

Mary Frampton's[2] Journal

. . . The unpopularity of the Duke of Wellington was extreme, so as to render his life in danger from the pressure of the crowd, stones being thrown at him, &c. The new police, established the preceding year to replace the old and useless watchmen, were set upon by the mob, aided by all the thieves and pickpockets in London, and many were much hurt. All these circumstances occasioned serious alarms, lest there should be danger, not to the King's person, but of bloodshed amongst the crowd, if he and the Queen went, as was intended, to dine at the city feast on the 9th of November. The dinner was consequently given up, which caused intense disappointment to the city, where the outcry was immense, and the Ministry much blamed, others, however, saying that the precaution was necessary. A large body of troops was moved to the capital, and the good conduct and forbearance of the new police was such that, although much of the popular cry was directed against them, the order they maintained was so universally acknowledged that these very attacks established them as the most useful defence of the metropolis. As the month advanced it became very gloomy, more than its proverbial horrors ever displayed before. An universal spirit of dissatisfaction pervaded every class. The plentiful harvest, good potato crop, remarkably fine autumn weather without frost to impede the labours of husbandry, appeared to have no effect in lessening the murmurs of discontent; whilst incendiaries, whose steps could not be traced, spread rapidly from Kent – where the setting fire to corn-stacks, barns, &c., first began in the month of October – to the adjacent counties. These incendiarisms were in general unconnected with the riotous mobs which nearly at the same time assembled, breaking and destroying machinery used in husbandry, paper-mills, &c., and also surrounding gentlemens' houses, extorting money and demanding an increase of wages. These mobs rose very unexpectedly, and spread with alarming rapidity.

On the 22nd of November the first risings took place in this county. Mr Portman immediately promised to raise the wages of his labourers, and by doing this without concert with other gentlemen, greatly increased their difficulties. My brother, Frampton, harangued the people at Bere Regis, and argued with them on the impropriety of their conduct, refusing to concede to their demands whilst asked with menaces. This spirited conduct caused him to be very unpopular, and threats were issued against him and his house.

November 28th. – Notice was received of an intended rising of the people at the adjacent villages of Winfrith, Wool, and Lulworth – the latter six miles off – which took place on the 30th. My brother, Mr Frampton, was joined very early on that morning by a large body of farmers, &c., from his immediate neighbourhood, as well as some from a distance, all special constables, amounting to upwards of 150, armed only with a short staff, the pattern for which had been sent by order of Government to equip what was called the Constabulary force. The numbers increased as they rode on towards Winfrith, where the clergyman was unpopular, and his premises supposed to be in danger. The mob, urged on from behind hedges, &c., by a number of women and children, advanced rather respectfully, and with their hats in their hands, to demand increase of wages, but would not listen to the request that they would disperse. The Riot Act was read. They still urged forwards, and came close up to Mr Frampton's horse; he then collared one man, but in giving him in charge he slipped from his captors by leaving his smock-frock in their hands. Another mob from Lulworth were said to be advancing, and as the first mob seemed to have dispersed, Mr F. was going, almost alone, to speak to them when he was cautioned to beware, as the others had retreated only to advance again with more effect in the rear. The whole body of the constabulary then advanced with Mr Frampton, and, after an ineffectual parley, charged them, when three men were taken, and were conveyed by my brother and his son Henry, and a part of the constabulary force, to Dorchester, and committed to gaol. I was at Moreton that day with Lady Harriot F. Our gentlemen returned about six o'clock; they described the mob they had encountered as being in general very fine-looking young men, and particularly well-dressed, as if they had put on their best clothes for the occasion. That night James Shirley and I sat up at Moreton. Many threats had been reported to us as having been made in the course of the day, and, during the dispersion of the mob, against Mr Frampton's person and property, but no fire took place on his estate. There was one announced to us watchers, but not being very near Moreton, we had nothing to do but to lament over the wickedness which occasioned that and so many other incendiary fires. It subsequently proved to have been a hayrick at the village of Preston, between Moreton and Weymouth, which had been set on fire; but though one man was strongly suspected, no legal proof against him could be procured.

There were no soldiers in the county, all having been sent towards London, Wiltshire, and Hampshire, where the riots raged first; and in the beginning of December hourly accounts of the assembling of mobs, for the purpose of breaking thrashing-machines, increase of wages, and extorting money, &c., arrived. Under these circumstances, it was judged necessary to block up all the lower windows of Moreton House, as well as all the doors, with the exception of that to the offices. The Mayor of Dorchester ordered the staff of Dorset Militia to go to Moreton to defend the house, nightly patrols were established, and Mr Frampton or his son sat up alternately for many nights. My sister-in-law also took her turn in sitting up with another woman, Lady Harriot saying that they were more watchful than men. Spies were certainly sent from the rioters to see the state of the house, &c.

London being comparatively, indeed really, tranquil, and large bodies of troops in the adjacent counties, my niece, Louisa F., was sent by her father and mother to accompany her cousins, the Lady Strangeways, to London, to be out of the way of alarm.

Charles Greville's Journal

November 25th. – The accounts from the country on the 23rd were so bad that a Cabinet sat all the morning, and concerted a proclamation offering large rewards for the discovery of offenders, rioters, or burners. Half the Cabinet walked to St. James's, where I went with the draft proclamation in my pocket, and we held a Council in the King's room to approve it. . . .

November 28th. – The Duke of Wellington, who as soon as he was out of office repaired to Hants, and exerted himself as Lord-Lieutenant to suppress the disorders, returned yesterday, having done much good, and communicated largely with the Secretary of State. The Government are full of compliments and respects to him, and the Chancellor wrote him a letter entreating he would name any gentleman to be added to the Special Commission which was going down to the county over which he 'so happily presided'. He named three.

There has been nothing new within these three days, but the alarm is still very great, and the general agitation which pervades men's minds unlike what I have ever seen. Reform, economy, echoed backwards and forwards, the doubts, the hopes and the fears of those who have anything to lose, the uncertainty of everybody's future condition, the immense interests at stake, the magnitude and imminence of the danger, all contribute to produce a nervous excitement, which extends to all classes – to almost every individual. . . .

December 1st. – The last two or three days have produced no remarkable outrages, and though the state of the country is still dreadful, it is rather better on the whole than it was; but London is like the capital of a country desolated by cruel war or foreign invasion, and we are always looking for reports of battles, burnings, and other disorders. Wherever there has been anything like fighting, the mob has always been beaten, and has shown the greatest cowardice. They do not, however, seem to have been actuated by a very ferocious spirit; and considering the disorders of the times, it is remarkable that they have not been more violent and rapacious. Lord Craven, who is just of age, with three or four more young Lords, his friends, defeated and dispersed them in Hampshire. They broke into the Duke of Beaufort's house at Heythrop, but he and his sons got them out without mischief, and afterwards took some of them. On Monday as the field which had been out with the King's hounds were returning to town, they were summoned to assist in quelling a riot at Woburn, which they did; the gentlemen charged and broke the people, and took some of them, and fortunately some troops came up to secure the prisoners. The alarm, however, still continues, and a feverish anxiety about the future universally prevails, for no man can foresee what course events will take, nor how his own individual circumstances may be affected by them.

Georgiana Ellis to Caroline Lascelles, 1 December

. . . We had Lord Clifden, Mr Sharpe, Sir Robert Wilson, Mr Byng and Mr Wall at dinner. The latter was in despair at Lord Clifden's notions of Reform. It is quite extraordinary how this question is gaining every day; it is scarcely any longer a question whether you are for, or against, reform, but what sort of reform you prefer. Poor Mr Wall is altogether in a most desponding state since his expedition into Hampshire. He talks as if it was all over with the landed property. His view is by far the most melancholy I have yet heard; is not from fear of the disturbances, which in that part of the country are nearly put down, but from the belief of the disaffected state of feeling among the lower orders. There is certainly one very strong case; that of Sir Thomas Baring, who for 20 years has devoted his time and his fortune for the good of the poor in his neighbourhood, and who has found them all going against him. I hear Ld. Melbourne is, however, in much better spirits and thinks all going on better. I am delighted to hear of Ld Harewood having approved of Ld Grey. It appears to me of all governments the one he ought to support, as it is influenced by no other feeling but that of doing what is best for the country. . . .

Notes

1. The Arbuthnots had a farm at Woodford in Northamptonshire.
2. Mary Frampton (1773–1846) was the daughter of a prosperous country gentleman in Dorset. She was unmarried.

CHAPTER FOUR

The Battle Joined, March 1831

During the winter of 1830–1, as the government took measures to deal with the disorders in the agricultural counties, a sub-committee of four of its members held meetings to draw up a plan to put into effect its major policy of parliamentary reform. The country expected Grey to propose a scheme that would put an end to violent agitation by satisfying reasonable demands for change while maintaining the substance of the constitution, and Grey was determined to go no further along the road towards democracy than was necessary. As the sub-committee put it in its report, submitted to the Prime Minister in mid-January, their aim was, 'to effect such a permanent settlement of this great and important question, as will no longer render its agitation subservient to the designs of the factious and discontented – but by its wise and comprehensive provisions inspire all classes of the community with a conviction that their rights and privileges are at length duly served and consolidated'. Their measure would not 'merely be considered a bare redemption of their pledges to their sovereign and the country' in order 'to evade or stifle the general demand for a complete alteration of the existing system'. It was, as Grey had instructed them at the outset of their deliberations, to be a settlement of the question for the foreseeable future, which would put an end to the agitation for reform and allow the government to give its attention to other matters.

The reform plan was based on proposals put forward by Lord John Russell, with modifications in detail suggested by his three colleagues on the sub-committee, Lord Duncannon, Lord Durham, and Sir James Graham. The basis of the scheme was that, while representation was not to be merely 'numerical' – in proportion to population – the right of electing members should bear some relation to the size and importance of different areas, and that individuals should qualify for the exercise of the franchise in the constituencies in some way that was broadly uniform over the country and related to some kind of propertied status. In the event, it was proposed that all existing parliamentary boroughs with populations of less than 2,000 would lose their individual representations, being absorbed into their counties, and those with populations between 2,000 and 4,000 would be restricted to a single member rather than two, as was the norm before 1832. This freed 168 seats (a quarter of the House of Commons) for redistribution, partly to the major (but not all) manufacturing and commercial towns, and partly to the larger counties. The aim was to preserve a balance between 'interests' – agriculture, trade, industry, and the professions – by selecting places that could be regarded as represenative of the major economic and social elements in the nation, and, above all, to ensure the sanctity of property as the basis of political rights. Individuals would qualify for the right to vote in either a county or borough by the ownership or occupation of property – landed property in the counties, or household property of a certain value (houses rated to local taxes at a value of £10 per annum or above) in the boroughs. Other sections of the proposed scheme dealt with the methods of holding elections and were designed to reduce corruption and expense in electioneering.

The details of the scheme were kept a close secret during the spring, while Grey secured the king's approval and the government prepared for the parliamentary battle. Resistance was certain, not only from members who represented seats due to be abolished, most of whom, whether intentionally on the government's part or not, sat on the Tory benches, but also from men of wealth and property in many counties who disliked the erosion of the political power of their class by the admission of urban and middle-class interests to the charmed circle.

Essentially, however, the opposition was to come from the Tories on party political grounds: the reform battle was fought between the two opposed parties who together now formed almost the whole House of Commons. In this battle the government was at a disadvantage. The Whigs had beaten Wellington and taken office not because they were the majority party in the Commons, and certainly not because they had been chosen by the country, but because Wellington's support had split and public opinion had deserted him. The disclosure by Lord John Russell on 1 March 1831 of the details of the Reform Bill would reunite much of the old Tory party in opposition to it. The descriptions by various observers of the debate on the second reading make it plain that the majority of members were astonished by the scope of the Bill, to the extent of derision in some cases. The second reading was eventually carried, but only by a single vote, to scenes of excitement hardly paralleled in the chamber since the time of Charles I and Cromwell. When the committee stage, of examination of the Bill clause by clause, began, it was clear that the opposition would be strong enough to amend it almost out of existence. The battle for the second reading was won, but the war had hardly started; and the war was to be fought not only in the Houses of Parliament but on the streets of the kingdom.

The Times *cautions against universal suffrage, 9 December 1830*

We are haters of all monopolies, and among others of a monopoly of the elective franchise, by such a (miscalled) reform of Parliament as would introduce into the constituent body, by means of universal suffrage, the mass, and with the mass the dregs, of the existing population.

That species of reform of Parliament would be a monopoly of power, and, consequently, of everything to the appropriation of which unreflecting power could be rendered applicable, by the numerical majority of the people – in other words, by the mob.

We are staunch friends to a broad and fundamental reform; and if enemies to universal suffrage, or to the establishment of a low qualification for the great mass of electors, it is because such a principle would be, in effect, a *narrowing* of the representative system, by the virtual exclusion of all influence derived from property, and an absolute surrender of the commonwealth to a single class – a class moved to frequent warfare against every other, by the extremes of destitution and desperation acting upon incurable ignorance, prejudice, and distrust. . . .

As for the admission of *mere* 'numbers' into the state, not qualified or distinguished by any further claims, the constitution of England exhibits no such tendency. The electors for towns where apprenticeship forms a qualification, have a stake in the country through that skill and that evidence of honest and reputable conduct, both of which constitute their property, and without which they could not have obtained the freedom of their respective trades, or been permitted to earn the wages of art and industry. Even the potwalloper, the lowest, meanest, and most worthless of electors, has a constructive interest in the borough for which he votes, through the period during which he has been connected with it, and does not countenance the principle of naked numbers.

If a class of electors be desired, less open to corruption than a large majority of those who now possess that privilege, the standard of qualification ought to be raised, not reduced . . . property, no matter under what name, must be admitted. . . .

The Times *calls for reform, 1 March 1831*[1]

We are arrived now at the grand crisis for which the country has been so long preparing itself – a reform, or a dissolution within a few days or hours! – a reform, or the immediate reappearance of those who resist the just demands of the nation before their constituents! But it is impossible that the reform should not be admitted: for, if rejected, it is obvious that all connexion whatever between the men from thenceforth assembling themselves in Westminster, and the people of England, is at an end! They are unknown to us! They have no kind of connexion or sympathy with us! They cannot be Englishmen! They cannot have heard of what is passing in the country: – the millions of voices calling for reform – the millions of signatures attached to petitions with the same demand, and sent down to that house! All England wants reform: who are they to oppose it? . . .

Hobhouse's Recollections

At last came the great day – Tuesday, March 1. I went to the House at twelve o'clock, and found all the benches, high and low, on all sides, patched with names. With much difficulty I got a vacant space on the fourth bench, nearly behind the Speaker, almost amongst the Opposition and the Anti-Reformers.

Lord John Russell began his speech at six o'clock. Never shall I forget the astonishment of my neighbours as he developed his plan. Indeed, all the House seemed perfectly astounded; and when he read the long list of the boroughs to be either wholly or partially disfranchised there was a sort of wild ironical laughter, mixed with expressions of delight from the ex-Ministers, who seemed to think themselves sure of recovering their places again immediately. Our own friends were not so well pleased. Baring Wall, turning to me, said, 'They are mad! they are mad!' and others made use of similar exclamations, – all but Sir Robert Peel; he looked serious and angry, as if he had discovered that the Ministers, by the boldness of their measure, had secured the support of the country. Lord John seemed rather to play with the fears of his audience; and, after detailing some clauses which seemed to complete the scheme, smiled and paused, and said, 'More yet.' This 'more,' so well as I recollect, was

Schedule B, which took away one member from some boroughs that returned two previously. When Lord John sat down, we of the Mountain cheered long and loud; although there was hardly one of us that believed such a scheme could, by any possibility, become the law of the land.

Sir John Sebright seconded the motion in a short speech. Poor Sir Robert Inglis made a long Anti-Reform speech, and called the Ministerial plan a revolution. Lord Althorp spoke out manfully; Lord L. Gower treated us to some 'prose run mad' for an hour or two; and Hume adjourned the debate at half-past twelve o'clock. We all huddled away, not knowing what to think – the Anti-Reformers chuckling with delight at what they supposed was a suicidal project, and the friends of Ministers in a sort of wonderment. I recollect that a very good man, Mr John Smith, a brother of Lord Carrington's, caused much amusement by saying that Russell's speech made his hair stand on end.

Sir Robert Peel, with his usual quickness and sagacity, took care at the end of the debate to ask for an explanation of the £10 qualification for householders in towns, which certainly partook more of disfranchisement than any other reform, and was calculated to make the whole plan unpopular.

Burdett and I agreed there was very little chance of the measure being carried, and that a revolution would be the consequence. We thought our Westminster friends would oppose the £10 qualification clause; but we were wrong, for we found all our supporters delighted with the Bill.

Le Marchant's Memoir of John Charles Viscount Althorp, *March 1831*

By this time the excitement in the country had greatly increased, as appeared in the extension of the Political Unions and the violence of their proceedings; but among the higher classes this feeling showed itself so faintly that the Ministers were suspected of doubting its existence, and fears were entertained that their Bill would not be strong enough to satisfy the country. Even on the very day that it was to be brought forward, these apprehensions prevailed at Brooks's, where the general despondency was alarmingly ominous of an approaching failure. The secret was so well kept that although Lord Lowther, a very adroit intriguer, had contrived almost at the last hour to learn some of the leading provisions of the Bill, when he mentioned them no one believed him.

This memorable debate, unexampled in modern times both for its length and importance, began at a few minutes before five o'clock. There was a large concourse of people both in Palace Yard and the approaches to the House, and they respectfully fell back to make a passage for Lord Althorp, who had walked from Downing Street with Lord John Russell. As far as I could judge (being in the crowd), the general interest was in Lord Althorp, Lord John being then so little known that few persons noticed him. I followed them into the House, where they at once took their seats next to each other in the middle of the Ministerial Bench. Lord John looked very pale and subdued. He cast occasional glances at the immense array of the Opposition in front of him, and then spoke to Lord Althorp, as if commenting on the disagreeable contrast it presented to its appearance when the Whigs sat there. He had indeed abundant reason to feel that he was about to address an audience of which a large majority were, either from principle or prejudice, his decided opponents. Lord Althorp was calm and thoughtful as usual.

Lord John Russell spoke for rather more than two hours. His speech, though highly praised by the country at the time, has been censured by Radical writers as not equal to the occasion. It appeared to me admirably fitted to obtain what he aimed at – the success of his measure. His constitutional argument, on which he perhaps dwelt too long, called forth a slight degree of languor and impatience, and yet it served to increase the effect of his announcement of Schedule A. This came with an absolutely electrifying shock. Loud cheers burst at once from the Ministerial Benches, but these were answered by equally loud shouts of derision from the Opposition, and this conflict lasted through the whole enumeration of the boroughs in the two Schedules. It was difficult to say on which side the voices predominated.

It was for the peroration of the speech that Lord John Russell had reserved his best powers, and a more noble and convincing plea for Reform had not been heard for many years within the walls of the House. It stamped him as a statesman, an orator, and a patriot, but it fell on ears deafened by the effect of the Schedules, and he sat down *in a profound silence.*

It was the opinion of Lord Brougham that if Sir Robert Peel had now risen and said that he would not discuss so revolutionary and so mad a proposal, and had insisted on immediately dividing the House, the Bill would have been rejected: and in the general confusion at the moment this might certainly have happened; but then a far more revolutionary Bill would have been the inevitable result. But Sir Robert was in no frame of mind to risk so hazardous an experiment. Lord Althorp, who watched him as he sat opposite, told me that during the introductory part of Lord John's speech his features expressed only astonishment and contempt, but as the plan was unfolded he looked more and more cast down, and at last he held his hands before his face as if unable to control his emotions. He foresaw the imminent danger of his party. Not so his followers, who were clamorous and confident. Sir Henry Hardinge went so far as to say to those around him, that as soon as the plan had been ventilated, public indignation would drive the Ministers from office.

After a few remarks from Sir John Sebright, to second Lord John's motion, Sir Robert Inglis rose in reply, and this was a signal for a general rush of members into the lobby, where they collected in groups to discuss the Bill. In my attempts to learn the opinions of the Liberal members, I found none of mark unreservedly in its favour. There seemed to be a general impression, extending to those who had called for increased energy on the part of the Ministers, that they had now gone too far. Some of those most advanced in their views confessed that they were quite bewildered, and must have time to make up their minds. Mr Hudson

Gurney, a very clever and original thinker, who could not be counted on beforehand by either party, surprised me by saying, that he had no doubt. 'I consider it,' he observed, 'an honour to the age for any Administration to have proposed this Bill, not that there is a chance of these men carrying it. Only Oliver Cromwell could do that. But if the Bill should pass, I ask where are the men to govern the country?'

The interest of the night was certainly transferred from the House to the lobby, and the latter was in proportion far the most crowded. Neither Sir Robert Inglis, who consumed a couple of hours in delivering an elaborate pamphlet against all Reform, nor Mr Horace Twiss, who declaimed in the same spirit against the principles of the Bill, were men to obtain attention in such a crisis. A partial restoration of order took place, when Lord Althorp, seeing the general desire for an adjournment, rose to close the debate. His speech was not of a character to find a place in history, for independently of his defects as a speaker, he had ceded to Lord John all the opportunity of distinction to be gained that night by a member of the Government. He spoke only because his position as Leader, and his personal weight both in the House and the country, made an early expression of opinion from him on this momentous question absolutely necessary. He said what he really felt with his usual plainness, and at the same time so earnestly, and so resolutely, as to fix the minds of many timid, honest reformers who generally sought his pilotage on the political waters. Much that fell from him was repeated in more eloquent language by some of the speakers later in the debate, with great effect. It was at a crisis like this that his intervention was of importance, and some of the ablest members of the House, such as Mr Brougham at one time and Sir Francis Baring at another, have told me that his decision and the correctness of his judgment alone fully entitled him to the authority which he exercised over his followers, so that he was in fact one of the safest of leaders. The House adjourned before midnight.

Undecided as the reception of the Ministerial measure was in appearance, I believe the Ministers were satisfied. They had gained a commanding position. They had struck the members of the Opposition with terror, and this was pretty sure to be followed by the support of their own party. They might fail in the first onset, but they saw victory before them at a distance. Reform indeed was virtually carried.

Princess Lieven to her brother Alexander, 2 March

I was absolutely stupefied when I learnt the extent of the Reform Bill. The most absolute secrecy had been maintained on the subject until the last moment. It is said that the House was quite taken by surprise; the Whigs are astonished, the Radicals delighted, the Tories indignant. This was the first impression of Lord John Russell's speech, who was entrusted with explaining the Government Bill. I saw Lord Grey when the first report of what had passed in the House was brought to him. He believed – or said he did – that it was a great triumph, & repeated with self-satisfaction, 'I have kept my word with the nation.' It was impossible for me not to express my regret. The Ultra-Tories, under the presidency of the Duke of Cumberland, have just been called together. The Duke went with the determination not to consent to any amendment, except such a one as would absolutely destroy the Bill. I do not yet know what line the late Ministers propose to adopt; I shall only hear this evening, too late to tell you in this letter. Everybody is lost in amazement and dumbfoundered, the friends of the Ministry included – but it is admitted that the Bill bears examination – contains many useful things. I have had neither the time nor the courage to read it. Its leading features have scared me completely: 168 members are unseated, sixty boroughs disfranchised, eight more members allotted to London & proportionately to the large towns and counties, the total number of members reduced by sixty or more, & septennial Parliaments maintained – the two last being the only good features of the Bill. . . .

Thomas Creevey to Miss Ord[2]

3 March

Well, what think you of our Reform plan? My raptures with it encrease every hour, & my astonishment at its boldness. It was all very well for an historian like Thomas Creevey to lay down the law, as he did in his pamphlet, that all these rotten nomination boroughs were modern usurpations, or that the *communities* of all substantial boroughs were by law the real electors; but here is a little fellow not weighing above 8 stone – Lord John Russell by name – who, without talking of law or anything else, creates in fact a perfectly new House of Commons, quite in conformity to the original formation of that body. . . . What a coup it is! It is its *boldness* that makes its success so certain. . . . A week or ten days must elapse before the Bill is printed and ready for a 2nd reading; by that time the country will be in a flame from one end to the other in favour of the measure. . . . I saw the stately Buckingham going down to the Lords just now. I wonder how he likes the boroughs of Buckingham and St. Mawe's being bowled out. He would never have been a duke without them, and can there be a better reason for their destruction?

5 March

. . . Well, our Reform rises in publick affection every instant. . . . To think of dear Aldborough and Orford, both belonging to Lord Hertford, and purchased at a great price, being clearly bowled out, without a word of with your leave or by your leave. Aye, and not only that such proprietors are destitute of all means of self-defence, but they are treated as *criminals* by the whole country for making any fight on their own behalf. . . . At Crocky's, even the boroughmongers admitted that their representative, Croker, had made a damned rum figure. Poor Billy Holmes! Both he and Croker will have but a slender chance of being M.P.'s again under our restored constitution. In short, Bessy, there is no end to the fun and confusion that this measure scatters far and near into by far the most corrupt, insolent, shameless, profligate gang that this country contains. They are all dead men by this Bill, never to rise again, and their occupation is dead also. . . . To be sure the poor devils who stick to the wreck will have mobbing enough from out of doors before the business is over. . . .

Charles Greville's Journal, *7 March*

Nothing talked of, thought of, dreamt of, but Reform. Every creature one meets asks, What is said now? How will it go? What is the last news? What do *you* think? and so it is from morning till night, in the streets, in the clubs, and in private houses. Yesterday morning met Hobhouse; told him how well I heard he had spoken, and asked him what he thought of Peel's speech; he said it was brilliant, imposing, but not much in it. Everybody cries up (more than usual) the speeches on their own side, and despises those on the other, which is peculiarly absurd, because the speaking has been very good, and there is so much to be said on both sides that the speech of an adversary may be applauded without any admission of his being in the right. Hobhouse told me he had at first been afraid that his constituents would disapprove this measure, as so many of them would be disfranchised, but that they had behaved nobly and were quite content and ready to make any sacrifices for such an object. I asked him if he thought it would be carried; he said he did not like to think it would not, for he was desirous of keeping what he had, and he was persuaded he should lose it if the Bill was rejected. I said it was an unlucky dilemma when one-half of the world thought like him and the other half were equally convinced that if it be carried they shall lose everything.

The Times, *7 March*

We receive daily communications from correspondents, calling for a general illumination: some recommending it this evening, when Their Majesties go to Covent-garden Theatre; others, on the evening subsequent to leave being obtained to bring the Reform Bill into Parliament. We see no impropriety, still less any cause of alarm, in this public expression of rational joy at a measure which we look upon as certain to produce a great moral, as well as political, regeneration among the people of Great Britain. There are, however, some persons who are frightened out of their wits at any demonstration of popular feeling; and there are also mischievous wretches who would gladly avail themselves of any little disturbance incidental to the most harmless assemblages of the multitude, in order to convert it into an argument of the danger of a general tumult. To take away all pretence of alarm from one party, or mischief-making from the other, it may, perhaps, be expedient to delay the illumination till after the second reading of the Bill. This time cannot be very distant. . . .

Hobhouse's Recollections

9 March
Lord John Russell closed the debate by an excellent speech at exactly twenty-five minutes to one o'clock on the morning of March 10; the Speaker put the question, that 'LEAVE BE GIVEN TO BRING IN A BILL TO AMEND THE REPRESENTATION OF THE PEOPLE IN ENGLAND AND WALES'. The friends of the Bill gave a great shout for the 'AYES', and only two 'NOES' were heard. 'And I have lived to witness this – *the greatest event, for good or for evil, that has occurred since the Revolution of 1688; in some respects greater even than that.*' This was the entry I made in my diary. The Irish and Scottish Reform Bills were also brought in after short debates, which lasted till three in the morning.

10 March
The feeling in the country is all but unanimous in favour of Reform. Never before were the Whigs bold, nor the Reformers prudent. The King answered the City Address yesterday in most decisive terms. . . .

Charles Greville's Journal

11 March
It is curious to see the change of opinion as to the passing of this Bill. The other day nobody would hear of the possibility of it, now everybody is beginning to think it will be carried. The tactics of the Opposition have been very bad, for they ought to have come to a division immediately, when I think Government would have been beaten, but it was pretty certain that if they gave time to the country to declare itself the meetings and addresses would fix the wavering and decide the doubtful. There certainly never was anything like the unanimity which pervades the country on the subject, and though I do not think they will break out into rebellion if it is lost, it is impossible not to see that the feeling for it (kept alive as it will be by every sort of excitement) must prevail, and that if this particular Bill is not carried some other must very like it, and which, if it is much short of this, will only leave a peg to hang fresh discussions upon. The Government is desperate and sees no chance of safety but from their success in the measure, but I have my doubts whether they will render themselves immortal by it. It is quite impossible to guess at its effects at present upon the House of Commons in the first return which may be made under it, but if a vast difference is not made, and if it shall still leave to property and personal influence any great extent of power, the Tory party, which is sure to be revived, will in all probability be too strong for the Reforming Whigs. The Duke of Wellington expected to gain strength by passing the Catholic question, whereas he was ruined by it.

15 March
It is universally believed that this Bill will pass, except by some of the

ultras against it, or by the fools. But what next? That nobody can tell, though to see the exultation of the Government none would imagine they saw their way clearly to a result of wonderful good. I have little doubt that it will be read a second time, and be a good deal battled in Committee. Although they are determined to carry it through the Committee with a high hand, and not to suffer any alterations, probably some sort of compromise in matters of inferior moment will be made. But when it comes into operation how disappointed everybody will be, and first of all the people; their imaginations are raised to the highest pitch, but they will open their eyes very wide when they find no sort of advantage accruing to them, when they are deprived of much of the expense and more of the excitement of elections, and see a House of Commons constructed after their own hearts, which will probably be an assembly in all respects inferior to the present. Then they will not be satisfied, and as it will be impossible to go back, there will be plenty of agitators who will preach that we have not gone far enough; and if a Reformed Parliament does not do all that popular clamour shall demand, it will be treated with very little ceremony. If, however, it be true that the tendency of this Bill will be to throw power into the hands of the landed interest, we shall have a great Tory party, which will be selfish, bigoted, and ignorant, and a Radical party, while the Whig party, who will have carried the measure, will sink into insignificance. Such present themselves to my mind as possible alternatives, as far as it is practicable to take anything like a view of probabilities in the chaos and confusion that mighty alterations like these produce.

I dined with Lord Grey on Sunday; they are all in high spirits. . . .

17 March
The Reform Bill is just printed, and already are the various objections raised against different parts of it, sufficient to show that it will be pulled to pieces in Committee. Both parties confident of success on the second reading, but the country *will* have it; there is a determination on the subject, and a unanimity perfectly marvellous, and no demonstration of the unfitness of any of its parts will be of any avail; some of its details may be corrected and amended, but substantially it must pass pretty much as it is. . . .

Hobhouse's Recollections

21 March
Lord J. Russell moved the second reading of his Reform Bill in the House this evening, and the debate went on till past two in the morning.

22 March
The debate on the Reform Bill was resumed. The rumours were rather more in favour of our success than they had previously been. Hume and Holmes compared lists, and brought them almost to an equality. But some

votes were still doubtful. Acland, as usual, spoke at two, amidst loud roars of Question! Russell replied, and Peel looked as if he was going to speak, but we prepared to give him a reception on both sides had he done so unfair a thing.

The gallery was cleared, and at exactly three minutes to three in the morning the Speaker put the question on Sir Richard Vyvyan's amendment, 'That the Bill be read a second time this day six months.' The shouts of Ayes and of Noes were tremendous.

For some time we in the House appeared the strongest, but by degrees our ranks were thinned, and we thought we were beaten. Lord Maitland ran up to me and told me the numbers in the lobby were 309, but shortly after he returned, pale and breathless, and said, 'You have it.' . . . And so we had, for there were only 301 against us; and when the Tellers approached the table, and ours were on the right, we burst into tumults of delight, clapping hands, waving hats, and shouting lustily with all our might. I was in raptures – not foolish, I hope; for I said and thought that the vote had saved the country. I crossed the House, and shook hands with Althorp, Graham, and Russell, all of whom seemed delighted with the measure. The defeated party put a good face on the matter, and, as William Peel said to me, bore their beating with good humour.

23 March
Passed the day in giving and receiving congratulations.

Thomas Creevey to Miss Ord, Brooks's, 23 March

Majority for our Bill

1

Devilish near, was it not? Yesterday I was of opinion that to *lose* the question by one would have been the best thing for us; but I don't think so now. . . . Everybody likes winning, and it keeps people's spirits up. . . . I went into Crocky's after the opera, being determined to wait the result, and there were quantities of people in the same mind, friends and foes, but we were all as amicable and merry as we could be. A little before five [a.m.] our minds were relieved by the arrival of members without end – friends and foes – and I must say (with the exception of young Jack Shelley) the same good temper and fun were visible on both sides.

26 March
. . . I wish you could have been with me when I entered our Premier's drawing-room last night. I was rather early, and he was standing alone with his back to a fire – the best dressed, the handsomest, and apparently the happiest man in all his royal master's dominions. . . . Lady Grey was as proud of my lord's speech as she ought to be, and *she*, too, looked as handsome and happy as ever she could be. . . .

T.B. Macaulay to Thomas Flower Ellis, 30 March

Dear Ellis,

I have little news for you, except what you will learn from the papers as well as from me. It is clear that the Reform Bill must pass, either in this or in another Parliament. The majority of one does not appear to me, as it does to you, by any means inauspicious. We should perhaps have had a better plea for a dissolution if the majority had been the other way. But surely a dissolution under such circumstances would have been a most alarming thing. If there should be a dissolution now there will not be that ferocity in the public mind which there would have been if the House of Commons had refused to entertain the Bill at all. – I confess that, till we had a majority, I was half inclined to tremble at the storm which we had raised. At present I think that we are absolutely certain of victory, and of victory without commotion.

Such a scene as the division of last Tuesday I never saw, and never expect to see again. If I should live fifty years the impression of it will be as fresh and sharp in my mind as if it had just taken place. It was like seeing Caesar stabbed in the Senate House, or seeing Oliver taking the mace from the table, a sight to be seen only once and never to be forgotten. The crowd overflowed the House in every part. When the Strangers were cleared out and the doors locked we had six hundred and eight members present, more by fifty five than ever were at a division before. The Ayes and Noes were like two vollies of cannon from opposite sides of a field of battle. When the opposition went out into the lobby, – an operation by the bye which took up twenty minutes or more, – we spread ourselves over the benches on both sides of the House. For there were many of us who had not been able to find a seat during the evening. When the doors were shut we began to speculate on our numbers. Everybody was desponding. 'We have lost it. We are only two hundred and eighty at most. I do not think we are two hundred and fifty. They are three hundred. Alderman Thompson has counted them. He says they are two hundred and ninety nine.' This was the talk on our benches. I wonder that men who have been long in parliament do not acquire a better coup d'oeil for numbers. The House when only the Ayes were in it looked to me a very fair house, – much fuller than it generally is even on debates of considerable interest. I had no hope however of three hundred. As the tellers passed along our lowest row on the left hand side the interest was insupportable, – two hundred and ninety one: – two hundred and ninety two: – we were all standing up and stretching forward, telling with the tellers. At three hundred there was a short cry of joy, at three hundred and two another – suppressed however in a moment. For we did not yet know what the hostile force might be. We knew however that we could not be severely beaten. The doors were thrown open and in they came. Each of them as he entered brought some different report of their numbers. It must have been impossible, as you may conceive, in the lobby, crowded as they must have been, to form any exact estimate. First we heard that they were three hundred and three – then the number rose to three hundred and ten, then went down to three hundred and seven. Alexander Baring told me that he had counted and that they were three hundred and four. We were all breathless with anxiety, when Charles Wood who stood near the door jumped on a bench and cried out. 'They are only three hundred and one.' We set up a shout that you might have heard to Charing Cross – waving our hats – stamping against the floor and clapping our hands. The tellers scarcely got through the crowd: – for the house was thronged up to the table, and all the floor was fluctuating with heads like the pit of a theatre. But you might have heard a pin drop as Duncannon read the numbers. Then again the shouts broke out – and many of us shed tears – I could scarcely refrain. And the jaw of Peel fell; and the face of Twiss was as the face of a damned soul; and Herries looked like Judas taking his neck-cloth off for the last operation. We shook hands and clapped each other on the back, and went out laughing, crying, and huzzaing into the lobby. And no sooner were the outer doors opened than another shout answered that within the house. All the passages and the stairs into the waiting rooms were thronged by people who had waited till four in the morning to know the issue. We passed through a narrow lane between two thick masses of them; and all the way down they were shouting and waving their hats; till we got into the open air. I called a cabriolet – and the first thing the driver asked was, 'Is the Bill carried? – 'Yes, by one.' 'Thank God for it, Sir.' And away I rode to Grey's (*sic*) Inn – and so ended a scene which will probably never be equalled till the reformed Parliament wants reforming; and that I hope will not be till the days of our grandchildren. . . .

Mrs Arbuthnot's Journal, *29 March*

The Govt carried their second reading of the Bill by 1, in the fullest House ever remembered. We had 301 and they had 302. I never remember any question that excited such intense interest. The Govt were struggling for their places & the Opposition for existence, for those who oppose the Bill feel that, if it is carried, the whole frame of society in England will be destroyed. This feeling is shared by many who support the Bill, who do it from cowardice, fear of their constituents and a belief that, in the Committee, the Bill will be either so modified as to become inoffensive or that it will be thrown out there. Our hope now is to throw it out in the Committee; but the misfortune is that the Ministers have made the most unsparing use of the King's name and, having obtained his sanction to the Bill, it becomes next to impossible to oppose *all* reform, which, after all, is the only *principle* to go upon. I do not mean that it is not possible to suggest a thousand trifling improvements for diminishing expense at elections, preventing bribery &, when it is detected, transferring the franchise to large towns; but the moment the *principle* is admitted that you have *a right* to take the franchise from one town which has committed no offence & transfer it to another, I cannot see upon what *principle* you can ever stop while there is a town unrepresented with 100 inhabitants more than one with representatives. Sir Robert Peel feels very strongly that the

King, having so far sanctioned the measure as to allow it to be introduced, has rendered it very difficult for any minister to prevent all change in the representation.

Our difficulties in opposing reform are, however, all aggravated by Peel's character. If the Conservative Party felt they could rely upon him, they wd fight the battle; but they cannot. They know he will yield some points on reform, & the consequence is they all have their own crochets, all want to gain popularity with their constituents by advocating at once that which, from Peel's nature, they feel will be yielded sooner or later.

On the Govt side the party are united, zealous, active & using every engine to carry this mischievous Bill, the members of Govt because they think it will save their places, the radicals because they see clearly that, this Bill carried, the game will be in their hands.

On our side we are at *sixes & sevens*. The Duke, stout & determined against reform, says he cannot lead & direct the party because he is not in the House of Commons, where the battle must be fought; Peel, saying he does not wish to return to office while he enjoys the discomfiture of the Ministers in all their measures, treats all the Tory party with arrogance & insolence, affects to consider himself as an *individual* & not the leader of the party, & has hitherto positively rejected all the advances of the ultra-Tories who now desire nothing better than to make up past differences & unite cordially with us. . . .

The Duke repeated his opinion last night in the H. of Lords that the House of Commons deserved well of the country instead of all the abuse now heaped upon it, & his conviction that the Govt cd not be carried on in a House constructed after the fashion of this Bill. Some people think him indiscreet in asserting again his strong feeling against reform; & he told me he was aware that this opinion shut the door to his return to office, but he said it was his opinion, his firm & honest conviction, that he never wd come into office to propose a reform founded upon principles of spoliation & violence which, in its consequences, must be destructive to the country, and that he thought it more frank and manly to state his opinion openly in his place & not allow it to be supposed he had changed or wd change.

I don't know whether it is *politic*, but I am sure such sentiments are worthy of his frank and noble character. I have never seen him so disturbed and put out as by this reform question. He thinks, if carried, that a revolution is inevitable, that a reformed House of Commons will immediately attack the tithes & the West Indies, that all property will become insecure, that the Funds will fall, the revenue not be paid & that, when once we get into financial difficulties, our whole frame will be dislocated & destroyed! And for what is all this risk to be run? To keep an incapable Ministry in their place, many of whom are frightened at their own bugbear. Brougham's account of his colleagues is that Ld Grey is in his dotage led by Ld Durham, that Lord Althorpe is a blockhead, Sir James Graham a puppy and, as to the Duke of Richmond, he has not brains enough to fill the smallest thimble that ever fitted the smallest lady's finger. He has made divers attempts to enter into communication with the

Duke in order to secure the Woolsack, come what may; but the Duke has paid no attention to his advances.

Lord Grey affects to think his Bill the most perfect thing that ever was & the salvation of the country. They don't, however, talk quite so boldly about the King as they did. We have good reason to believe they sounded him as to a dissolution when they got their majority of *one* & found he wd not do it, and they have since complained bitterly of the people in his Household who are opposed to their interests; that is to say, who don't wish to see the Crown pulled off the King's head.

The Duke of Wellington to Mr Gleig,[3] 11 April

MY DEAR SIR,

It is curious enough that I who have been the greatest reformer on earth should be held up as an enemy to *all* reform. This assertion is neither more nor less than one of the lying cries of to-day. If by Reform is meant Parliamentary Reform, or a change in the mode or system of representation, what I have said is that I never heard of a plan that was safe or practicable that would give satisfaction, and that while I was in office I should oppose myself to reform in Parliament. This was in answer to Lord Grey on the first day of the session.

I am still of the same opinion. I think that Parliament has done its duty. But constituted as Parliament is – having in it as a member every man noted in the country for his fortune, his talents, his science, his industry, or his influence; the first men of all professions, in all branches of trade and manufacture connected with our colonies and settlements abroad; and representing, as it does, all the states of the United Kingdom – the government of the country is still a difficult task. To conduct the government will be impossible, if by Reform the House of Commons should be brought to a greater degree under popular influence. Yet let those who wish for Reform reflect for a moment where we should all stand if we were to lose for a day the protection of government. That is the ground on which I stand in respect to the question in general of Reform in Parliament. I have more experience in the government of this country than any man now alive, as well as in foreign countries. I have no borough influence to lose; and I hate the whole concern too much to think of endeavouring to gain any. Ask the gentlemen of the Cinque Ports whether I have ever troubled any of them. On the other hand, I know that I should be very popular in the country if I would pretend to alter my opinion, and alter my course; and I know that I exclude myself from political power by persevering in the course which I have taken.

But nothing shall induce me to utter a word, either in public or private, that I don't believe to be true. If it is God's will that this great country should be destroyed, and that mankind should be deprived of this last asylum of peace and happiness, be it so. But as long as I can raise my voice, I will do so against the infatuated madness of the day.

In respect to details, it has always appeared to me that the first step upon this subject was the most important. We talk of unrepresented great towns. There are towns which have all the benefit of being governed by the system of the British Constitution without the evil of elections. Look at Scotland! Does Scotland suffer because it has not the benefit of riotous elections? I think that Reform in Scotland would be, and I am certain would be thought, a grievance by many in that country. I can answer for there being many respectable men in Manchester, and I believe there are some in Birmingham and Leeds, who are adverse to a change.

But how is this change to be made? Either by adding to the number of the representatives in Parliament from England! or by disfranchising what are called the rotten boroughs! The first cannot be done without a departure from the basis, and a breach of the Acts, of Union – and mind! a serious departure and breach of those Acts, inasmuch as the limits of the extension could not be less than from fifteen to twenty towns.

The last would be, in my opinion, a violation of the first and most important principle of the Constitution, for no valid reason, and upon no ground whatever, excepting a popular cry and an apprehension of the consequences of resisting it. But this is not all. I confess that I see in thirty members for rotten boroughs, thirty men, I don't care of what party, who would preserve the state of property as it is: who would maintain by their votes the Church of England, its possessions, its churches and universities; all our great institutions and corporations; the union with Scotland and Ireland; the dominion of the country over its foreign colonies and possessions; the national honour abroad, and its good faith with the King's subjects at home. I see men at the back of the government to enable it to protect individuals and their property against the injustices of the times, which would sacrifice all rights and all property to a description of plunder called general convenience and utility. I think that it is the presence of this description of men in Parliament, with the country gentlemen, and the great merchants, bankers and manufacturers, which constitutes the great difference between the House of Commons and those assemblies abroad called Chambers of Deputies. It is by means of the representatives of the close corporations that the great proprietors of the country participate in political power. I don't think that we could spare thirty or forty of these representatives, or with advantage exchange them for thirty or forty members elected for the great towns by any new system.

I am certain that the country would be injured by depriving men of great property of political power; besides the injury done to it by exposing the House of Commons to a greater degree of popular influence.

You will observe that I have now considered only the smallest of all reforms – a reform which would satisfy nobody; yet it cannot be adopted without a serious departure from principle (principle in the maintenance of which the smallest as well as the greatest of us is interested), and by incurring all the risks of these misfortunes which all wish to avoid.

I tell you that we must not risk our great institutions and large properties, personal as well as real. If we do, there is not a man of this generation so young, so old, so rich, so poor, so bold, so timid, as that he will not feel the consequences of this rashness. This opinion is founded, not on reasoning only, but on experience; and I shall never cease to declare it.

Believe me, &c.,
WELLINGTON

Alexander Somerville's[4] Autobiography of a Working Man

The majority of *one* for the second reading of the Reform Bill was celebrated throughout the kingdom by a mixture of illumination and darkness, lighted windows and broken glass, bell-ringing and prohibitions of bell-ringing – by rejoicing and rioting, strange to behold, and still more strange to think upon. There abounded in all extravagance the liberal joy that the reformers were triumphant, associated with the most resolute tyranny to compel the anti-reformers to put on signs of rejoicing when they felt no joy. In Edinburgh the Lord Provost, head of the city magistracy, and the other members of the anti-reform corporation, were solicited by the inhabitants to proclaim a general illumination. They refused: but seeing, as evening came on, the general preparations for it, and the threatening aspect of the street mobs, they assented that the town should be lighted, and proclaimed accordingly. To many householders, who were willing to be guided by them, and by them only, the published authority came too late. They knew nothing of it, and remained in darkness. Others who were deep in political grief at hearing of the majority of *one* against rotten boroughs, resolved to keep their houses in gloom, and to sit within and mourn. Unfortunately for those of darkness and sorrow who lived in Herriot Row and Abercromby Place (spacious lines of first-class houses fronting to the Macadamized road-way newly laid with loose stones, and to the Queen-street Gardens, with their iron railing), the Lord Provost, an unwilling man to light his windows, lived there. Stones were thrown and his glass was broken. The sound of crashing glass and the facility of getting missiles to throw whetted the appetite of the ten thousand headed mob – a little taste of window breaking to it, being not unlike a little taste of worrying to the wild beast – and so to the work of destruction the mob rolled like a sea, and roared like storms meeting upon rocks and seas. It proclaimed itself the enemy of anti-reformers and of glass. Like tides about Cape Horn where contrary winds meet tides, as banded constables meet mobs to beat them back, this human sea, storm risen, rounded the Royal Circus, Moray-place, Queen-street, Charlotte and St. Andrew's Squares, through the long streets which join the eastern and western boundaries of the New Town together; and with wrath where it flowed and wreck where it ebbed, bore upon its surf the sea-weed that knew not whither it was carried.

I was a piece of its sea-weed. I was now for the first time tossed upon the waves of a popular commotion. At the beginning there was a pleasing sense of newness. Even the first sound of breaking glass was not unmusical. Combativeness and distructiveness were charmed. But, as dash went the stones, smash fell the glass, and crash came the window frames – slash, smash, crash, from nine o'clock to near midnight, reflection arose and asked seriously and severely what this meant; was it reform? was it popular liberty?

Many thousands of others who were there must have asked themselves the same questions; yet still the cry was, 'Up with reform light, down with tory darkness!' And unilluminated tories, masters and servants, male and female, aged and youthful; even the infant tories in their mothers' arms came to the windows, holding candles, all they had in their houses, twinkling feebly on the face of night, to let the mob see that toryism was smiling, was joyful; happy, very happy, at the advent of reform, and the majority of *one*. But those signs of truce came too late. Reform would hold no truce until anti-reform windows were broken.

The Tory newspapers proclaimed this outrage to be the first fruits of reform. And when, a few days after, at the election, another mob threatened to throw the Lord Provost over the North Bridge, and pursued him with a purpose of mischief until he took refuge in a shop in Leith-street, from which he was carried away, so the story went, barrelled up in a hogshead; they promised the country in general, and the city of Edinburgh in particular, a continuance and extension of such riots at all future elections. The reform newspapers were content to say that the riots reflected no discredit on reformers, the rioters were only 'the *blackguards* of the town.'

In subsequent years I have often reflected upon this word 'blackguard', as applied to political glass-breakers. Whatever unsolved problems we might suggest in social and political philosophy about the term, I believe that there is now one problem solved by experience, which was hidden in futurity then – namely, that the greater the number of men enfranchised, the smaller is the number of 'blackguards'.

Notes

1. Lord John Russell was to introduce the Reform Bill in the House of Commons on 1 March.
2. Thomas Creevey (1768–1838) the diarist, wit and Whig politician, was an admirer of Lord Grey. Miss Ord was his step-daughter.
3. The Reverend G.R. Gleig (1796–1888), Chaplain-General of the forces, served as a young man under Wellington in the Peninsula and became a close friend. He took Holy Orders in 1820 and published a biography of the duke in 1862.
4. Somerville was a labourer at a nursery garden near Edinburgh in 1831; in 1832 he enlisted as a trooper in the Scots Greys. His *Autobiography of a Working Man* was published in 1848.

CHAPTER FIVE

The People Decide, April–May 1831

On 19 April the government was defeated by eight votes on an amendment, moved by General Gascoyne, Tory member for Liverpool, declaring that the number of members to represent England and Wales should not be reduced. Ministers had proposed to do so in order to allow a larger share of representation to Scotland and Ireland. The amendment was intended to wreck one of the major features of the Bill, but it also foreshadowed the likely fate of many others. The Cabinet decided to dissolve Parliament and hold a general election to put the question before the country, confident, after the many demonstrations of support that had accompanied the second-reading debate, that the new House of Commons would reflect public opinion and give a large majority for reform.

The king, however, objected to submitting the decision to a virtual referendum of the country, since it was clear that the election would be fought almost everywhere on the issue of reform. It was virtually unprecedented at that time for general elections to be used as a means of mobilizing public opinion behind a particular measure. Ministers themselves were reluctant to endorse that principle, but there seemed to be no other way to save the Bill. William IV had to give way, but he refused at first to go to Westminster in person to dissolve Parliament, in order to show his lack of enthusiasm. However, the opposition in both Houses made the mistake of trying to prevent the dissolution by moving addresses to the throne against it. The king was more enraged at this attempted interference with his prerogative rights than he was with his ministers for compelling him, and there followed the famous episode in which he hastily robed and prepared himself to rush to the House of Lords, as he said in a hackney carriage if the state coach was not ready, and entered the chamber amid unprecedented scenes of disorder, described by Charles Greville and by the Lord Chancellor, Brougham. His arrival put an end to the spectacle and Parliament was dissolved, to the joy of reformers everywhere who promptly, but mistakenly, assumed that the incident demonstrated the king's enthusiastic support for reform. *The Times* even proposed a public subscription to put up a monument to him to commemorate the occasion, and ingenious manufacturers set to work to produce souvenirs. In London crowds turned out to pursue the popular pastime of breaking the windows of houses belonging to opponents of reform, especially the Duke of Wellington's. The untimely death of the duchess, whose body lay in the house that very evening, did not prevent them. Small wonder that the duke foretold revolution.

The elections turned out even more favourably for the government than was expected. The counties elected supporters of reform almost to a man, showing that even under the old system the most independent of members, as the 'knights of the shire' were reputed to be, could not resist the tide of public opinion. 'England is gone perfectly mad', Mrs Arbuthnot declared. Only in the greater number of 'pocket' boroughs did the Tory opposition keep a foothold, but the government's majority in the Commons was now so overwhelming that the second Reform Bill, differing slightly in detail from the first, passed through all its stages there with no real difficulty despite Tory resistance. The opposition was demoralized, Peel almost abandoning his followers to fight a hopeless battle without him. On 7 September the Bill passed its final stages in the Commons.

The war was only beginning. The question on everyone's lips was 'What will the Lords do now?' It took the next nine months for the question to be answered.

Charles Greville's Journal, 24 April

At Newmarket all last week, and returned to town last night to hear from those who saw them the extraordinary scenes in both Houses of Parliament (the day before) which closed the eventful week. The Reform battle began again on Monday last. The night before I went out of town I met Duncannon, and walked with him up Regent Street, when he told me that he did not believe the Ministers would be beaten, but if they were they should certainly dissolve instantly; that *he* should have liked to dissolve long ago, but they owed it to their friends not to have recourse to a dissolution if they could help it. On Monday General Gascoyne moved that the Committee should be instructed not to reduce the members of the House of Commons, and this was carried after two nights' debate by eight. The dissolution was then decided upon. Meanwhile Lord Wharncliffe gave notice of a motion to address the King not to dissolve Parliament, and this was to have come on on Friday. On Thursday the Ministers were again beaten in the House of Commons on a question of adjournment, and on Friday morning they got the King to go down and prorogue Parliament in person the same day. This *coup d'état* was so sudden that nobody was aware of it till within two or three hours of the time, and many not at all. They told him that the cream-coloured horses could not be got ready, when he said, 'Then I will go with anybody else's horses.' Somebody went off in a carriage to the Tower to fetch the Crown, and they collected such attendants as they could find to go with his Majesty. The Houses met at one or two o'clock. In the House of Commons Sir R Vyvyan made a furious speech, attacking the Government on every point, and (excited as he was) it was very well done. The Ministers made no reply, but Sir Francis Burdett and Tennyson endeavoured to interrupt with calls to order, and when the Speaker decided that Vyvyan was not out of order Tennyson disputed his opinion, which enraged the Speaker, and soon after called up Peel, for whom he was resolved to procure a hearing. The scene then resembled that which took place on Lord North's resignation in 1782, for Althorp (I think) moved that Burdett should be heard, and the Speaker said that 'Peel was in possession of the House to speak on that motion.' He made a very violent speech, attacking the Government for their incompetence, folly, and recklessness, and treated them with the utmost asperity and contempt. In the midst of his speech the guns announced the arrival of the King, and at each explosion the Government gave a loud cheer, and Peel was still speaking in the midst of every sort of noise and tumult when the Usher of the Black Rod knocked at the door to summon the Commons to the House of Peers. There the proceedings were if possible still more violent and outrageous; those who were present tell me it resembled nothing but what we read of the 'Serment du Jeu de Paume,' and the whole scene was as much like the preparatory days of a revolution as can well be imagined. Wharncliffe was to have moved an address to the Crown against dissolving Parliament, and this motion the Ministers were resolved should not come on, but he contrived to bring it on so far as to get it put upon the Journals. The Duke of Richmond endeavoured to prevent any speaking by raising points of order, and moving that the Lords should take their regular places (in separate ranks), which, however, is impossible at a royal sitting, because the cross benches are removed; this put Lord Londonderry in such a fury that he rose, roared, gesticulated, held up his whip, and four or five Lords held him down by the tail of his coat to prevent his flying on somebody. Lord Lyndhurst was equally furious, and some sharp words passed which were not distinctly heard. In the midst of all the din Lord Mansfield rose and obtained a hearing. Wharncliffe said to him, 'For God's sake, Mansfield, take care what you are about, and don't disgrace us more in the state we are in.' 'Don't be afraid,' he said; 'I will say nothing that will alarm you;' and accordingly he pronounced a trimming philippic on the Government, which, delivered as it was in an imposing manner, attired in his robes, and with the greatest energy and excitation, was prodigiously effective. While he was still speaking the King arrived, but he did not desist even while his Majesty was entering the House of Lords, nor till he approached the throne; and while the King was ascending the steps the hoarse voice of Lord Londonderry was heard crying 'Hear, hear, hear!' The King from the robing-room heard the noise, and asked what it all meant. The conduct of the Chancellor was most extraordinary, skipping in and out of the House and making most extraordinary speeches. In the midst of the uproar he went out of the House, when Lord Shaftesbury was moved into the chair. In the middle of the debate Brougham again came in and said 'it was most extraordinary that the King's undoubted right to dissolve Parliament should be questioned at a moment when the House of Commons had taken the unprecedented course of stopping the supplies,' and having so said (which was a lie) he flounced out of the House to receive the King on his arrival. The King ought not properly to have worn the Crown, never having been crowned; but when he was in the robing-room he said to Lord Hastings, 'Lord Hastings, I wear the Crown; where is it?' It was brought to him, and when Lord Hastings was going to put it on his head he said, 'Nobody shall put the Crown on my head but myself.' He put it on, and then turned to Lord Grey and said, 'Now, my Lord, the coronation is over.' George Villiers said that in his life he never saw such a scene, and as he looked at the King upon the throne with the Crown loose upon his head, and the tall, grim figure of Lord Grey close beside him with the sword of state in his hand, it was as if the King had got his executioner by his side, and the whole picture looked strikingly typical of his and our future destinies.

Such has been the termination of this Parliament and of the first act of the new Ministerial drama; there never was a Government ousted with more ignominy than the last, nor a Ministry that came in with higher pretensions, greater professions, and better prospects than the present. . . .

Hobhouse's Recollections, *22 April*

Parliament was dissolved in the *Gazette* of April 23. The news from the country was very encouraging, and the greatest enthusiasm prevailed in the metropolis. A Westminster meeting took place in Covent Garden, to address His Majesty and thank him for dissolving the Parliament. It was one of the largest meetings I ever saw assembled in that place, where I had seen so many crowds. Sir Francis Burdett and myself were received as in days of yore. Our speeches were rather peppery, it must be confessed, but they suited the taste of the day.

The next day I attended a meeting at the Crown and Anchor, for establishing a Fund to assist Reform candidates. I proposed the plan agreed upon; we formed a Committee on the spot. Edward Ellice gave me the list of certain influential members of Brooks's Club who had put down their names for sums amounting already to £15,000, a good deal of which had been disposed of in procuring seats for some good men and true. This appeared somewhat in contradiction to the principles on which we put forward our political pretensions; but we were obliged to fight our opponents with their own weapons, no other mode of warfare would have had the slightest chance of success. Subscriptions poured in by sums amounting to thousands of pounds.

May 2nd. Sir Francis Burdett and myself went in procession to Covent Garden. Our reception was very gratifying; and we ascended the hustings amidst such thunders of applause as have been seldom heard even there.

Thomas Creevey to Miss Ord, 23 April

. . . Nothing could exceed the firmness and conduct altogether of our Sovereign yesterday. I know from Lord Grey that, when the latter stated the inconvenience that might arise from proroguing by commission, but added that it was quite out of the question to ask his Majesty to prorogue in person, the King replied: – 'My lord, I'll go, if I go in a hackney coach!'

The Times *proposes a monument to William IV on the dissolution of Parliament, 28 April*

It has been suggested that some memorial of a peoples gratitude should be raised on the present occasion to the patriot King, who has referred it – so far as those abuses which it is meant to correct will suffer it to be referred – to the British nation, whether it will have a reformed or a corrupt House of Commons – a legislative body purely chosen by the people, or one nominated in part by the Peers. The money might soon be raised. What shall the memorial be? The public sees that colossal figure, at the south-east corner of Hyde-park, cast from the cannon which was won by our gallant troops in a series of continental battles. We care not whether it is well or ill devised, but the motive was a noble one. Why might not some work of art of a similar kind be erected at the north-east corner of the same Park, looking towards Oxford-street? It is as proper to record by a lasting testimony the triumphs obtained over domestic, as over our foreign foes, – the victories of our King, as of our most celebrated General. The uniformity of the Park, with respect to its ornaments, would thus be preserved. We should like to write the inscription.

The Times, *26 April*

We mentioned some time since the activity of our manufacturers in preparing a handkerchief, representing, in a very clever allegorical illustration, the friends and enemies of reform. We have since been favoured with a view of some gown pieces, made of cotton, and intended for the humbler classes, in which the head of William IV, with a crown and anchor, has been most ingeniously worked. From the skilful way in which the devices are managed, the effect is as pleasing as striking; there is not the least inelegance about it.

Benjamin Haydon's Autobiography, *28 April*

There was an illumination last night. The mob broke all the windows which had no lights. They began breaking the Duke [of Wellington]'s but when the butler came out and told them the Duchess was lying dead in the house, they stopped. There is something affecting in the conqueror of Napoleon appealing for pity to a people he had saved.

Letters from the Duke of Wellington to Mrs Arbuthnot

Stratfield Saye, 28 April
. . . I learn from John that the Mob attacked my House and broke about thirty windows. He fired two Blunderbusses in the Air from the Top of the House, and they went off. I write to desire that the Parish may be sued for the Value of the Damage done. . . .

29 April
. . . I think that my Servant John saved my House, or the Lives of many of the Mob – possibly both – by firing as he did. They certainly intended to destroy the House, and did not care one Pin for the poor Duchess being dead in the House. . . .

1 May

Matters appear to be going on as badly as possible. It may be relied upon
that we shall have a Revolution. I have never doubted the Inclination and
disposition of the lower Orders of the People. I told you years ago that the
people are rotten to the Core. You'll find that it is true. They are not
bloodthirsty, but they are desirous of Plunder. They will plunder, destroy
and annihilate all Property in the Country. The Majority of them will then
starve; and we shall witness scenes such as have never yet occurred in any
part of the World.

It is quite impossible that this Country can maintain half its people upon
any system whatever excepting that on which we are going on at present.

I told you likewise that the Upper Orders and the Gentry were not
prepared or in a state to resist the attack upon Property which would be
made. They are demoralized equally with the Lower orders, but in a
contrary Sense. The lower orders are audacious and excited by a thirst for
Plunder; the Upper Orders Timid, and excited alone by a thirst for
Popularity. Even those defeated at this moment in their objects would
walk on all fours to please the Mob and regain their Seats! . . .

Princess Lieven to Alexander, 3 May

. . . The elections in England have taken a startling turn; for the most part
they are Radical, & go infinitely beyond all that either the lovers or even
the authors of Reform could ever have anticipated. The reaction against
the Bill, which everyone imagined would spread rapidly, was suddenly cut
short by the dissolution of Parliament. Then from the moment that the
country saw that the King lent himself to the measure, & regarded it with
favour, there was no way of raising a cry against Reform. It was long
doubtful whether the King wished for Reform *à outrance*, but there is no
longer any room for doubt, & this has inspired the Liberal party with fresh
energy.

I am greatly concerned at all that has happened; & I could not forbear to
say to Lord Grey, in reply to some words of triumph of his on the
elections, that he would long for his enemies when he found himself face
to face with his new friends. Lord Grey is possessed by a demon of
incredible madness. Very few persons of weight share his illusions, &
quite a string of the Whigs themselves are taking steps to prevent the Bill
being presented again in the same shape as that of the rejected measure.
There is, too, serious alarm at the Jacobin tendency displayed in some
quarters; it is easy to rouse such a feeling, but very difficult to keep it in
check later on. Ministers want to gain popularity for themselves & for the
King; they have got it, but at the expense of England's happiness. . . .

The King has been greatly annoyed by the disturbances which marked
the illuminations for the dissolution of Parliament. The Tories refused to
illuminate – so all the windows of their houses were broken by the mob,
& they were forced to sleep in fresh air. This is a nice state of
things. . . .

Lady Lyttelton to the Hon. Mrs Pole-Carew, Hagley, 9 May

. . . Well as I say, then, all outward show is peaceful. But what a worry within! What a simmering and inch by inch wearing out of one! Now I suppose you know what is happening in your old *patria cara*. Parliament was dissolved, and a great cry arose in all parts of this country [Worcestershire] in favour of some reform candidate being proposed, and against Colonel Lygon, who has always voted against every kind and degree of reform. The cry increased and at last grew to such a pitch that the people by thousands were up in every town, on the roads, in the streets, looking out and enquiring 'who will stand?' No candidate, however, appeared. Certain squires kept meeting, writing, wishing and talking about it, but none of them would 'bell the cat.' A Mr ——, a very unpopular and questionable hop merchant, came forward, but withdrew again. One feared one thing and another another, and all the time the middle and lower ranks were growing louder and more dogged in their opinion and determination. When one morning, April 26, I went in to visit Lord L. in his dressing-room. 'I have a bold thought,' said he. 'What is it?' said I. 'I have thought of a candidate. Your brother Frederick.' So then you may imagine, perhaps, my terror, my remonstrances, my entreaties, my arguments, my sickness. All in vain. His Lordship was sure it would do – sure it would take – sure he would take the consequences – sure he did not care if anybody found fault – it was the best thing to be done. It should be done. I meantime kept life in my body by thinking that of course Fritz would refuse; that *his* head was cool, that it would come to nothing – that perhaps Lord L. would think better of it when his beard was off. Not a word of it all happened. Lord L. persevered – was off by two o'clock for Althorp – found Fritz, taking snuff over his own comfortable fireside. Fritz accepted, published his address, came here, and has been (whatever may be the final result) a candidate of most unparalleled popularity – was met by 20,000 people at Dudley, is dragged through every town, cheered by every voice, and not allowed to spend one farthing, happen what may. He stands avowedly and in earnest for this Parliament *only*, and on no ground of course but his pledge to vote for the Reform Bill. The other party are working very hard against him, and Colonel Lygon spends I don't know what. £2,000 a day *before* the poll opened! But yet we are very sanguine.

Now, don't suppose that it is a wish to see Fritz M.P. for the county, or a desire for the Reform Bill, that makes poor dear Bessy [the Hon. Mrs F. Spencer] and me so dreadfully anxious and eager. No, my dear. It is that this very daring plan will, *if it fails*, bring such a storm about us of anger and disappointment from all my family – my *unconsulted*, and prudent, and Ministerial, and very calm and measuring family! Only think of having to go to town (bad enough at any rate!) defeated, having got the *Chancellor of the Exchequer's brother* defeated, by mere hot-headedness and injudiciousness, and all the sins *most* visited by the world's anger! Oh!!! Meantime if it were not for that, it would be some fun. We read (I must not say *write*) such good squibs and verses, and we have such good accounts of Fritz's speaking, and such comical stories are happening every hour. But alas! alas! why is Hagley Hall like the Escurial? Because it is a gridiron, *I* say, and so does poor Bessy, my *fellow steak*. I must go to her now, and try to make each other worse. Lord L. is at Worcester, sitting hidden in a corner of an inn to hear news. . . .

The Duke of Wellington to Lord Melville,[1] Walmer Castle, 30 May

. . . I think that the government election under the excitement occasioned by King William's dissolution of Parliament in person, and by his Majesty's eagerness in the cause manifested by his declaration that he would go in a hackney-coach rather than not appear, has given his monarchy a shake from which it will not recover during his reign. The alteration of numbers has been double what it has been in any former general election, and the language on hustings, at election dinners, &c., shows that there is now as much of subversive opinion in Parliament as we can well stagger under.

I don't in general take a gloomy view of things; but I confess that, knowing all that I do, I cannot see what is to save Church, or property, or colonies, or union with Ireland, or eventually monarchy, if the Reform Bill passes. It will be what Mr Hume calls 'a bloodless revolution.' There will be, there can be, no resistance. But we shall be destroyed one after the other, very much in the order that I have mentioned, by due course of law.

Princess Lieven to Alexander, Richmond, 11 May

. . . There is a curious point to be noted in what is passing now in England. On the Continent the source of all Radical ideas are the schools – the universities and their students propagate republicanism; while in this country the only resistance which the proposals for Reform have met with comes from the three universities of the Empire – Oxford, Cambridge, & Dublin. The universities have unanimously elected anti-Reformers. One would say then, that here it is the most educated party which repels any so-called improvement of the method of representation. This fact has made a strong impression. The King himself, among others, has said when giving his assent to the new elections that he would regard the choice made by the universities as the touchstone of the saner portion of his subjects. . . .

Charles Greville's Journal

11 May

The elections are going on universally in favour of Reform; the great interests in the counties are everywhere broken, and old connexions dissevered. In Worcestershire Captain Spencer, who has nothing to do with the county, and was brought there by his brother-in-law, Lord Lyttelton, has beaten Lygon, backed by all the wealth of his family; the Manners have withdrawn from Leicestershire and Cambridgeshire, and Lord E Somerset from Gloucestershire; Lord Worcester too is beaten at Monmouth. Everywhere the tide is irresistible; all considerations are sacrificed to the success of the measure. At the last Essex election Colonel Tyrrell saved Western, who would have been beaten by Long Wellesley, and now Western has coalesced with Wellesley against Tyrrell, and will throw him out. In Northamptonshire Althorp had pledged himself to Cartwright not to bring forward another candidate on his side, and Milton joins him and stands. The state of excitement, doubt, and apprehension which prevails will not quickly subside, for the battle is only beginning; when the Bill is carried we must prepare for the second act.

14 May
The elections are still going for Reform. They count upon a majority of 140 in the House of Commons, but the Tories meditate resistance in the House of Lords, which it is to be hoped will be fruitless, and it is probable the Peers will trot round as they did about the Catholic question when it comes to the point.

Mrs Arbuthnot's Journal

16 May
. . . The Duke has lost heart entirely. He thinks the revolution is begun and that nothing can save us; that, in the artificial state in which England is, nothing can enable her to exist in her glory but maintaining her establishments in Church and State; that this is now impossible. The King & his Govt are, he says, leagued with the mob to overturn the existing institutions; that, in truth, the Govt are now in the hands of the mob, for he says, they will not be able to manage their new Parliament or direct the storm which they have raised, and he foresees nothing but civil war & convulsions.

8 June
. . . The elections are over and we have got about 275 staunch anti-reformers. With such a body and with the great majority of the House of Lords I am persuaded, if we only fight boldly and argue the Bill upon its merits or, rather, demerits, we shall still avoid a revolution. The Bill is in itself so preposterous, so unjust, so utterly useless to procure the objects which the Govt *say* they have, and so impossible in its details to carry into execution, that I expect it will be entirely altered & rendered quite innocent before it comes out of the committees of Lords & Commons.

The Govt have certainly acted thro'out a most wicked and unjustifiable part. They have pursued as Ministers (when their business is to uphold the King's authority and to protect his subjects) all the line of conduct which they practised when an opposition; a reckless determination to carry their own objects at every risk, & the same custom of appealing to the worst passions of the people to gain an advantage without ever considering how those passions were to [be] allayed. They brought forward their Reform Bill because, having failed in all their proposed taxes, they felt themselves becoming contemptible in the House & despised in the country. They therefore made it radical & violent and then, by means of the Press, roused the people throughout the country into a positive frenzy of desire for its success. They encouraged every species of violence, connived at, if they did not cause, an order for an illumination in London, & gave no protection to those who, because they did not choose to illuminate, had their windows broken & their property destroyed; and, by the writings in their papers persuaded the people all over the country that *the King* was most anxious for the Bill and that, if it was carried, they wd have bread & meat at half the price they now pay. To such an extent does this delusion go, that I have heard of servants who will only hire themselves for six months *because, at the end of that time, the Reform Bill will have passed.*

But England is gone perfectly mad and, in their desire to have this nonsensical Bill (whose authors don't pretend it will in reality do any thing for the People) the people overlook every other object. In Cumberland they prefer a Mr. Blamire as their Member, who is a seller of fat cattle at Liverpool and has hardly a qualification, & they throw out Ld Lowther, who will have 50,000 a year in the county, who takes the most active interest in their local concerns & is an excellent man of business. In Lancashire they threw out Mr. Wilson Patten, who they acknowledge is the best county member they ever had, & take a Mr. Heywood, a banker who knows nothing of Parliament or anything but his shop. In Essex they thro' out Col: Tyrell, an excellent, honourable man, & choose Long Wellesley, a man no gentleman speaks to & so overhead & ears in debt that he was at Calais till the election was over, & the sheriff who returned him had his hands full of writs against him. Such it has been all over the country, & all this for a Bill that has not common sense in it & that wd put us down on a par with the nonsensical constitutions of France & Spain.

Still, I feel if the Opposition are *ably led* we shall be strong enough to prevent mischief. It is rumoured the Govt will make 30 Peers to force the measure through the House of Lords. I don't believe 30 wd be enough & I can hardly think they will venture on such a proceeding. Without it, the Duke of Wellington, if he manages adroitly, will carry any measure he pleases. In the Commons we have 270 men who, we have every reason to believe, will attend with all the warmth & earnestness & regularity of men who feel that their lives & properties are at stake, & there are, besides, many others, new men & honest men who will be biassed by speeches & open to conviction as to the absurdity of many of the promises of the Bill & the dangerous tendency of admitting such a principle of spoliation. But all will depend upon *the leading* our party has, & there, I fear, is our weak point. If we had Mr. Perceval or Lord Londonderry I shd have no fears; the spirit & energy of one, the gentlemanlike mind, conciliatory manners & perfect temper of the other, wd unite, wd either of them unite, our jarring elements. But, alas! I fear we have none such among us now.

The Ultra-Tories are willing & most anxious to be entirely reunited with us; but, unhappily, both the Duke and Peel feel so bitterly the treatment they received from them while they were in office that neither, in their hearts, have forgiven it. . . .

Charles Greville's Journal, *23 June*

The King opened Parliament on Tuesday, with a greater crowd assembled to see him pass than was ever congregated before, and the House of Lords was so full of ladies that the Peers could not find places. The Speech was long, but good, and such as to preclude the possibility of an amendment. There was, however, a long discussion in each House, and the greatest bitterness and violence evinced in both – every promise of a stormy session. Lord Lansdowne said to the King, 'I am afraid, sir, you won't be able to *see* the Commons.' 'Never mind,' said he; 'they shall *hear* me, I promise you,' and accordingly he thundered forth the Speech so that not a word was lost. . . .

Hobhouse's Recollections

23 June
For the first time in my life I attended the Speaker of the House of Commons with the Address to the King. We mustered at the House in considerable numbers, 130 or 140. Our Ministers were in their livery, and looked very menial.

I thought the King looked ill. His answer, as usual, was short. He was very attentive to our address, and seemed to wish to show by his movements that he understood and approved of what he heard.

When the Speaker put the address into the King's hand, he knelt on one knee before the throne so that his head was not much above the footstool. This looked a little like Persian adoration, I thought. We all backed out of the room in a throng, the effect of which was not imposing but ridiculous. The King is a good King, the best we ever had.

24 June
This was the day fixed for the introduction of the second Reform Bill, and, although I went down earlier than usual, I found every place taken; and I heard that all the Opposition benches had been occupied since eight in the morning. Being at prayers, however, I did get a seat on the right, below the gangway, amongst the Irish Members. Lord John Russell began his speech at half-past five. He spoke two hours on introducing his new Bill, which seemed to differ very little from the old Bill. Part of his speech was, I thought, good – part of it not so happy. He did not spare the new moderate Reformers, and Peel and Chandos, with their associates, looked a little uncomfortable.

The eccentric Colonel Sibthorp, and Mr. Conolly, M.P. for Donegal, and Lord Stormont were amongst the most obstreperous of the minority. Charles Ross, as usual, was providing materials, fetching books and paper, for Peel. He looked more than usually disconcerted, when Russell mentioned that St. Germans was to be added to the schedule of boroughs to be disfranchised.

Sir Robert Peel followed Russell in a half-angry tone. He promised a division on the second reading, and spoke out most decisively against the Bill, so that, coupling this with the threatening aspect of the Lords, we all expected a most severe struggle.

Charles Greville on the progress of the second Reform Bill

June 25th. – John Russell brought in his Bill last night, in a good speech as his friends, and a dull one as his enemies, say. . . .

July 8th. – The second reading of the Reform Bill was carried at five in the morning by 136 majority, somewhat greater than the Opposition had reckoned on. Peel made a powerful speech, but not so good as either of his others on Reform. . . .

July 14th. – The effects of Peel's leaving the [Tory] party to shift for itself were exhibited the night before last. He went away (there was no reason why he should not, except that he should have stayed to *manage* the debate and keep his people in order), and the consequence was that they went on in a vexatious squabble of repeated adjournments till eight o'clock in the morning, when Government at last beat them. The Opposition gradually dwindled down to twenty-five people, . . . while the Government kept 180 together to the last; between parties so animated and so led there can be no doubt on which side will be the success. The Government were in high spirits at the result, and thought the fatigue well repaid by the display of devotion on the part of their friends and of factious obstinacy on that of their enemies. After these two nights it is impossible not to consider the Tory party as having ceased to exist for all the practical and legitimate ends of political association – that is, as far as the House of Commons is concerned, where after all the battle must be fought. There is still a rabble of Opposition, tossed about by every wind of folly and passion, . . . but for a grave, deliberative, efficient Opposition there seem to be no longer the elements, or they are so scattered and disunited that they never can come together, and the only man who might have collected, and formed, and directed them begs leave to be excused. It is a wretched state of things and can portend no good. If there had not been prognostications of ruin and destruction to the State in all times, proceeding from all parties, which the event has universally falsified, I should believe that the consummation of evil was really at hand; as it is I cannot feel that certainty of destruction that many do, though I think we are more seriously menaced than ever we were before, because the danger is of a very different description. But there is an elasticity in the institutions of this country, which may rise up for the purpose of checking these proceedings, and in the very uncertainty of what may be produced and engendered by such measures there is hope of salvation.

July 31st. – Althorp raised a terrible storm on Friday by proposing that the House should sit on Saturday. They spent six hours debating the question, which might have been occupied in the business; so that, although they did not sit yesterday, they gained nothing and made bad blood. . . . John Russell is ill, nearly done up with fatigue and exertion and the bad atmosphere he breathes for several hours every night. . . .

August 11th. – . . . Nothing remarkable in the Commons but Lord John Russell's declaration that 'this Bill would not be final if it was not found to work as well as the people desired,' which is sufficiently impudent considering that hitherto they have always pretended that it was to be final, and that it was made so comprehensive only that it might be so; this has been one of their grand arguments, and now we are never to sit down and rest, but go on changing till we get a good fit, and that for a country which will have been made so fidgetty that it won't stand still to be measured. Hardinge, whom I found at dinner at the Athenaeum yesterday, told me he was convinced that a revolution in this country was inevitable; and such is the opinion of others who support this Bill, not because they think concession will avert it, but will let it come more gradually and with less violence. I have always been convinced that the country was in no danger of revolution, and still believe that if one does come it will be from the passing of this Bill, which will introduce the principle of change and whet the appetites of those who never will be satisfied with any existing order of things; or if it follows the rejection of this Bill, which I doubt, it will be owing to the concentration of all the forces that are opposed to our present institutions, and the divisions, jealousies, rivalships, and consequent weakness of all those who ought to defend them. God knows how it will all end. . . .

Lord Althorp to his father, Earl Spencer, 26 August

I have lately been a very bad correspondent; but, since I have taken the management of the Reform Bill into my own hands, I have been so overwhelmed with Work that I have not had a moment to spare. We are going on slowly, but well, in the House of Commons. I fear, however, we have but little chance in the House of Lords, making allowance even for any number of Coronation Peers which is consistent with decency. The danger from the rejection of the Bill, and consequent dissolution of the Ministry, is great; but the relief to me will be so enormous, that my patriotism is not sufficient to induce me to look forward to it with any other feeling but that of hope. I do not indeed consider the danger to be so great as some other people do. It will undoubtedly be very difficult to govern; but the people are so accustomed to obedience to the law, that I do not apprehend any actual tumult. I keep quite well. I was knocked up a good deal last night, for I had to speak so very often, and in consequence I think I may have been in bed a quarter of an hour or so before I went to sleep; except in this instance, I fall asleep the instant I am in bed, and do not wake till I am called. . . .

Le Marchant's Memoir of Althorp, *22 September*

The next day nearly two hundred members, with Lord Althorp and Lord John Russell at their head, the latter bearing the Reform Bill in his hand, appeared at the bar of the House of Lords. A large attendance of Peers, besides an absolute throng of strangers, showed that they were expected. It was difficult to say whether Lord John delivered his message, or the Lord Chancellor communicated it, to the House with the greater solemnity of tone and manner. Hansard truly observes 'that these words of mere form and ceremony, which no one perhaps ever thought of listening to before, were on this occasion heard with breathless attention.' The evident impression made by the scene on the Tory Peers present, encouraged Ministers to think more favourably of their prospects. The Second Reading was fixed for the 22nd instant.

Out of the House, the cause of Reform now stood on the highest pinnacle of the public favour; the people regarded the Bill as safe; a general illumination to celebrate the passing of it in the Commons took place in London with the sanction of the Lord Mayor, and no public event in my day, since the battle of Waterloo, has called forth such warm and general expressions of delight. Unfortunately, in these rejoicings the populace forgot the respect due to the hero of Waterloo. His windows, and those of some of his political friends, were broken, much to the regret of the Ministers. Among the higher classes, both in London and the Provinces, there was of course no lack of dinners and after-dinner speeches. The banquet given by the Reform members, at the Thatched House, on the 26th, to Lord Althorp and Lord John Russell, probably far excelled all the other entertainments of a similar character. It was attended by almost every supporter of the Bill in the House, Sir Francis Burdett officiating as Chairman, in which capacity he was almost unrivalled. When Lord Althorp entered the room, he was almost oppressed by the congratulations and thanks of the company, as if all of them were under personal obligations to him; and the praise he afterwards received from the Chair seemed to find an echo in every heart. He wrote to his father that even at Northampton he had never met with such a welcome. His short speech in reply was so vehemently cheered that I am tempted to insert it here: –

I have never been ambitious of power, or of high degree, but I have been, and am still, ambitious of that popularity which is the true result of an honest and consistent discharge of public duty. With this ambition, you will judge what my feelings are on the present occasion, when I am honoured by such a mark of distinction from gentlemen who have been selected from the body of my fellow-countrymen as the known and avowed supporters of those measures upon which – it is vain to conceal the fact – the happiness, the prosperity, and the future welfare of the country depend. I hope I am not vain when I say, that I do feel proud, in the highest degree, of such a proof of your approbation. I hope and trust I have done my best. I am sure I have endeavoured to do so with regard to the great measure of Reform; but if that measure has at least to a great extent succeeded, how has that happy result been attained? It has been attained by your assistance and by the support of the people of England; and I should be wanting in justice if I did not say, that such a result could not have been attained except by the most extraordinary and unparalleled exertion on your part, by the steady attendance of the gentlemen I have now the honour of addressing, during a long and tedious sitting, throughout the whole of which we were compelled to present to our enemies such a front as proved to them, that, though they might protract the struggle, they never could hope to gain the slightest advantage in the contest.

The evening passed off with great spirit. 'God save the King' was of course enthusiastically received, and the whole of the company joined in the chorus –

Confound their politics,
Frustrate their knavish tricks.

The King, I have no doubt, was highly pleased with the account; and it may here be mentioned that pains were taken that he should be made fully acquainted with any circumstances likely to strengthen his interest in Reform.

These manifestations of the feelings of the country were misunderstood by the Peers. A large majority of them, whilst admitting the general excitement, attributed it to the inflammatory arts of the Ministry, assisted by the commercial distress at home and political disturbances abroad, with the removal of which they confidently expected popular opinion would return to its former channels. Parliamentary Reform had few cordial supporters even among the Whig Peers. Lord Carnarvon, a violent Whig, had always been opposed to it, and so was Lord Grenville. Independently of party spirit, which in the Lords had more of personal feeling than in the Commons, the whole body of the Tory Peers had an inherent and honest aversion to any great constitutional changes. Unlike the Anti-Reformers in the House of Commons, they were in a very decided majority; and, conscious of their strength, to yield against their own convictions to what they deemed the revolutionary policy of the Commons, appeared to them a mean betrayal of their legislative functions.

Unfortunately the Duke of Wellington, so wise in most respects, was slow in discovering the signs of the times; and it is not surprising that, under such a leader, still possessing almost unbounded influence, the largest section of the Peerage was predetermined to reject the Bill.

The Duke of Wellington to Lord Cowley,[2] *London, 15 July*

MY DEAR HENRY,

Having heard it doubted whether you would be in England at the period at which the Reform Bill will come up to the House of Lords, I write you one word upon the subject. The bill is now in the Committee in the House of Commons. It was brought to that stage by a considerable majority for such a bill; and its provisions are carried by one not much diminished in numbers.

It is true that the progress of the Committee is but slow, and I think it probable that the bill will not get through the House of Commons in the month of July. But we must expect it in the House of Lords early in August, and the second reading, upon which the House will have to determine, shortly afterwards.

I don't know whether you have considered the subject, or have made up your mind upon the course which you will pursue upon it.

It is not denied that the object of the bill is to overturn every existing interest and influence in the country, and to establish something else instead, of the working of which we may judge, not alone by what we see in France and other countries, but by what we see in those places in this country in which the system now to be generally established throughout the country has long existed, such as Westminster, Southwark, Preston, &c. The King's ministers in the House of Lords have never been able to state by what influence they expected to carry on the King's business in Parliament, in the reformed Parliament; and I don't believe that there is a man in England who does not think that this Reform must lead to the total extinction of the power and of the property of this country. Some, that is to say nine-tenths of all the proprietors whether of real or personal property, the members of the learned professions, the ecclesiastical, political, commercial and banking establishments, look with apprehension and dread at the consequences. Others, that is to say the mob, the Radicals, the Dissenters from the Church of all religious persuasions, hail the measure as the commencement of a new era of destruction and plunder. The ministers and their adherents in both Houses of Parliament alone deny its consequences. But they do so only in public discussion. In private many of those who vote and will vote for the measure lament its consequences; some even I know who are members of the Cabinet. You will say that it is extraordinary that such a measure should be carried under such circumstances. Carried I hope it will not be. I think that the House of Lords will be true to itself, and will enable us yet to save the country.

I conclude that you read the newspapers, and I will advert only generally to the arguments on this question. Nobody denies the existence of the anomalies and abuses in the details of the existing system of representation, and everybody admits that Parliament, as now constituted, has deserved well of the country, and that we have here a government which has made us the richest and most powerful state in Europe, has enabled us to overcome the greatest difficulties that any country ever had to encounter, and, if men could know when they were happy, has made us the happiest people on earth.

But we are told that the people are dissatisfied with the system of representation and that it must be changed, or we shall have a revolution by force.

Now it is one of the curious circumstances attending this country, and shows in the strongest manner the power of Parliament as now constituted, that however frequent the changes, convulsions, and revolutions in this country, they have always been made by Parliament. For instance, the Reformation and all its conformations? Parliament. The Commonwealth? Parliament. The Restoration? Parliament. The Revolution? Parliament. The succession of the House of Hanover? Parliament. I don't fear a revolution by force. I know that the government and the law are too strong for any combination of force by the people. We have daily examples of the defeat of such combinations. At all events, I know that this Reform must bring with it ruin to all our establishments, institutions, fortunes, and power; and if we are to fall, I prefer to fall in defence of the constitution and institutions as now established than by the lingering operation of a modern revolutionary system to be established in this country by the Reform Bill.

I should be sorry that you were absent from the House of Lords when the House will discuss this bill; and I therefore earnestly urge you to commence your journey for your return, as soon as possible after you will receive this letter, so as to be here as early as possible in August.

Believe me, &c.,
WELLINGTON

Notes

1. Robert Saunders Dundas (1771–1851), 2nd Viscount Melville, a Tory politician.
2. Henry Wellesley (1773–1847), 1st Baron Cowley, was Wellington's youngest brother. He was ambassador to Vienna in 1831.

CHAPTER SIX

Crisis in the Lords, September 1831–April 1832

After the second Reform Bill had passed through the House of Commons in the autumn of 1831, the House of Lords became the centre of attention for the next six months. The Duke of Wellington was confident that the government would not get the Bill through the Upper House without a substantial creation of additional peerages to swamp the opposition, and he felt that the king's dislike of such a step and what he thought was the cooling of popular enthusiasm would play into the hands of the Tories. Macaulay, however, feared that defeat in the Lords would set off revolution and urged that the ministers must not retreat. Even Charles Greville who had deep misgivings about reform thought that it must be granted in some shape. The leading opposition peers met at Apsley House to discuss their tactics and, despite a drunken scene in which Lords Eldon and Kenyon and the Duke of Cumberland disgraced themselves, they agreed Wellington's proposal to oppose the principle of reform on the second reading in the hope of substantial amendments at the committee stage. Wellington was less optimistic in private, and the recurrence of attacks on Apsley House showed that the hero of Waterloo was still the target of popular anger.

The soldier in him was revived by the prospect of battle, and he used every resource to muster his troops for the second reading debate. The Howard sisters followed the debate closely, and Harriet herself attended one of the five evenings which it occupied. The opposition's victory by an unexpected majority of forty-one at seven o'clock in the morning on the sixth day threw the country into consternation. It was clear that if the Bill was to pass without serious amendment the government would have to create at least sixty peers. Attention was particularly drawn, by *The Times* and other newspapers, to the votes of the bishops which had practically determined the outcome. Urged on by the popular press and by radical orators, anger turned against those who were held responsible for thwarting the people's wishes. At Derby, Nottingham and Bristol violent riots resulted in widespread destruction and several deaths, and on 5 November several of the more unpopular bishops, including those of Exeter and Worcester, were burnt in effigy in place of Guy Fawkes. The *Poor Man's Guardian* published a vivid account of one such event at Huddersfield which was accompanied by violent radical speeches. London was defended by strong forces of troops and the new Metropolitan Police, whose dispositions were advised by the Duke of Wellington. The duke also wrote to the king to express alarm at the activities of the popular Political Unions (headed by middle-class reformers and radicals like Thomas Attwood, the Birmingham banker) and in particular at the supposed threat that they were preparing to arm themselves. Even in the normally tranquil county of Dorset, Mary Frampton and her friends witnessed rioting and disturbances, spreading from the county by-election which returned an anti-reformer, Lord Ashley, against the Whig candidate, William Ponsonby, by a majority of 36 in a poll of 3,658. Her relatives in the north Midlands also sent her graphic accounts of the rioting in Derbyshire and Nottinghamshire. It seemed as though the revolution foretold by Wellington was about to break out, while, as J.W. Croker observed, the only way to avert it seemed to be to pass a reform bill which would itself be 'a revolution gradually accomplished *by due form of law*'. The outbreak in Sunderland of what was to become a fearsome and widespread epidemic of cholera at this very moment completed the picture of approaching doom. At the turn of the year the Duke of Rutland was fortifying Belvoir Castle and arming and training his servants. If ever nineteenth-century Britain came close to revolution, it was during that winter.

There followed an attempt, led by a Yorkshire peer Lord Wharncliffe and a few other 'waverers' from the opposition side, to find a compromise solution that would allow a moderated reform bill to pass by agreement between the government and the opposition. It stood little chance: Grey and the Cabinet felt themselves bound by their pledges to the public and by the overwhelming result of the recent general election to stick to 'the whole Bill, and nothing but the Bill', and Wharncliffe failed to deliver any substantial support for a compromise from the other side.

The winter months were taken up in discussions among the Whigs and in the press about the extent to which new peers must be made. Grey was as reluctant as anyone on either side to force the king against his wishes or to destroy the powers of the House of Lords by such means, and was plagued by divisions in his Cabinet as to whether, and on what scale, new peerages must be resorted to. In the end, a retreat by some of the bishops and others under the pressure of fear or persuasion secured the passage of the Bill by nine votes on 14 April. It was not, however, the end.

T.B. Macaulay to Hannah Macaulay, 13 September

My love,

I am in high spirits at the thought of soon seeing you all in London and of being again one of a family – and of a family which I love so much. It is well that one has something to love in private life. For the aspect of public affairs is very menacing – fearful, I think, beyond what people in general imagine. Three weeks however will probably settle the whole, and bring to an issue the question, Reform or Revolution. One or the other I am certain that we must and shall have. I assure you that the violence of the people, the bigotry of the Lords, and the stupidity and weakness of the ministers, alarm me so much that even my rest is disturbed by vexation and uneasy forebodings – not for myself; for I may gain and cannot lose – but for this noble country which seems likely to be ruined without the miserable consolation of being ruined by great men. All seems fair as yet, and will seem fair for a fortnight longer. But I know the danger from information more accurate and certain than, I believe, any body not in power possesses – and I know, what our men in power do not know, how terrible the danger is.

All this is strictly confidential. I called on Lord Lansdowne on Sunday. He told me distinctly that he expected the bill to be lost in the Lords, and that if it were lost the ministers must go out. I told him with as much strength of expression as was suited to the nature [of] our connection, and to his age and rank, that if the ministers receded before the Lords, they and the Whig party were lost – that nothing remained but an insolent oligarchy on the one side and infuriated people on the other – that Lord Grey and his colleagues would become as odious and more contemptible than Peel and the Duke of Wellington. 'What could be done?' 'Make more peers,' said I. Lord Lansdowne objected to such a course with the feeling natural to a nobleman of such ancient descent and such high rank. But why did not they think of all this earlier? Why put their hand to the plough and look back? Why begin to build without counting the cost of finishing? Why raise the public appetite, and then baulk it?

I told him that the House of Commons would address the King against a Tory ministry. I feel assured that it would do so. I feel assured that if those who are bidden will not come, the highways and hedges will be ransacked to form a reforming ministry. To one thing my mind is made up. If no body else will move an address to the Crown against a Tory ministry, – I will. –

This is all strictly secret. I cannot tell you how it vexes and alarms me. Kindest love to all.
Ever yours my dearest
T B M.

To Hannah Macaulay, 15 September

. . . We are to have a magnificent dinner in a week or ten days to commemorate the passing of the Bill through the Commons. There will be three hundred Members or thereabouts present. It will cost us, I am sorry to say, three pounds a piece. We are to dine in Stationers' Hall, the Company having lent it to us for the occasion. The Landlord of the Albion Tavern is to furnish the dinner; and, by all that I can hear of that eminent person, we may think ourselves very lucky to get off for £3 each. Every thing is to be in the first style. Sir Francis Burdett is to take the chair. The Newspapers will be full of it, no doubt, whenever it does take place. There is to be a table for the reporters. . . .

Charles Greville's Journal

17 September

Reform, which has subsided into a calm for some time past, is approaching its termination in the House of Commons, and as it gets near the period of a fresh campaign, and a more arduous though a shorter one, agitation is a little reviving. The 'Times' and other violent newspapers are moving heaven and earth to stir up the country and intimidate the Peers, many of whom are frightened enough already. The general opinion at present is that the Peers created at the coronation will not be enough to carry the Bill (they are a set of horrid rubbish most of them), but that no more will be made at present; that the Opposition, if united, will be strong enough to throw out the Bill, but that they are so divided in opinion whether to oppose the Bill on the second reading or in Committee that this dissension will very likely enable it to pass. Up to this time there has been no meeting, and nothing has been agreed upon, but there would have been one convened by the Duke of Wellington but for Lady Mornington's death, and this week they will arrange their plan of operations. From what Sefton says (who knows and thinks only as Brougham and Grey direct him) I conclude that the Government are resolved the Bill shall pass, and that if it is thrown out they will do what the Tories recommended, and make as many Peers as may be sufficient, for he said the other day he would rather it was thrown out on the second reading than pass by a small majority. With this resolution (which after having gone so far is not unwise) and the feeling out of doors, pass it must, and so sure are Government of it that they have begun to divide the counties, and have set up an office with clerks, maps, &c., in the Council Office, and there the Committee sit every day. . . .

22 September
There was a dinner at Apsley House yesterday; the Cabinet of Opposition, to discuss matters before having a general meeting. At this dinner there were sixteen or seventeen present, all the leading anti-Reformers of the Peers. They agreed to oppose the second reading. Dudley, who was there, told me it was tragedy first and farce afterwards; for Eldon and Kenyon, who had dined with the Duke of Cumberland, came in after dinner. Chairs were placed for them on each side of the Duke, and after he had explained to them what they had been discussing, and what had been agreed upon, Kenyon made a long speech on the first reading of the Bill, in which it was soon apparent that he was very drunk, for he talked exceeding nonsense, wandered from one topic to another, and repeated the same things over and over again. When he had done Eldon made a speech on the second reading, and appeared to be equally drunk, only, Lord Bathurst told me, Kenyon in his drunkenness talked nonsense, but Eldon sense. Dudley said it was not that they were as drunk as lords and gentlemen sometimes are, but they were drunk like porters. Lyndhurst was not there, though invited. He dined at Holland House. It is pretty clear, however, that he will vote for the second reading, for his wife is determined he shall. I saw her yesterday, and she is full of pique and resentment against the Opposition and the Duke, half real and half pretended, and chatters away about Lyndhurst's not being their cat's paw, and that if they choose to abandon him, they must not expect him to sacrifice himself for them. The pretexts she takes are, that they would not go to the House of Lords on Tuesday and support him against Brougham on the Bankruptcy Bill, and that the Duke of Wellington wrote to her and *desired* her to influence her husband in the matter of Reform. The first is a joke, the second there might be a little in, for vanity is always uppermost, but they have both some motive of interest, which they will pursue in whatever way they best can. The excuse they make is that they want to conceal their strength from the Government, and accordingly the Duke of Wellington has not yet entered any of his proxies. The truth is that I am by no means sure *now* that it is safe or prudent to oppose the second reading,

and though I think it very doubtful if any practicable alteration will be made in Committee, it will be better to take that chance, and the chance of an accommodation and compromise between the two parties and the two Houses, then to attack it in front. It is clear that Government are resolved to carry the Bill, and equally clear that no means they can adopt would be unpopular. They are averse to making more Peers if they can help it, and would rather go quietly on, without any fresh changes, and I believe they are conscientiously persuaded that this Bill is the least democratical Bill it is possible to get the country to accept, and that if offered in time this one will be accepted. I had heard before that the country is not enamoured of this Bill, but I fear that it is true that they are only indifferent to the Conservative clauses of it (if I may so term them), and for that reason it may be doubtful whether there would not be such a clamour raised in the event of the rejection of this Bill as would compel the Ministers to make a new one, more objectionable than the old. If its passing clearly appears to be inevitable, why, the sooner it is done the better, for at least one immense object will be gained in putting an end to agitation, and restoring the country to good-humour, and it is desirable that the House of Lords should stand as well with the people as it can. It is better, as Burke says, 'to do early, and from foresight, that which we may be obliged to do from necessity at last.' I am not more delighted with Reform than I have ever been, but it is the part of prudence to take into consideration the present and the future, and not to harp upon the past. It matters not how the country has been worked up to its present state, if a calm observation convinces us that the spirit that has been raised cannot be allayed, and that is very clear to me.

24 September
On Monday the battle begins in the House of Lords, and up to this time nobody knows how it will go, each party being confident, but opinion generally in favour of the Bill being thrown out. There is nothing more curious in this question than the fact that it is almost impossible to find anybody who is satisfied with the part he himself takes upon it, and that it is generally looked upon as a choice of evils, in which the only thing to do is to choose the least. The Reformers say, You had better pass the Bill or you will have a worse. The moderate anti-Reformers would be glad to suffer the second reading to pass and alter it in Committee, but they do not dare do so, because the sulky, stupid, obstinate High Tories declare that they will throw the whole thing up, and not attempt to alter the Bill if it passes the second reading. Every man seems tossed about by opposite considerations and the necessity of accommodating his own conduct to the caprices, passions, and follies of others.

J.W. Croker's[1] diary, Walmer, 21 September

We found the Duke with only Cooke, whom his Grace had asked to meet me, but he had come down on Thursday.
    I find the Duke well in health and I may say in *spirits*, though he is very

grave. Some of this seriousness, which is remarkable, is no doubt attributable to the death of the Duchess; but it is also considerably increased by, and deducible from, his anxiety about public affairs. He looks upon the result of the general election as decisive in favour of the Ministers' Reform Bill, and in that Bill he sees, as I have always done, nothing but revolution. His opinion is that the Bill may be considered as passed, and that the revolution has already begun its march, and will be accomplished, whether a little sooner or later, without violence or bloodshed, unless indeed, there happen to be one or two assassinations, as of himself or Peel, which he thinks not improbable. He tells me that he had a few days ago a letter from a man who gave a name and date, apprising him that it was intended on the meeting of Parliament to attempt to shoot him from a crowd which would be assembled in Palace Yard. This letter he thought it right to send to Sir Richard Birnie, who had that very day returned a very flippant answer, making light, or rather, nothing of the matter, and saying that, if anything were intended, the Duke would not have been forewarned. The Duke answered him gravely that he must know that the last observation was not correct; that Cato Street and the intended proceedings on Lord Mayor's Day had (as well as some other attempts) been made known by anonymous information; but, at all events, that as the man gave a name, *Will. Sidmouth*, and a date, *Cheapside*, Sir Richard should have at least inquired whether there was any such person before he had sent such an offhand answer. This letter he wrote on Wednesday, and has not yet had an answer. He went on, in reference to the revolutionary aspect and prospect of the times, to say that, in the general state of disorganization and contempt of all authority which the Ministers had excited and kept up to secure their party triumph, there was no doubt a danger that they might be suddenly overborne by the irregular power they had called into action; but the great body of the nation was sound enough, he thought, to prevent any immediate violence. As the revolutionists are now all with the Ministry and enjoying a common triumph, I think this ferment will pass away; but its effect will remain, and grow gradually and quietly more and more destructive of our old constitution. First, all reverence for old authorities, even for the House of Commons itself, has received an irrecoverable shock, and then the composition of the new House of Commons, which will only change to become worse, will render government by royal authority impracticable. So it will go down step by step, quicker or faster, as temporary circumstances may direct, but the result will be that at last we shall have a revolution gradually accomplished *by due form of law*!

The Duke of Wellington to Lady Shelley

London, 24 September
My dear Lady Shelley,
    You will see that the Reform Bill has at last come up to the House of Lords, and it will come under discussion upon the Second Reading on

Monday, October 3. Of course we are looking very anxiously after numbers.

What do you say to Lord Gage? I heard some time ago that he entertained a very sensible opinion upon this subject; and thought that if the Bill should pass, the government of the country would become impracticable. Does he think so still? Could you insinuate to him to come up and vote against the Bill, or to give his proxy against it?

I know that you are a *sensible* woman, and will manage the affair with discretion.

Believe me, ever yours most affectionately,
Wellington

London, 1 October
My dear Lady Shelley,

You are delightful. I have not time to say more. You may rely upon it that we shall have no difficulty if we reject the Bill. . . .

Correspondence of the Howard sisters: Georgiana to Caroline

Dover House, 3 October

. . . We are just come to town for this eventful time. It will be intensely interesting. I cannot help feeling very confident that it will be carried; partly I believe from thinking it will be too terrible if it is not, and therefore disliking to think of the possibility. My husband, who has been going over the lists of the Peers, thinks it will be carried by a very small majority. Lord Mulgrave, who has been equally busy on the subject, is on the contrary very desponding. He came down to Roehampton yesterday with a very melancholy view of the state of things. What added to it, was the account of the Dorsetshire election, which surprised every body, tho' it had been expected to be a hard contest. It was thought however that the anti-reformers had made their great push yesterday and that William (Ponsonby) will get it up to-day. I am afraid he is not personally very popular. . . . Of late the only subject of conversation has been, how this or that Peer would vote, and one is told of the strangest changes; such as that Ld Howe would vote for it! I believe many are frightened and would gladly retract, but then they are usually too deeply engaged. We are to dine early to-day; the evening without any tidings will appear very long, and one would wish oneself there very much, among the many ladies who nightly attend. . . .

[Added in a P.S.] I am afraid I have been too sanguine; it does not look well and my husband is more alarmed. They are 17 ahead in proxies, and will be more. Ly Holland has just been and tries to be in spirits. Mr. Wood says at this moment there is a majority of one in our favour, but is not very good authority from seeing things too much *en beau*. I have also seen Harriet; she says the other side are *so* confident. The impression now is that it will be lost by a few.

Wednesday evening

. . . These 2 days have resembled each other very much; the same conjectures and the same topics, the same hours for dinner and the same for sitting up. Neither of the debates appear to have been particularly lively. The account we heard of Ld Grey was that he had spoken admirably. I find however there is a difference of opinion . . . some thinking it quite his best, others looking upon it as rather feeble. Ld Wharncliffe spoke best on the other side. . . . Last night Ld Winchelsea spoke in a violent manner, imprecated a great deal; his vote had been reckoned doubtful, but he declared against the bill. Then followed Ld Harrowby, and his party extol his speech quite up to the skies, and say it is quite unanswerable. I must confess that in a little bulletin my husband sends us, he was represented as twaddling and quite an old woman, tho' he afterwards thought some parts good. Still, I was surprised to find when I went out and saw Tories, that it was quite *the* speech. Ld Melbourne spoke well, but not enough or sufficiently to the subject. The Duke of Wellington was admitted to be indifferent. It has been very comfortable having Mama, Blanche and Harriet here. We drink tea, get a little acct. at 10 o'clock and part at $\frac{1}{2}$ past 12. My Sposo came home about that time both nights, rather before it was over; the heat they say is very great, and I am afraid he may suffer by this attendance. . . .

1 o'clock (a.m.)

My husband not come yet; his account is, that Lord Lansdowne has spoken *quite admirably*; Lord Dudley, before, made a long, clever, bitter speech, but it was difficult to hear. When he wrote, Lord Londonderry was speaking much louder and more absurdly than ever. Mama, Blanche and Mrs. Lamb came here 1st, then dear George, then George Lamb, then Lord Granville, who only arrived to-day from Paris, all very much pleased with Lord Lansdowne; then Harriet, all in black, and very pale, with a very bad headache, partly from the heat, and partly, she said, from the loudness of Lord Londonderry and Lord Winchelsea. She was very glad to have been however, and said it was very exciting and interesting. . . . There had been some little squabble between the Duke of Wellington and Lord Holland, early, on a petition. She thought Lord H. seemed very violent and Papa interposed. Ld Haddington was going to speak when she came away; he votes against after much indecision. . . . He (Lord Dover) got home at about $\frac{1}{2}$ past 1, quite enchanted with the debate. Lord Radnor made a very amusing speech; he thought Lord Lansdowne better than he had ever heard him; quite excellent. Papa's little historical speech was very well done. It looks bad as far as the division is concerned; all the changes being against. Lord Waldegrave has declared himself and resigns his lordship of the Bedchamber. The consequences are most unpleasant to think of, whether the feeling of the people is shewn in the refusal to pay taxes, or in riots. They expect the debate to continue over to-night. . . .

Harriet to Caroline, Hamilton Place, 6 October

... I should have had a delicious evening last night, but for the atmosphere unsweet and the excessive heat, which gave me a violent headache. I went at ½ past 3 with George and Morpeth to the House of Lords, the 1st time I had ever done it, and staid till 11, – a long time, but nothing to some of the ladies who go every night and stay to the end. Lady Jersey was seated among the reporters, who I am persuaded she believes all to be in love with her. I never was more entertained; there was a great deal of lively talk upon petitions. Lord Grey's manner is very fine, but over haughty, and I think I see his great vanity constantly piercing. Lord Holland was very violent – gesticulation, that must make it immense physical labour, and Lord Goderich is the same in this respect; it would be dreadful to come within the *ricoché* of his strong arm. Papa said a few words very well, and hardly gave one time to be nervous. The Chancellor is delightful in his serious manner; the jokes and satire are hardly fair on such earnest subjects. After the Order of the day Lord Dudley spoke, I believe very well; it was deep, bitter and epigrammatic, when one caught some of the sounds of his many voices, but this was seldom.

I was pretty well placed next to Ly Clanricarde; we had a wall to lean against and saw very well when standing up, but as I said before, it made me very ill indeed, and it is melancholy and humiliating not to be able to do these things with impunity. I went with Ly Harrowby and Ly G. Wortley to drink tea. We found Ly Jersey, Ly Salisbury, Ly Lyndhurst and Ld Forester, so that I felt very out of my water. There were about 40 women; a terrible number. I think Ly Clanricarde a very clever person with *un esprit très mâle*. She wishes the Bill success, liking the Ministers, but does not at all approve of the Bill, which surprised me.

Georgiana to Caroline, Dover House, 8 October

... 41! the greatest number that had been thought possible by our side. We were quite prepared for losing it by a considerable majority, tho' the Bishops had not been reckoned upon as all going against, which with the exception of 2 they did, on the Archbishop of Canterbury declaring himself. It will be trying to you, hearing the shout of triumph, but they will be short and one cannot envy them their feelings. Most of them are I believe frightened to death at their own success. I cannot feel depressed and I do not think my husband is so; he thinks they will, and what I care for more, that they ought to stay in; and as long as they do, I believe the danger is kept off, and the carrying of the Bill only deferred. It was exciting too, hearing of Brougham's speech, the finest thing that ever was heard. My husband says it was the general feeling, and that too much praise cannot be given to it. He thought it very judicious as well as clever; therefore do not believe the enemy's story should they attempt to deny it. ...

Charles Greville's Journal, *10 October*

Yesterday morning the newspapers (all in black) announced the defeat of
the Reform Bill by a majority of forty-one, at seven o'clock on Saturday
morning, after five nights' debating. By all accounts the debate was a
magnificent display, and incomparably superior to that in the House of
Commons, but the reports convey no idea of it. The great speakers on
either side were:– Lords Grey, Lansdowne, Goderich, Plunket, and the
Chancellor, for the Bill; against it, Lords Wharncliffe (who moved the
amendment), Harrowby, Carnarvon, Dudley, Wynford, and Lyndhurst.
The Duke of Wellington's speech was exceedingly bad; he is in fact, and
has proved it in repeated instances, unequal to argue a great constitutional
question. He has neither the command of language, the power of reasoning, nor the knowledge requisite for such an effort. Lord Harrowby's
speech was amazingly fine, and delivered with great effect; and the last
night the Chancellor is said to have surpassed all his former exploits,
Lyndhurst to have been nearly as good, and Lord Grey very great in reply.
There was no excitement in London the following day, and nothing
particular happened but the Chancellor being drawn from Downing Street
to Berkeley Square in his carriage by a very poor mob. The majority was
much greater than anybody expected, and it is to be hoped may be
productive of good by showing the necessity of a compromise; for no
Minister can make sixty Peers, which Lord Grey must do to carry this Bill;
it would be to create another House of Lords. Nobody knows what the
Ministers would do, but it was thought they would not resign. A meeting
of members of the House of Commons was held under the auspices of
Ebrington to agree upon a resolution of confidence in the Government this
day. The majority and the magnificent display of eloquence and ability in
the House of Lords must exalt the character and dignity of that House,
and I hope increase its efficacy for good purposes and for resistance to this
Bill. It may be hoped too that the apathy of the capital may have some
effect in the country, though the unions, which are so well disciplined and
under the control of their orators, will make a stir. On the whole I rejoice
at this result, though I had taken fright before, and thought it better the
Bill should be read a second time than be thrown out by a very small
majority.

While the debates have been going on there have been two elections,
one of the Lord Mayor in the City, which the Reformers have carried after
a sharp contest, and the contest for Dorsetshire between Ponsonby and
Ashley, which is not yet over. Ponsonby had a week's start of his
opponent, notwithstanding which it is so severe that they have been for
some days within ten or fifteen of each other, and (what is remarkable) the
anti-Reformer is the popular candidate, and has got all the mob with him.
This certainly is indicative of some *change*, though not of a *reaction*, in
public opinion. There is no longer the same vehemence of desire for this
Bill, and I doubt whether all the efforts of the press will be able to
stimulate the people again to the same pitch of excitement.

Letters from Harriot G. Mundy to Lady H. Frampton, Markeaton (near Derby)

9 October, Sunday 8 a.m.
MY DEAR MOTHER,

Since writing the enclosed we have had direful events, but I am thankful to say that nothing serious has happened excepting breaking all the windows. Last night, just as we were nearly all in bed, and Mr. W.M. and I quite so, a large mob came from Derby (having just heard of the failure of the Reform Bill), and surrounded the house, shouting and halloaing, and smashed all our windows, and broke in many doors and frames of windows. Luckily we were very strong in point of men-servants, and Godfrey Mundy is here, but I must say they did not show much inclination to enter. We are going to send off for troops to Nottingham – sixteen miles – which is our nearest point, so expect to be quite strong and secure before night.

You need not be the least alarmed, as we are all quite well, and I only write because you may have worse accounts by the newspapers.

12 October
MY DEAREST MOTHER,

We have not been visited again, for which we cannot be too thankful, as I have no dependence on the strength of our fortifications or on our forty men, if they really chose to attack us with all their force, for we have no military guard, and a superabundant quantity of windows, principally without frames, which by no means increase their power of resisting a mob. I have now been *four* nights without undressing, but I get so tired that I sleep quite as comfortably lying on my bed as I ever did, and by that means am all ready for any alarm. We have had one or two, but fortunately they proved false ones. Mr. W. Mundy comes to bed for a couple of hours at six o'clock, when it is broad daylight. I hope he will not suffer, but it is a terrible strain on his mind, having everything to do and his father to manage completely; he asks his son 50,000 questions where one would be quite sufficient, and about nothing at all just in the midst of all his bustle. However, his temper is proof against everything, and he is as cool and quiet as possible. We hear that Derby was very quiet last night, and that some of the people are *going* to work again as usual, but we cannot feel at all secure yet, as if the refractory people are dispersed and driven out of the town, they are very likely to form into parties and annoy the country. I am happy to say that Godfrey will not leave us till to-morrow, but what we shall do when he is gone I cannot think. The worst of being so near the town is that one hears the shouting and halloaing of the people and any guns that are fired, which is very disagreeable, as one never knows whether they may not be at the door the next minute. If my brother Henry was not captain in the yeomanry, I should invite him here to help defend us.

13 October

MY DEAR MOTHER,

We are more comfortable as far as the present is concerned, but have not a very agreeable prospect for the winter. Some fresh troops have arrived from Sheffield, and we are lent some yeomanry from Staffordshire, so that the town is kept very quiet, as they relieve one another, and take it by turns to patrol the streets. We have not been attacked again, and are tolerably defended, as I must say the tenants and labourers came to our aid instantly – many even on Saturday night – and have stood very firm ever since. With *them* Mr. Mundy is very much liked, as he is so very kind and liberal about their rent and money matters, and they understand him. Mr. W. Mundy is extremely popular, and always has been so. Only think of poor Mrs. Wilmot at Chaddesden (née Mundy of Shipley) hearing the mob halloo out when they threw a stone up to the nursery where her three poor little children – the eldest not three years old – were all crying from fright, 'I wonder how many of those little brats we've squashed now?' I undressed *nearly* for the first time last night, but I cannot help being in a great fuss about Mr. W.M., which prevents me from going to bed as the rest have done all the time. All the neighbouring counties are inclined to be uproarious, but I hope we may get some troops stationed at Derby. The Duke of Devonshire is come down to stay in case we want our Lord Lieutenant. Godfrey Mundy goes to-day.

The Times, 10 October

Our paper of today is dedicated to the description of that just indignation which is felt by the British people on the rejection of their Reform Bill! Every where they are in movement: we can hardly sum up the various constituent bodies that are appointing meetings, and the rapidity of the proceeding is no less remarkable. The remedy will be applied almost as soon as the blow is struck. Re-action indeed! Yes, there is a re-action! That is, the same action of insisting upon Reform is repeated, but with ten times greater zeal and determination. In looking over the elements of which the fatal majority is composed, attention fixes first, and principally, on the Bishops. These reverend Lords have more to do with the people than the other Peers: their functions, and those of their less elevated brethren, are discharged with and among the people; and yet through them it is, that a bill for the establishment of the people's rights has been lost; for had they voted on the other side, twenty in number, the division would have been about equal. . . .

Hobhouse's Recollections, *12 October*

I went to Court to present addresses from the electors assembled at the Crown and Anchor, the parishioners of St. Anne's, Westminster, and other large bodies of Metropolitan electors. I was surprised on going into the streets to find the shops shut, and a great many ill-looking and ill-dressed people standing about. There was something in the look and manners of the crowds which, I confess, I did not like.

In Bond Street I saw a large placard with this inscription: '199 *versus* 22,000,000!' and I went into the house to persuade the shopman to take it down. He was a shoemaker, and, though very civil, was very firm, and refused to remove the placard, saying he had only done as others had done. When I told him who I was, he said, 'Oh, I know you very well'; but he still declined to follow my advice.

There was a strong force of police and of Horse Guards near St. James's Palace. A line of the latter was drawn across Pall Mall to keep off a crowd, whose banners I saw beyond the soldiers, and whose shouts I heard. Processions paraded the Mall, which might have been seen by the King from the Palace windows. The parishioners from St. Pancras had, besides their banners, two red caps of liberty, and they huzzaed lustily; but I saw no violence of any kind, nor heard of any disaster. . . .

I went to the House of Commons through masses of people, who were noisy enough, but not mischievous. I was much vexed, however, to hear that the Duke of Wellington's windows had been broken, and that Lord Londonderry had been wounded by a stone. These occurrences were too true, and disgraceful enough. At the House of Commons I heard Lord Althorp and Lord John Russell complained of as having inflamed the populace by the answers which they had given to the addresses from the Birmingham Union. A day or two before it was asserted that the rejection of the Bill had caused no excitement.

The Duke of Wellington to Mrs Arbuthnot, London, 12 October

I inclose you a Note which I wrote you this morning before you set out for Oatlands. But just as I was about to send it a Mob surrounded my House, upon which they commenced an attack with Stones which lasted 50 Minutes in broad daylight before any assistance came. They broke all the Windows on the lower floor looking towards Rotten Row, a great Number in my Room in which I was sitting, some in the Secretary's Room, and some in the Drawing Room above Stairs. All the blank windows fronting towards the Park and Piccadilly are likewise broken. They did not attempt to break into the Garden. We had Men with fire Arms ready to receive them.

They are quiet now; but there is a considerable body in the Park about the Statue, and another attack is threatened for this evening. However, I do not fear it.

My Garden and the Area between my Room and the Garden are filled with Stones. The Principal fire was directed upon my Room, which they reached easily from the Road.

It is now five o'clock and beginning to rain a little; and I conclude that the Gentlemen will now go to their Dinners!

Plate 1   Charles, 2nd Earl Grey, *c*. 1828. Prime Minister, 1830–4

Plate 2 King William IV

Plate 3 Arthur Wellesley, 1st Duke of Wellington, *c.* 1827

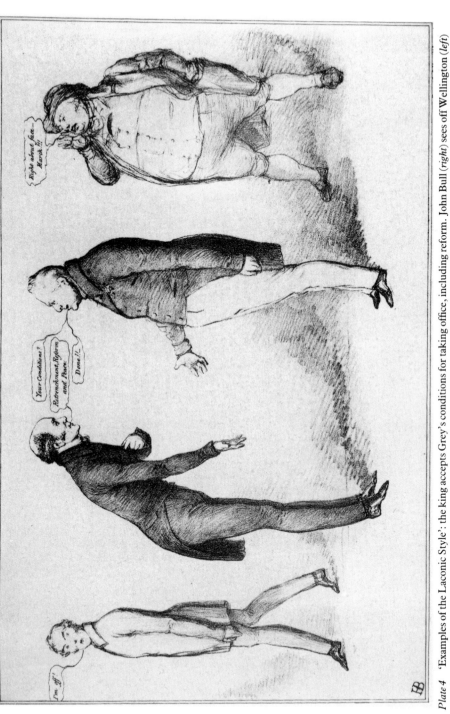

Plate 4 'Examples of the Laconic Style': the king accepts Grey's conditions for taking office, including reform. John Bull (*right*) sees off Wellington (*left*)

Plate 5 The House of Lords: William IV prorogues parliament, April 1831

Plate 6 'Handwriting upon the Wall': 'HB' satirizes the king's puzzled attitude towards reform, May 1831

Plate 7 'A Political Union': John Bull angrily drags on Lord Grey who is forced to pull along the reluctant William IV

Plate 8 'Captain Swing', from a contemporary print

Plate 9   Sir Robert Peel, 1838

Plate 10 Henry, 1st Baron Brougham and Vaux. Lord Chancellor, 1830–4

Plate 11   Lord Althorp. Leader of the House of Commons, 1830–4

TAKING AN AIRING IN HYDE PARK

A PORTRAIT

Framed but not yet Glazed

Plate 12 'Framed but not yet glazed': Wellington looks through the broken windows of Apsley House

Plate 13 'Up and Down'. The end of the 'Days of May', 1832: John Bull puts his weight under Grey's end of the political see-saw to push Wellington down

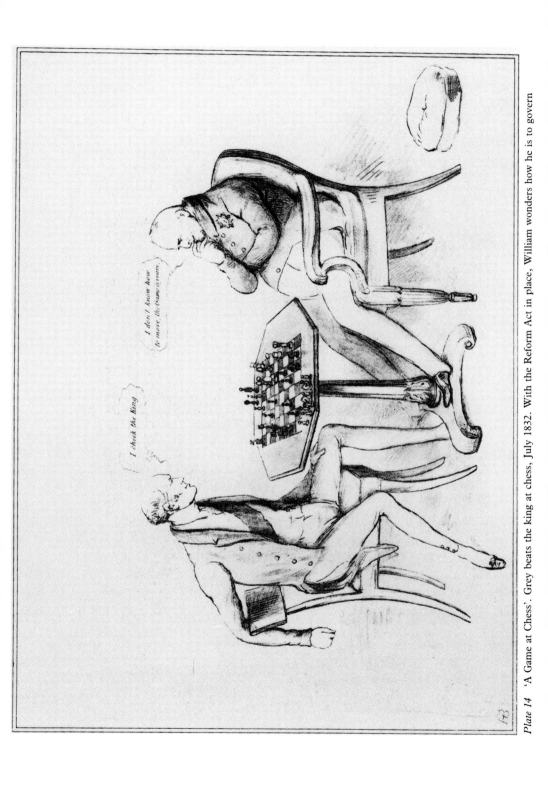

Plate 14 'A Game at Chess'. Grey beats the king at chess, July 1832. With the Reform Act in place, William wonders how he is to govern

Plate 15 'March of Reform': the new members arrive to take their seats in the first reformed parliament, March 1833

Charles Greville's Journal, *15 October*

. . . With a yelling majority in the House, and a desperate press out of it, they go on in their reckless course without fear or shame. Lord Harrowby made a speech in the House of Lords, and declared his conviction that the time was come for effecting a Reform, and that he would support one to a certain extent, which he specified. In the House he was coolly received, and the 'Times' hardly deigned to notice what he said. Parliament is to be up on Thursday next, and will probably not meet till January, when of course the first thing done will be to bring in the Bill again. What, then, is gained? For as Ministers take every opportunity of declaring that they will accept nothing less efficient (as they call it) than the present Bill, no compromise can be looked for. Lord Harrowby is the only man who has said what he will do, and probably he goes further than the bulk of his party would approve of; and yet he is far behind the Ministerial plan. So that there seems little prospect of getting off for less than the old Bill, for the Opposition will hardly venture to stop the next *in limine* as they did this. I do not see why they should hope to amend the next Bill in Committee any more than the last, and the division which they dreaded the other day is not less likely, and would not be less fatal upon another occasion. If, then, it is to pass at last, it comes back to what I thought before, that it might as well have passed at first as at last, and the excitement consequent on its rejection have been spared, as well as the odium which has accrued to the Peers, which will not be forgotten or laid aside.

The Dorsetshire election promises to end in favour of Ashley, and there will be a contest for Cambridgeshire, which may also end in favour of the anti-Reform candidate. These victories I really believe to be unfortunate, for they are taken (I am arguing as if they were won, though, with regard to the first, it is the same thing by contrast with the last election) by the Tories and anti-Reform champions as undoubted proofs of the reaction of public opinion, and they are thereby encouraged to persevere in opposition under the false notion that this supposed reaction will every day gain ground. I wish it were so with all my soul, but believe it is no such thing, and that although there may be fewer friends to *the Bill* than there were, particularly among the agriculturists, Reform is not a whit less popular with the mass of the people in the manufacturing districts, throughout the unions, and generally amongst all classes and in all parts of the country. When I see men, and those in very great numbers, of the highest birth, of immense fortunes, of undoubted integrity and acknowledged talents, zealously and conscientiously supporting this measure, I own I am lost in astonishment, and even doubt; for I can't help asking myself whether it is possible that such men would be the advocates of measures fraught with all the peril we ascribe to these, whether we are not in reality mistaken, and labouring under groundless alarm generated by habitual prejudices and erroneous calculations. But often as this doubt comes across my mind, it is always dispelled by a reference to and comparison of the arguments on both sides, and by the lessons which all that I have ever read and all the conclusions I have been able to drawn [sic] from the study of history have impressed on my mind. I believe these measures full of danger, but that the manner in which they have been introduced, discussed, defended, and supported is more dangerous still. The total unsettlement of men's minds, the bringing into contempt all the institutions which have been hitherto venerated, the aggrandisement of the power of the people, the embodying and recognition of popular authority, the use and abuse of the King's name, the truckling to the press, are things so subversive of government, so prejudicial to order and tranquillity, so encouraging to sedition and disaffection, that I do not see the possibility of the country settling down into that calm and undisturbed state in which it was before this question was mooted, and without which there can be no happiness or security to the community. A thousand mushroom orators and politicians have sprung up all over the country, each big with his own ephemeral importance, and every one of whom fancies himself fit to govern the nation. Amongst them are some men of active and powerful minds, and nothing is less probable than that these spirits of mischief and misrule will be content to subside into their original nothingness, and retire after the victory has been gained into the obscurity from which they emerged.

Mrs Mundy to Lady H. Frampton, Markeaton, 15 October

MY DEAR MOTHER, – After my letter was gone to the post I received yours. We perceive that you do not think much of our mob, which considering your own troubles last year is not surprising, but I assure you that our situation was rather terrific, and, indeed, we do not think ourselves as extraordinarily out of the reach of a second edition yet. Conceive how horrid it was on Sunday morning, just as we had finished our doleful breakfast, having been up all night, and having the yells of the multitude and the crash of windows, and doors still ringing in our ears, to have a gentleman (Mr Meynell) ride up, saying that he was just come from Derby (where he expected to have been annihilated by the mob, as they threatened him, and told him that they should visit him), that they had forced the town gaol and liberated twenty-three prisoners, were proceeding to the county gaol, which he feared could not resist long, and were then coming on to us to Kedleston (Lord Scarsdale's), and to his place. We distinctly heard the shouts of the mob, not having a window or shutter whole, and if they had come at that moment we could not have offered the slightest defence or resistance, as the whole of the lower rooms were open, and anybody could have walked into them as easily as possible. Fortunately the gaoler made a gallant defence, which delayed the rioters until the dragoons arrived from Nottingham, which was only just in time, as they were preparing to scale the walls, and if so, or they had attacked it with powder, it must have given way.

To-day a detachment of the 18th Foot arrived from Manchester, so we feel tolerably secure, and privately we attribute these to my uncle Ilchester's great kindness in speaking to Lord Melbourne, as I am sure that his and Lord Lansdowne's mention of us makes them think less lightly of our situation, and we feel very grateful in consequence. We are very thankful for our preservation, as you may believe, for the Nottingham rioters plundered much more; and at Colwick, near Nottingham – Mr. Musters' place – they entered, seized the furniture and pictures, which they made into a bonfire before the door, and utterly ruined it. Only Mrs. Musters and her daughter were at home. Mrs Musters was ill in bed, and she was obliged to be carried out of the house and laid under a bush for safety. This is dreadfully brutal for an English mob, and makes one's prospects sadly gloomy. They say that Mr Musters was *excessively* unpopular, and that if he had been found at the moment, he would certainly have been murdered. . . .

William Mundy to Lady H. Frampton, Markeaton, 20 October

MY DEAR LADY HARRIOT, I want to tell you how much interested I have been about the progress of your election, more particularly from having been present at the last, and now I must congratulate you upon its successful termination. We are beginning to breathe again after the last turmoil, which has now quite subsided; and as I hope and believe that we shall have some troops at Derby through the winter, I have no doubt we shall remain quiet. As Harriot has already described the whole to you, I will not recur to it again further than to express my admiration of her coolness and composure throughout the bustle. She was of essential use by giving me some hints which were of great value at the time, and altogether behaved just as I expected she would do in any emergency. I am happy to say that she does not seem to have suffered from the alarm. It is surprising that Derby should have been almost the only place in the kingdom to riot on this occasion, which I can only attribute to the constant excitement in which the inhabitants have been kept by the Radical party, by holding no end of public meetings, getting up petitions upon all occasions, &c., so that they were ready charged for an explosion. I hope Mr Frampton thinks we did right in not firing upon the mob the other night, taken by surprise and unprepared as we were for such an attack; as my idea is, that it is not well to begin a fire unless one is prepared to keep up a brisk one, and with the few guns and pistols we could muster at the moment it would have been impossible to defend all the doors and windows if they had been determined to force an entrance, though the first man who *entered* I should certainly have shot.

I am now told that many of these rascals themselves repent having visited us, and regret that they did not go to Lord Scarsdale's instead, before the Hussars arrived to impede their further operations. . . .

Lady Shelley to Mrs Arbuthnot, Maresfield (circa *21 October*)

MY DEAR MRS ARBUTHNOT,

. . .The rejection of the Bill has given me new life, provided your friends (don't scold) the *asinine* Tories (their new name), will be rational, and meet the moderate Reformers without any consideration of self-interest. These people overthrew the Duke's Government and gave us up a prey to the Radical support to which Lord Grey was forced to have recourse if he intended to be Minister. From Lord Grey's birth, *party*, and not the good of his country, has been his idol; he clings to it still. But times are changed since Foxites and Pittites were distinctions, and there must be a corresponding change in political morality, or men like the Duke, who think only of their country's good, can never remain at the helm. Whig and Tory are at an end, and we must have only Conservative reformers and Radical reformers. I *think* it is not too late to save the country; but unless some kind of Reform Bill is passed this Session, a Bill which *ought to satisfy* those who don't want plunder – it is all over. In Lancashire all business is at a stand-still – in *suspense* – as our agent says. If the Bill had passed the Lords, there would have been an immediate withdrawal of capital from trade. As it is, they will wait for another Session before emigration, so if a moderate Bill is passed all will be well. In this part of the county no one is for the *Bill*, I believe; yet all are in favour of some Reform, tho' it is very little talked or thought of. . . .

Mrs Arbuthnot's Journal, *23 October*

The Ministers did everything they could by their speeches & by their Press to excite riots all over the country upon the rejection of the Bill, but they failed entirely. The only places where there were disturbances were Derby & Nottingham &, to shew what the supporters of the Bill are at Derby, their first object was to break open the jail & let out the felons; & at Nottingham, besides burning down the Castle, they attacked the house of Mr. Musters in the neighbourhood, a gentleman not in Parliament & no way connected with politics, completely destroyed it & *stole* all the plate, jewels & valuables they c^d lay their hands on. But Nottingham is blessed with a dissenting Corporation who are reformers & did not choose to let the soldiers & constables go to the assistance of Mr. Musters.

In London there were no disturbances for three days. At the end of that time the King came to London and held a levée, upon which the radicals got up processions with addresses & the mob broke the windows of several houses. They broke all the Duke of Wellington's windows in broad daylight &, tho' the Ministers were informed that there was an intention of attacking his house, there was not a single policeman came till the mob had been throwing stones for 55 minutes, & then not one man was taken up. And afterwards Ld Melbourne & Mr. Lamb pretended to be *very sorry*! They nearly broke the Duke's head, for a stone went within an inch of him. Luckily he had put up outside shutters to his gallery windows or all his fine pictures w^d have been spoiled. Lord Grey, riding by his house two days before, expressed great vexation at his having put up outside shutters & said no windows w^d be broke.

The Ministers pretended to be frightened to death at the idea of the Bill being thrown out and said they sh^d not know how to restrain the despair of the people; & the Lord Advocate talked so much of a rebellion in Scotland that Chas's regt was sent off at an hour's warning from Winchester to Edinburgh. But it turns out the people are perfectly tranquil & take the loss of the Bill with a calmness & resignation very vexatious to the Gov^t. Chas writes us word the people of Edinburgh only desire *to be let alone*, and all over the country they are evidently tired of the Bill. . . .

Lord Ellenborough's diary, 31 October

I think from what I see reported as taking place at the several meetings that there is a more decided tendency to revolution than there yet has been. The revolutionists speak out more – they aim directly *at the Church* – and what must be the fate of the Church when by the Reform Bill the power of legislating for it is placed in the hands of the Dissenters who constitute the majority of that class to which the elective franchise is to be given? The Ministers are willing to receive the assistance of the revolutionists in order to produce terror & thus carry the Bill by which they are to stand or fall. The revolutionists take the assistance of the Ministers, using them as their tools, to effect an object which, once gained, gives them in its results all they want. The Ministers imagine they can resist the torrent when they please – but they are creating a power over which they will have no controul.

In the course of the day I heard that the mob had fired from the windows on the occasion of Sir C. Wetherall's entrance into Bristol (as Recorder I believe) & killed seven of the 14th Dr[agoons]. The subsequent account was that 65 houses were burnt, & the firing was going on when the coach came away. This is the most serious event which has occurred. I fear there are very few Troops at Bristol. Only 2 Troops of the 14th are there.

At 20 minutes after 10 I received a note from Mr. Edwards who is in Cheltenham, in reply to my enquiry respecting the latest news from Bristol. The worst seems to be past. The citizens are forming themselves into a guard to protect property – but 100 houses have been burnt, amongst these the Bishop's Palace, the Custom House, the Mansion House and the three prisons. The counts from Bath are not favourable. An inn there has been nearly demolished. The crisis is arrived.

The Revd J.L. Jackson to C.B. Wollaston, Clifton

31 October

As reports may have reached Dorsetshire from Bristol, I now write to assure you and our other friends that at present we are unharmed by fire and the mob. I do not think that report could have gone beyond the horror of our actual condition last night. During the whole of Saturday Bristol was in a state of considerable ferment from the arrival of Sir C. Wetherall, the Recorder. In the evening the multitude assembled before the Mansion House in Queen Square, and smashed the windows by a volley of stones in the front of the building. The Recorder was then at dinner with the Mayor and Corporation; the people then went away. But yesterday morning when I was going down to Bristol to serve the church of a friend, I learnt that the populace had actually broken into the Mansion House, had forced the cellars and were destroying and gutting the house.

I proceeded to the church, which was at no great distance from the Mansion House, and went through the prayers, but whilst reading the Commandments I heard two distinct charges of pistol firings. In fact the military, two troops of horse, who had been summoned, then fired. The congregation became alarmed, and dispersed without my giving them a sermon, but only a few words of exhortation to repair quietly to their own homes, and look after their servants and dependents. I also quitted the church and walked home without receiving the slightest insult or interruption, but the knots of men standing about the streets were of the most awful character. Three individuals were killed by the soldiers and more wounded. In the afternoon we heard that the multitude was assembled in much greater masses, and about four o'clock we saw the new City and County Gaol in flames; afterwards the Bridewell and another prison in the Gloucester Road, about a mile from Bristol. In the course of the evening Queen's Square was fired and the Bishop's palace. Of Queen's Square two whole sides have been burnt down, including the Mansion House and what must be of irreparable loss to such a place as Bristol, the Custom House. The cathedral was preserved, and is still standing, but was attempted. Other property to an immense amount is also destroyed. This morning an actual slaughter has taken place; it is supposed, though of course nothing precise can be known at present, that above seventy persons have been killed, besides a large number who have been wounded. The military charged through some of the principal streets, cutting right and left. What will be the event of this evening and night I know not, but I believe that the events of yesterday will never be effaced from the recollection of my family while memory holds her place.

1 November
Thus far had I written yesterday when I was called to attend a meeting of the respectable inhabitants of Clifton for the defence of the place. About two hundred householders were enrolled and divided into four parties, each party under the command of half-pay officers. By this precaution we have slept last night securely in our beds, and Clifton, thank God, has been uninjured. Five houses had been particularly threatened by the incendiaries, and might now with many others have been smoking in flames. This mode of attack is tremendous, it is by applying phosphorus to the doors. Much praise and many obligations are due to the military for

their forbearance at first, and for their decision latterly. The magistrates, police, and constables were wholly inefficient. Indeed one of the worst features of many which are bad is the rotten state of the public mind, not only amongst the very low, but in the different gradations of society, even to the highest and most influential. It is a fact that the Bishop's palace was plundered and fired by not more than ten men and a rabble of mere boys. It is also a fact that the fires of Sunday night appeared to cause a degree of exultation amongst many not of the lowest class. Just as I am closing my letter I hear that two more fires occurred last night, and that they would certainly have been multiplied but for the presence of the military; also that Bath is in a considerable ferment. Of course reports will be exaggerated, but may God preserve us and our guilty Land! Our wretched Ministers have raised a storm which, I fear, it will not be in their power to direct or control.

Yours, &c.,

J.L. Jackson

Charles Greville's Journal, *11 November*

The country was beginning to slumber after the fatigues of Reform, when it was rattled up by the business of Bristol, which for brutal ferocity and wanton, unprovoked violence may vie with some of the worst scenes of the French Revolution, and may act as a damper to our national pride. The spirit which produced these atrocities was generated by Reform, but no pretext was afforded for their actual commission; it was a premature outbreaking of the thirst for plunder, and longing after havoc and destruction, which is the essence of Reform in the mind of the mob. The details are ample, and to be met with everywhere; nothing could exceed the ferocity of the populace, the imbecility of the magistracy, or the good conduct of the troops. More punishment was inflicted by them than has been generally known, and some hundreds were killed or severely wounded by the sabre. One body of dragoons pursued a rabble of colliers into the country, and covered the fields and roads with the bodies of wounded wretches, making a severe example of them. In London there would probably have been a great uproar and riot, but fortunately Melbourne, who was frightened to death at the Bristol affair, gave Lord Hill and Fitzroy Somerset *carte blanche*, and they made such a provision of military force in addition to the civil power that the malcontents were paralysed. The Bristol business has done some good, inasmuch as it has opened people's eyes (at least so it is said), but if we are to go on as we do with a mob-ridden Government and a foolish King, who renders himself subservient to all the wickedness and folly of his Ministers, where is the advantage of having people's eyes open, when seeing they will not perceive, and hearing they will not understand? Nothing was wanting to complete our situation but the addition of physical evil to our moral plague, and that is come in the shape of the cholera, which broke out at Sunderland a few days ago. To meet the exigency Government has formed another Board of Health, but without dissolving the first, though the second is intended to swallow up the first and leave it a mere nullity. Lord Lansdowne, who is President of the Council, an office which for once promises not to be a sinecure, has taken the opportunity to go to Bowood, and having come up (sent for express) on account of the cholera the day it was officially declared really to be that disease, he has trotted back to his house in the country.

Lord Fitzroy Somerset[2] to the Duke of Wellington, Horse Guards, 2 November

MY DEAR LORD,

The accounts received this morning from Bristol announce that all continued quiet there yesterday evening, and Sir Richard Jackson, who commands the troops, appeared to entertain no apprehension of a renewal of the riot. The destruction of property, however, is immense.

The language held at the late meeting in London, at which Sir Francis Burdett presided, will have attracted your attention. A meeting of the *useful classes* is summoned for Monday next to consider some very violent resolutions (to meet in White Conduit Fields); and the preparations which are being made for the meeting induce a belief that it may lead to the perpetration of some acts of violence. The military will therefore be held in a state of readiness, and the cavalry within an easy distance of London will be brought up as a reinforcement, as they were precisely at this time last year.

If at the breaking up of the meeting acts of violence shall be determined upon, the mob may proceed either to the City or to the west end of the town, the position of White Conduit Fields rendering their movement either to the one side or the other a matter of equal facility. In this uncertainty it appears to me that we cannot do more than hold our military force in readiness in their respective barracks or posts, to move when called upon. But I should very much like to be favoured with your ideas on the subject; and also upon the more general question of the defence of London in the event, which is not unlikely, of there being a riot with the view to the attack of obnoxious persons, the destruction of property, and the subsequent overthrow of the King's government. For such occurrences the military authorities should, in such times as the present, be prepared; and I feel confident that upon a matter of such moment you will, with your usual kindness, assist me with your invaluable advice and opinion.

The force we shall have in and about London on Monday next will be nearly as much as we could command upon the first occurrence of a serious disturbance, and will consist of

The 1st Life Guards, from Windsor to Hyde Park Riding House.

The 2nd Life Guards, Regent's Park Barracks.

The Blues, Hyde Park Barracks.

The 9th Lancers, King's Stables, Pimlico.

The 7th Dragoon Guards from Canterbury, to be cantoned near London, and to assemble either at the Obelisk or Vauxhall Bridge.

One squadron of the Greys from Hants and Sussex, to move up from Croydon to Vauxhall Bridge or some other convenient spot.

Four guns, Riding Establishment, St. John's Wood.

Four guns or more, Carlton House stables.

One Battalion of Foot Guards and detachment of Artillery, Tower.

Four battalions of Foot Guards, Portman Street Barracks, Knightsbridge Barracks, Mews Barracks, Westminster quarters and daily duties.

500 Marines from Woolwich, at Deptford Dockyard or the Obelisk. To these four guns might also be added.

This is all the force we can at present muster, and the garrisons of Portsmouth and Chatham are not so strong as they ought to be.

Your most faithful and affectionate,

Fitzroy Somerset.

Wellington to Lord Fitzroy Somerset, Sudbourne, November

MY DEAR LORD FITZROY,

I don't know what intelligence you have of plans for Monday, but if you know of no more than that there is to be a meeting on Monday in White Conduit Fields, I think that your preparations as detailed in your letter go too far. If you are to take up positions with your troops as often as the turbulent adherents of the government assemble a mob, you will soon wear them out.

I would bring the 1st Life Guards to be cantoned with their head at Knightsbridge, their rear at Brentford and Kew. The 9th Lancers doubled up at Kensington Barracks; and a strong post in the King's stables at Pimlico. The 7th Dragoon Guards to be cantoned with their head at the Obelisk, their rear at Blackheath. The Greys at Croydon.

The Marines in the barracks at Deptford or Woolwich.

Four guns, Carlton House stables.

Four guns, Riding Establishment, St. John's Wood.

Four guns to be in readiness at Woolwich, to come off to join the Marines.

The Guards in their respective barracks. The battalion in quarters doubled up at the Mews, or in Carlton House Riding-house, the Tiltyard, &c.

This places everything at your disposition and under cover.

The following are the great objects to be maintained: –

First, the Tower.

There are provisions in the Tower, I believe. But you must look to the communication with the Tower by water as well as by land; by water from above as well as from below bridge. With a view to command this communication, I recommend that a company from the Tower should be put into the Ordnance stores in Tooley Street.

I will advert to the land communication presently.

Secondly, the Bank of England.

The picquet in the Bank is full sufficient for its security. I desired some time ago that there should be provisions in the Bank. This ought to be taken care of.

Thirdly, the King's palaces, the Horse Guards, the Parliament House; the parks, particularly St. James's Park; the Mews Barracks; the Old Golden Cross, Charing Cross; the houses at the end of Whitehall, joining Parliament Street. A few men in these will enable you to command the whole space from Parliament Street to the Strand.

In case of alarm the troops at Knightsbridge and on the road to Windsor should double up at Pimlico and in Hyde Park Barracks.

Those on the Canterbury Road, and the Marines, and four guns from Woolwich, at the Obelisk. Those at Croydon at Vauxhall Bridge.

The guns in St. John's Wood, by the Riding Establishment, to Portman Street Barracks.

The police should seize for you certain prominent buildings in all parts of the town, such as the insurance office in Lower Regent Street, the church in Upper Regent Street, the church in the Strand, Somerset House in the Strand, Temple Bar, the turnpike house at the March-gate in Southwark, Bedlam, the Town House in the Borough, which commands the main street; the houses at the upper end of the approach from London Bridge.

All these will give you the command of the roads leading from St. James's Park (which ought to be the centre of your operations) to the Tower over Westminster and London Bridges; to the Bank by the same road; into the Strand and into the City. The police should likewise secure for you the possession of St. Paul's Church.

You would likewise be able by Regent Street to reach the north end of the town and the City Road.

I think that you ought to be prepared with the means of laying open any building which might be occupied and which might oppose the progress of the troops. Probably one of each of the four pieces of ordnance might be eighteen-pound iron carronades, such as we had with the army in Spain. They would lay open, in a minute, any house or church. Or you might have four of them at Carlton House stables, or at the Horse Guards.

Don't forget provisions for the troops in case you should turn them out. Plenty of biscuit and cheese will be sufficient, with the porter, which will not be wanting anywhere. But when once the troops quit their barracks those buildings will be best, excepting always the Mews; as you have not enough to leave men behind to take care of the barracks. You must be certain therefore of some means of giving food to the men and horses.

I believe that this is all that I have to suggest. It all goes to nothing excepting preparation, and the means of communicating with all parts of the town, particularly with those parts of which it is important to retain possession, and into which it will be important to penetrate.

I would recommend to you not to show a man till it should be necessary to act. I would keep the parks quite clear; lock up the gates, and drive out every person who should attempt to enter. If the troops are to be turned out, let it be to act; and that at once and efficiently.

Instead of having the alarm post of the troops on the Canterbury Road and from Woolwich, at the Obelisk, I would put them into the enclosure of Bedlam; and those at Vauxhall Bridge, into Vauxhall Gardens or the Vinegar Merchant's premises. It is a great object not to allow the mob to collect about the troops.

I shall be in London on Sunday.

Believe me, &c.,

WELLINGTON.

Mary Frampton's Journal

5 November

Various rumours spread of intended mischief on this night, but all passed quietly, and whether Lord Ashley's effigy, or that of Guy Fawkes was burnt, made happily no difference as to riot or confusion. The only difference was that no stuffed Guy Fawkes were brought to our door, as was the common custom of the day, and that the fireworks were more prolonged, lasting from dark until near midnight. Apprehensions had been entertained of riots, and the guard at the gaol was increased, and a day or two previously special constables had been sworn in and organized for the town, ready to be called upon if required. All the regular troops had quitted the barracks to go to Bristol, and at this time the safety of the county, as far as military were concerned, rested with the Yeomanry. As soon, however, as the riots at Bristol were quieted and a sufficient force fixed there, two troops of the 3rd Dragoons returned to their head-quarters at Dorchester.

On the morning of the 5th intelligence had been received that a mob from Poole were intending to attack Lord Eldon's place at Encombe, and also Corfe Castle. Mr Bond's troop of Yeomanry were in consequence called out, and stationed on and about the bridge at Wareham, thus effectually guarding the only approach from Poole to those places, excepting by sea, across Poole Harbour. All, however, passed off quietly, but the minds of the common people are wickedly excited by persons of a somewhat higher class going amongst them raising penny subscriptions to form a fund to pay Mr Ponsonby's expenses towards petitioning Parliament against Lord Ashley's return to Parliament, and talking the same language to induce them to give to it as was without scruple used to influence the votes and opinions of the mob in the two late contests, viz. that 'Reform' would give them meat as well as bread in abundance by paying only a quarter, if so much, of the present price for those articles. How can the poor resist such tempting language?

6 November

A good, well-printed paper has been sent out this day to contradict the falsehoods which have been printed and stuck about the town with a deep black border. This last was denominated the 'Black Lists;' it denounced the Lords and Bishops who voted against the Reform Bill as almost all pensioners of Government, and living on the taxes raised from the poor. Amongst the principal lies in this list was the assertion that all Lords-Lieutenants of Counties received large salaries, the amounts of which were I think stated, for their services instead of the honour being purely gratuitous, and indeed attended with expense to those holding it; but here again, how can the lower classes know whom to believe when such positive assertions are made? A letter from Bagshot mentions the alarm of the Bishop of Winchester, from threats having been made that his palace would be consumed, and in consequence troops were ordered there to guard the palace and himself and family.

The proclamation issued by Government, and the effect produced by the King himself coming suddenly to town without previous consultation with his Ministers, is likely to be useful, as there was a general idea spread amongst the lower orders that the King being in *favour* of Reform, they were supporting his wishes by their lawless endeavours to procure it, and that he would not allow the soldiers to act against them as they would cry out for 'The King and Reform.'

The Bishop of Exeter[3] to the Duke of Wellington, Exeter

5 November
MY LORD DUKE,
This place, I am sorry to say, is suffering from its vicinity to Bristol. Many of the miscreants who have escaped from the dragoons there are now here, and, joined to the dregs of this large population, exemplarily loyal as in the main it is, are exciting great alarm for the public peace. The most inflammatory bills have been freely circulated, calling on the populace to 'arm themselves, and imitate the heroic acts of the Bristol men to put down the *bloody usurpers*,' &c. As this day is always a day of licence it has been fixed upon for serious mischief. I am in hopes, however, that the preparations for resistance are such as to ensure the security of persons and property. I am myself especially threatened, and my house. But a threatened outrage rarely takes place, and I have taken such precautions as leave me nothing to apprehend for myself or my family.

I trouble your Grace with a letter, because I know your kindness would make you feel interested for me if the newspapers shall announce the expectation of mischief. I have also another reason – your Grace will, of course, be desirous to know the state of the county in every quarter, and it is the duty of all to assist in informing you.

There are strong indications of an expectation, if not of an actual plan, of insurrection against property among the lowest orders. This detestable Reform Bill has raised their hopes to the utmost. One of the papers dispersed in this place, headed 'The King and Reform,' invites the people to destroy the enemy, telling them that '*the price of provisions depends upon it.*' The effect is such, that almost all the artisans are in full hopes of an equalization of property, and hardly disguise their hopes. The principal iron manufacturer in this city (which is not a manufacturing place) told me to-day, that all his men, 100 in number, for the first time in his experience, refused to be sworn as special constables: they told him that 'they could not lose by a change.' Yet some of these fellows earn a guinea and a half per week – many, I believe most of them, a guinea. The principal builder in the place has met with a similar refusal.

At Plymouth and the neighbouring towns, including a population of more than 100,000, the spirit is tremendously bad. The shopkeepers are almost all Dissenters, and such is the rage on the question of Reform at Plymouth, that I have received from several quarters (the soberest and most respectable) the most earnest entreaties that I will not come there to consecrate a church, as I had engaged to do. They assure me that my own person, and the security of the public peace, would be in the greatest danger. Yet in my diocese generally – and I believe with the sole exception of Plymouth – I enjoy a very high degree of popular favour. I say this, your Grace will believe me, not from vanity, but because it is an ingredient in the case.

6 November
The night has gone off with little more excitement than is, I understand, usual on the 5th of November. As the populace has always been suffered to burn Guy Fawkes and the Pope, the magistrates very judiciously resolved not to interfere with their usual sport, and not to be inquisitive as to the additional figures they might choose to burn. This was communicated to me for my opinion, it being known that an effigy of myself, as well as of Lord Rolle, &c. had been prepared. I entirely concurred in the view taken by them; and expressed my *wish* that the burning should take place, for it seemed to me quite plain, that it was much better the effigies, as they were prepared, should be got rid of, else the peace would be endangered on some other night, when the authorities were less ready to meet the mischief. I mention this circumstance, that your Grace may not suppose, if you see any report of these matters in the newspapers, that it was weakness on the part of the magistracy which caused this illegal sport.

On the whole, the moral result of the intended mischief in this place is, I hope, very good. Though there were no regular troops at hand, the magistrates were able to prove their power at all times to collect force enough to put down the attempts of the mob.

It is a grievous reflection that a few demagogues, Lord —— at the head, have been able to pervert the feelings of a numerous portion of this county, which was, and I hope still is, essentially loyal. The farmers in several quarters have given strong indications of a return to common sense, and a dread of the Reform Bill.

I find that, individually, I stand the better with all here, except the mob, for my conduct on this question in Parliament.

I am, my Lord Duke, with the greatest respect,
    your Grace's most obliged and most faithful servant,
    H. EXETER.

Lady Lyttelton to her father, Earl Spencer, Hagley, 6 November

. . . The Worcester meeting went off beautifully; and if they *did* burn the Bishop and poor Lord Plymouth in the evening (as Lord L. heard they meant to do), it must have been a peaceful ceremony, for we heard nothing of any riot, in spite of Guy Fawkes and crackers into the bargain. Lord Lyttelton has a letter from the Bishop of Llandaff, who intends positively and without hesitation to vote for the Bill when it next comes on. His letter, as his always are, quite pleasant to read from the perfection of its language. He says he thinks many of his brethren will be taking his line. Lord Lyttelton has written word to Althorp of this vote gained. I hope he has heard of many others. . . .

The Poor Man's Guardian, *No. 22, Saturday 19 November*

BURNING A BISHOP IN EFFIGY!
Remember, remember,
The Fifth of November.
On the fifth of November the town of Huddersfield had the satisfaction of witnessing a ceremony of rather a novel description. Between fifteen and twenty thousand persons paraded the streets with an effigy of a Bishop (*as natural as life!*) and no funeral was ever conducted with greater awe and solemnity. When the procession reached the spacious and open square in the Market Place, all formed around the *Right Reverend Father in God*, and a person in priestly habiliments then delivered, in an audible and impressive manner, the following

FUNERAL ORATION!
Ho! all ye people of Huddersfield!
For, lo! and behold! here is a great, fat, bloated, blundering bishop, whom we have bartered for the poor, deluded, murdered Guy Faux! This is the last Fifth of November which shall constitute the anniversary of a bloody church and state conspiracy, in support of tithes, Easter offerings, oblations, obventions, and all the horrid and dreadful train of business, got up by the worse than devils, to deceive their dupes, for the purpose of rioting in holy luxury out of the *grindings* of our bones, to our utter ruin and past and present degradation.

And now, my friends and brethren, I have to inform you that on no future Fifth of November shall the country reverberate to the diabolical and nauseous rattling of the bells of old mother church, no more shall the disgusting and diabolical sound greet your ears, nor arouse your noble indignation, for now the great deceiver is going to his long home, and ye have all come to see him on his *long* journey, in the sure hope of a glorious change from rawhead and bloody bones, from a state worse than slavery to the old system of old England, with plenty of roast beef and plum pudding. Then with nine times nine, for the destruction of all monopolies – the new system – and fair play for the people, we hereby commit his infernal body to the flames, earth to earth, ashes to ashes, dust to dust, in the certain belief that eternal damnation will be his portion, and that he will never inherit a glorious resurrection.

> Good Lord! put down aristocrats,
> Let Boroughmongers be abhorred;
> And from all tithes and shovel hats
> Forthwith deliver us good Lord!

During the delivery of the oration, the most solemn silence was observed by the assembled multitude. No indication of levity was visible in the countenance of any of the *mourners*. The *veneration* and *affection*, now universally felt for the church, kept every man from laughing; though, to confess the truth, the rueful countenance of the Bishop, just before he was committed to the flames, made rather a ludicrous impression on the beholders. The good men of Huddersfield, however, were not to be *diverted* from their purpose by the dolorous countenance of the Bishop; and, as they were resolved to pursue the '*stern path of duty*,' they consigned him to the flames about 10 o'clock at night, after which the '*mob*' and '*populace*', as contradistinguished from the 'PEOPLE', quietly dispersed, and in less than fifteen minutes the streets were as clear as though nothing of an alarming nature had occurred.

> Religions are those codes and rules,
> Devised by PRIESTS to plunder FOOLS.

Lord Ellenborough's diary, 9 November

Egg the gunmaker told me yesterday that the price of musquets had risen from £1 to 25sh., that is, 25 per cent. There never was such a demand for them – a striking proof of the state of the publick mind.

James Milnes Gaskell[4] to his mother, Christ Church, 13 November

My dearest Mother,

Your last letter is very political; so are all other letters now, and so is all conversation here, for persons of all parties and opinions and persuasions, as far as I can learn, Whigs and Tories alike – Radicals we have none – agree in thinking the state of things most alarming, and I have not met one single person whose confidence in the Government is not shaken. I never had two opinions on the inexpediency of shortening Parlts or the criminality of forcing any measure, whether for good or for evil, upon an independent branch of the legislature; and I do think that if Ministers make 100 peers to carry the Reform Bill, i.e. if they incurred certain practical evil for the sake of possible theoretical good, they would be inviting as heavy a responsibility as ever rested on the head of a Minister.

We had an animated debate [at the Union] last Thursday upon Lowe's motion that the King would be justified in creating a sufficient number of peers to carry the Reform Bill. A great number of people spoke – among others, Herbert, Doyle and myself, almost all against the motion, and on dividing the numbers were, Ayes, four; Noes, ninety three; Majority, eighty nine.

With whomsoever I talk, I find myself disposed to look with an eye of pity on Lord Grey.

Your most affectionate son,

Milnes Gaskell

The Duke of Rutland to Lady Shelley, Belvoir Castle, 18 January 1832

. . . As to the Reform Bill! Lord Grey must go down in history as the rashest Minister who ever held the reins of State. If he makes the threatened batch of peers for one single vicious purpose he will be a fit subject for a Special Commission.

The juries at Nottingham have been summoned, and threatened, so as to mete out but very partial justice; and I am told the judges have proved themselves most miserable in their calling. Yet six men will be executed, and eight transported!

I am having all my labourers and servants drilled to the use of the great guns here. I have an artillery sergeant residing here for the winter, and we have drills every day. Last week I obtained a large supply of shot and ammunition from Woolwich. I am determined to make a good defence, if attacked.

Notes

1. Croker was visiting the Duke of Wellington at Walmer.
2. Lord Fitzroy James Henry Somerset (1788–1865), served with Wellington in the Peninsula and at Waterloo, later created Lord Raglan and commanded the British forces in the Crimean War. Secretary at the Horse Guards in 1831.
3. Henry Philpotts (1788–1869), Bishop of Exeter, a high Tory and high Churchman, fierce opponent of the Reform Bill in the House of Lords, for which he was burnt in effigy on 5 November 1831.
4. James Milnes Gaskell (1810–73), a friend of Gladstone and Arthur Hallam, was an undergraduate at Oxford 1829–31 and President of the Union 1831. He became MP for Much Wenlock in 1832 and retired in 1868.

CHAPTER SEVEN

'The Days of May', 1832

The winter months of 1831–2 were taken up with discussions among the Whig ministers and in the Press about the prospects for the Reform Bill in the House of Lords; the central question was whether Grey should seek the creation of additional peers to defeat the opposition, and if so, how many would be needed. Grey was as reluctant as anyone on either side to force the king against his wishes and equally averse to the creation of a large number of new peers, which would damage the prestige and authority of the Upper House, while the removal of men of property and family from the Commons might open the way to an increase in Radical support there. Nevertheless, he felt bound by his pledges to the people and by their support in the election of 1831 to persevere with 'the Bill, the whole Bill, and nothing but the Bill'. The attempt of a few 'Waverers' among the Tory peers, led by Lords Wharncliffe and Harrowby, to negotiate a compromise with the Government came to nothing and the parties were left in confrontation when the Lords began the second reading debate in early April. The 'Waverers' agreed to support this second reading, which passed on 14 April by nine votes, but when the committee stage began it quickly became apparent that the Bill's opponents were determined to emasculate it, clause by clause. On 7 May the Government was defeated on a Tory amendment which brought into question the main principles of the Bill. Grey and Brougham immediately sought an interview with the king at Windsor and requested authority to create whatever number of peers was necessary to pass it. The king answered that he preferred to accept the ministers' resignations and commissioned Wellington to form an alternative government.

Wellington's task was quickly shown to be impossible. He was prepared to take office to pass a more moderate reform bill in order to save the country, but Peel, the crucial figure in the House of Commons, refused to serve in any government which would propose a reform bill of any kind, remembering the furious attacks he had suffered in 1829 when he joined Wellington in forcing Catholic Emancipation on the king despite his own previous opposition to it. Not only did Peel's stubbornness wreck Wellington's attempt to form a Cabinet, but it highlighted what seemed to be a willingness by the duke to forego his avowed principles for the sake of office – unjust as that view was to a man whose motive was solely patriotic duty to his sovereign. Wellington's commission to form a government also aroused the country again, and as *The Times* reported in the middle of May, there was an organized and concerted run on the gold reserves of the Bank of England, under the slogan 'To stop the Duke, go for gold!' Even the loyalty of the troops was in question, should they be called on to act against the people. Within a week the duke surrendered his commission, Grey and his colleagues were recalled to the offices they had never in fact formally vacated, and the king gave Grey, in private, the assurance that he would create whatever number of peers was necessary to pass the Bill in the House of Lords. The country breathed relief as the Bill quickly went through its remaining stages, and to allow it to pass the third and final stage without allowing the recourse to new peerages Wellington and most of his friends withdrew from the House.

On 7 June the English Reform Act received the royal assent, followed shortly afterwards by those for Scotland and Ireland. The king, now thoroughly disillusioned with the ministers who he believed had forced his hand, refused to attend the Lords in person to give the royal assent, which was notified by commissioners to a House entirely empty on the Opposition side.

So the end of the crisis came with a whimper after all. How the Reform Act, later to be christened 'Great', would affect the government and people of Britain remained to be seen: the mood in June 1832 was one of relief that the crisis had passed without serious violence and revolution, rather than of optimism for the future. The future was, indeed, to show that not everyone who had fought for reform, or for the Bills, would gain what he or she had hoped for, at least in the short term. For Lord Grey and his followers, the passing of the Bills was an end in itself. No more could be expected. Looking back to the autumn of 1830 they were relieved that they had achieved what then seemed the primary objective: revolution had been averted.

Charles Greville's Journal

7 January 1832

. . . The question about the Peers is still under discussion; Lord Grey and the ultra party want to make a dozen *now*, the others want only to yield five or six. Lord Grey wrote to Palmerston saying the King had received his proposition (about the peers) very well, but desired to have his reasons in writing, and to-day at twelve there was to be another Cabinet on the subject, in order probably that 'the reasons' might go down by the post. The moderate party in the Cabinet consists of Lansdowne, Richmond, Palmerston, Melbourne, and Stanley. Palmerston and Melbourne, particularly the latter, are now heartily ashamed of the part they have taken about Reform. They detest and abhor the whole thing, and they find themselves unable to cope with the violent party, and consequently implicated in a continued series of measures which they disapprove; and they do not know what to do, whether to stay in and fight this unequal battle or resign. I told her [Lady Cowper] that nothing could justify their conduct, and their excuses were good for nothing; but that there was no use in resigning now. They might still do some good in the Cabinet; they could do none out of it. . . .

14 April

The Reform Bill (second reading) was carried this morning at seven o'clock in the House of Lords by a majority of nine. The House did not sit yesterday. The night before Phillpotts, the Bishop of Exeter, made a grand speech against the Bill, full of fire and venom, very able. It would be an injury to compare this man with Laud; he more resembles Gardiner; had he lived in those days he would have been just such another, boiling with ambition, an ardent temperament, and great talents. He has a desperate and a dreadful countenance, and looks like the man he is. The two last days gave plenty of reports of changes either way, but the majority has always looked like from seven to ten. The House will adjourn on

Wednesday, and go into Committee after Easter; and in the meantime what negotiations and what difficulties to get over! The Duke of Wellington and Lord Harrowby have had some good-humoured talk, and the former seems well disposed to join in amending the Bill, but the difficulty will be to bring these extreme and irritated parties to any agreement as to terms. The debate in the Lords, though not so good as last year, has been, as usual, much better than that in the Commons.

Brougham's account of the May crisis

8 May. We [Grey and Brougham] went to Windsor together, as the King had always required we should on any great emergency, and with the intention of asking for an unlimited creation of peers as the only means of carrying the Bill. We discussed on the way the names of those whom I had set down in my list, formed upon the principle of making the smallest possible permanent addition to the peerage; as by calling up eldest sons, by taking persons who had none, by selecting Scotch and Irish peers for British peerage, but also those not likely to have successors, to the number of eighty, which we considered might be required. He said, 'This is a strong measure to propose, reduce it how you will, and you must state it.' I said 'I had no objection to state the particulars, provided he would make the request and proposal.' 'No,' he said, 'it is your province officially, and you know the King required you to attend him on all such occasions.' I said, 'If it must be so, it must.' 'Of course,' he said, 'you speak in my name, as well as your own.' I said, 'And in that of the whole Ministry.' He said, 'Certainly, that is quite clear.' We laid our account with a refusal, though it did not seem quite certain. We expected, however, a very great reluctance and some delay. As soon as Grey had stated that we came humbly to advise his Majesty that he should accede to our prayer of having the means of carrying the Bill, the King said, 'What means?' I said, 'Sir, the only means; an addition to the House of Lords.' He said, 'That is a very serious matter;' and we both admitted that it was, and that unless quite convinced of its necessity, we never should think of recommending it. He then asked, 'What number would be required?' and I said, 'Sixty, or perhaps even eighty, for it must be done effectually, if at all.' He said 'that was a very large number indeed; was there ever such a thing done before?' I said, 'Never to that extent, or near it; Pitt had at different times made creations and promotions of much above one hundred, and Lord Oxford, in Queen Anne's time, had created twelve in order to pass one bill.' But I admitted these cases did not afford a precedent which went so far as this proposed creation. He said, 'Certainly nothing like it.' We continued to dwell on the necessity of the case, and our great reluctance to make such a request, and tender such advice to his Majesty. He said he must take time to consider well what we had laid before him; and when we saw Sir Herbert Taylor in the anteroom, while waiting for the carriage, and had some conversation with him, he said we were sure to have the King's answer to-morrow. Grey and I then set out, and on our way home had a wretched dinner at Hounslow, where he ate mutton-chops, and I insisted upon a broiled kidney being added to the poor repast. He laughed at me for being so easy and indifferent; and said 'he cared not for kidneys.' Nevertheless he ate them when they came. And we were in all the print-shops in a few days.

Next day the King sent an answer, accepting our resignation. . . .

Hobhouse's Recollections

7 May

The streets were placarded: 'Seventh of May,
                              Crisis Day'
– alluding to the debate in the Lords on committal of the Reform Bill.

I went to the House of Lords, and heard that Lord Lyndhurst had proposed to take the enfranchisement clauses of the Bill before the disfranchisement clauses; and that Lord Grey had declared such a course would be fatal to the Bill; that Lords Harrowby, Wharncliffe, and others had declared in favour of Lyndhurst; and that Ministers would be in a minority of 20 or 25 at the least. Nothing was more unexpected than this news.

A great many friends supposed that a creation of Peers was now inevitable; indeed, even the other side held the same language, and seemed afraid of their certain victory. The House divided, and, for the first time, I saw the division: Lyndhurst 151; Ministers 116.

Lord Grey then postponed the further consideration of the Bill until Thursday. Of this Lord Ellenborough complained, and said he was willing to admit the disfranchisement of 113 seats, and that he preferred household suffrage to the £10 qualification. This disclosure of the intention of the Tories to come in, and carry Whig Reform, drew forth a burst of eloquence from Lord Grey, who was loudly cheered by our friends, and then the House adjourned. I told several friends that Ministers were out. No one would believe me, but insisted that the King would create Peers. I told my wife with great glee, so far as I was concerned, that the Administration was at an end, for it had been beaten, and would resign.

8 May

I packed up my papers at the War Office to be ready for a start, for I felt sure all was over. At half-past two Lords Grey and Brougham went to the King at Windsor, with a proposal to create a sufficient number of Peers. Graham and Stanley and all seemed in good spirits, and said that, if the Tories had been paid for it, they could not have acted more for the country and the character of the Ministers. They did not seem to be sure, or indeed to care much, about the result of the proposal.

Lord Dover told me that Lord Grey had hesitated about proposing to make Peers, and preferred offering to resign. At last he was persuaded to take the other line.

9 May

Whilst I was getting up I received a note from Lord Durham marked 'Immediate.' It contained these words: 'Half-past nine. The King has refused to make Peers, and has accepted our resignation.'

After breakfast I went to Lord Durham's, and he showed me the note just arrived from Lord Grey. 'Dear Lambton, the King has accepted our resignations. Ever yours, G.'

We went to the Levee together. The only person, almost, to whom the King said nothing at the *entrée* Levee was the Duke of Wellington. The Duke of Richmond and Lord John Russell, standing by me, remarked it; and said the King was wretched, and angry with the Duke of Wellington. I said, 'Just the contrary; I would bet anything the Duke was Prime Minister.'

I talked with all the honest resigners, and shook hands with Lord Grey most warmly. He said to me, 'I could do nothing else; the Bill was taken out of my hands; I was no longer Minister.' We were all very merry, for undone dogs, as we were; and, when the Levee was over, the question was, what was the formality of resignation? No one seemed to know; but, at last, we were told that the King would see only those of the Cabinet who had particular business with him. Lords Grey, Lansdowne, Goderich, Palmerston, Duke of Richmond, and Lord Althorp went in one by one; and the Lord Chancellor came so late that some thought he was not coming at all. I was told that the King was very gracious, and wept, taking leave of Palmerston and Goderich, if not of others. He pressed Brougham and the Duke of Richmond to stay in office. The Duke of Richmond told me that he had got nothing by being in office, except the *entrée* for his two carriages. Lord John Russell told me he had been treated, before the Levee, with marked disrespect by the King, who did not speak to him, nor ask him to come in after the Levee. Nothing was known at Court about the new arrangements; but it appeared that Lord Lyndhurst was sent for after the Levee.

The House of Commons was very full. Ebrington gave notice of a call of the House, and an Address to the Crown, for the next day.

We adjourned, and I went to the Lords, where Lord Carnarvon was abusing Lord Grey *for deserting the King*!! Lord Grey made a very spirited answer, saying he would not consent to be the shadow of a Minister.

There was a great meeting at Brooks's, to consider Ebrington's Address. I had spoken to him about it, begging that it might be of a good decisive character, and that his speech would correspond with it. I told him, and Althorp too, that I did not approve of preaching patience, nor complimenting the King upon his conduct. Althorp replied that nothing should make him implicate the King.

I find the meeting at Brooks's was considered satisfactory. Ebrington, at first, proposed a milk-and-water Address, which was much improved upon.

Thomas Creevey to Miss Ord, Bury Street, 9 May

. . . Ladies, I have lost my Tower! *C'en est fait de nous*! Dead as mutton, every man John of us, so help me Jingo! You see, after our defeat in the Lords on Monday, a Cabinet was summoned for that night and the next day. The result was Grey and Brougham going down to Windsor yesterday at 3 o'clock to ask the King to create a sufficient number of peers in order to recover their ground and so secure the Bill, or, if he would not do that, to accept their resignation. They did not return till eleven; but by means of my faithful and active enquirer, [Lord] Sefton, who got to Crocky's a little past one, I found it was all over. The King had not even preserved his usual civility, had shown strong reluctance to the proposition, and concluded by saying that Lord Grey should have his answer on Thursday. He did not even offer the poor fellows any victuals, and they were obliged to put into port at the George posting-house at Hounslow, and so get some mutton chops. . . . Sefton was with Brougham a little after nine this morning, and during his stay a letter came from Grey to B. enclosing the Kings letter just received, in which his Majesty *accepts their* resignation. . . . Our beloved Billy cuts a damnable figure in this business, because he is clearly influenced by our defeat on Monday. He permitted the Duke of Cumberland to tell his friends that he would make no peers, and then the rats were in their old ranks again at once. All that *I* have to hope on this occasion is that there will be the same dawdling in making out my successor's patent as there was in making out mine. I regret certainly the loss of position and of doing agreeable things to myself with my official resources; but it was quite an unexpected windfall to me, has lasted much longer than I expected, and the recollection of the manner in which it fell to my lot will always be most agreeable to me. And so there's an end of the business, and it will never affect me more.

Lord Lyttelton to Lady Lyttelton

London, 9 May
. . . The King I hear was to be in town at twelve. Whether he is now – Good heavens! Here is Fritz come with the tremendous news of the King's refusal to make the Peers, and consequent acceptance of the Minister's resignation! Will there never be an honest King? And what is to betide us now that the King has stripped himself of all that incalculable power he possessed for our protection, and make the first person in the State the most hateful, and henceforward our principal weakness? To be sure the Ministers (of yesterday) stand higher than ever they did, since here is a complete justification of all that could be imputed to them; and it is possible their unblemished and noble characters may yet save us from a revolution. But God only knows. I see nothing distinctly, but all that I do see is most dark and ugly.

My Yeomanry Commission I shall probably, unless I find I cannot colourably, resign. For I certainly do not like to hold it for the purpose of forcing the people to submit to a Tory Ministry formed upon such principles and in consequence of such an intrigue as the present one. God grant that I may not be obliged to turn out again not merely for the suppression of a local riot.

10 May, three o'clock
. . . Returned from the Levee. The King looking as cool as ever; and he spoke for a minute, just to make a distinction, to Lord Radnor. What people these Kings are! It was said that Lord Harrowby had been sent for, but Fritz says it is the Duke of Wellington. Query. How many of ours would vote for *the* Bill brought in by His Grace? I know of two; Lord Radnor and Lord L[yttelton]. But how many more? Would not *he* have to make new Peers? Meantime the very Tories expect all kinds of confusion and difficulties, but say that *we* are answerable for leaving the country in such a state – and the King's for having allowed his name to be used to the lowest of the people, etc. All this is very pleasant in ordinary times, but now, too serious. . . .

The House was so crowded there was no moving about conveniently; and I could not see, from where I sat, the Episcopal bench. The heat was great, but not near equal, I think, to what it seemed in the House last October. Walked part of the way home with Lords Dartmouth and Aylesford. The latter was *shut out*, consequently there would have been 152. There must have been a great *Whip*. I talked amicably with Dartmouth, who gave me to understand that *many* (*i.e.*, he for one) would secede from the House if it was to be *swamped*. Truly (I *thought* – I did not *say* it), so much the better. . . .

11 May
. . . I am now sanguine about the result of all this commotion. Lord Grey remains at the helm, with his hands much strengthened for good purposes after the Reform Bill has been passed, and it will have been passed now by so clear a majority of the people, as distinguished from the populace, that it will be better received and be more final. . . .

Hobhouse's Recollections

Thursday 10 May
Ebrington introduced his motion with a good strong speech. Baring made a clever, unfair speech, and moved the negative, calling on Lord Althorp to tell what his advice to the King had been. Althorp rose, and, in the most impressive manner, plainly and resolutely, said that Baring knew what the advice had been; but, if he wished to be told, it was this: to create a sufficient number of Peers to carry the Reform Bill, in an efficient form, through the other House of Parliament.

Here the most tremendous cheers burst from all quarters of the House, and lasted louder and longer than I ever recollect to have heard; indeed, the spirit of the Reformers was up during the whole debate, and evidently cowed the other side, and gave the lie to the rumour of our apostacy.

Peel was very feeble, and felt it, as did the House; he said nothing about Reform. O'Connell handled him roughly. Macaulay made a good speech; but, as Burdett said, too like Coachmakers' Hall. We then divided, thinking we had a majority of at least a hundred; but we came in 288, the numbers inside being 208. The Opposition, particularly Lord Chandos, cheered as if they had gained a victory; and Sir Richard Vyvyan, amidst the laughter of us and ours, talked of the smallness of our majority. We went away, well pleased, about twelve o'clock.

Friday 11 May
Rumours that Peel and the Duke of Wellington are in negotiation with Lord Lyndhurst; the greatest possible excitement prevailing everywhere. A large Westminster meeting at Crown and Anchor, and meetings in the City. At House of Commons very sharp debates on presenting petitions, and everything announcing some crisis. The Duke of Wellington said to be Minister.

Saturday 12 May
For a short time at W.O. [War Office]. Sir James Graham called out under the window that everything was settled, and that the Duke of Wellington was Minister; Baring Chancellor of the Exchequer; Murray, Hardinge, etc., in office; and Parliament to be dissolved on Monday.

I went to Lord Grey, and saw him for a short time. He spoke to me about his resignation, and seemed very much affected by the tributes of esteem and respect offered to him from every part of the country. He told me that a Birmingham man had burst into tears before him; he said that Reform of Parliament was, in his view, like Catholic Emancipation, the removal of a stumbling-block, and not a cure for all evils. He had done his best to pass the measure, and when he failed, went out.

Sunday 13 May
It seems the Duke of Wellington is the chief, or, at least, the framer of the Ministry; and, from something that A. Baring said to me on Friday, I think *he* is Chancellor of the Exchequer. In the meantime the spirit is roused all over the country, and seems likely to end in mischief. I saw Tavistock to-day, and walked a good deal with him; he is completely benighted, I think, and supposes everything is to go off quietly. Peel, Croker, and Goulburn, all have declined office under the Tory Reformers; for it now turns out we are to have the Bill and the Duke of Wellington!!! Almost incredible; but true.

I went to a meeting at Brooks's where Lord Ebrington proposed another Address to the Crown, against the Duke of Wellington, but he eventually withdrew his proposal. The truth was, many of our people were afraid of a dissolution, and thought an Address would bring it on. I was afraid that, if we relaxed, the people would distrust us; and, besides, the Tories would find means to fritter away our opposition.

I had a letter from Sir Herbert Taylor to-day, expressing the King's regret at losing my services, and his satisfaction with my civility, etc., and appointing me to call on him the next day.

Monday 14 May

At half-past two I went to St. James's, and had my audience of resignation. The King was extremely civil; calling me 'My good friend,' 'My dear sir,' etc. He told me he knew I had too much property to lose, to wish for, or assist, any attempts at convulsion. I said, 'Your Majesty has not a more loyal subject than myself.' He replied, 'I know it.'

He then talked of various matters, of my father, of his intimacy with Lord Sidmouth, of the way in which it began. He said Sidmouth was a good speaker, and an agreeable man, but not a Minister of great capacity. I told him of my father being present when Pitt made his first speech at the Bar. We then talked of the cholera, which, he said, he did not think had been bad in London; then asked whether I had a house in Wiltshire, and where I should settle in the summer; then, about the James Hays, and other trifling matters.

In conclusion, he said, 'I will not take up more of your time; I have now seen you in public and in private, and I hope I may be permitted, occasionally, to keep up our acquaintance.' I replied that he was very condescending, and bowed *backwards* out of the room. He was looking well, and in good spirits; and, when I told him so, he said, 'Thank God, I was never better in my life.' I thought he seemed pleased to be rid of his Whig tutors.

At House of Commons. Call of the House not enforced. Lord Ebrington, on London petition, commenced a fire on the Duke of Wellington, for accepting office to carry the Reform Bill. He called it a violation of public morality. Macaulay spoke much to the same purpose; T. Duncombe was more explicit, and spared no epithet of contempt. Peel was there, but said nothing, looking most miserable. Baring tried his hand, very badly: it appeared he was mouthpiece to Wellington. He was received with horse-laughter when he declared that the Bill must pass, and that Wellington was justified in passing it. The debate was most triumphant, if debate it can be called.

I came away at half-past seven. It appears the debate went on, afterwards, until eleven; and that the Wellingtonians were so chapfallen that Burdett, Hume, and O'Connell recommended a cessation of hostilities, for the sake of a reconciliation between the King and the Whigs.

But the 'coup de grâce' was given to the *phantom* Ministry by Inglis, who declared against such a dereliction of public honour; and Wynne also said, if the Bill was to be carried, it ought to be carried by the Whigs. Even Hunt owned that nothing but the return of Lord Grey could tranquillise the country. Baring made a second speech in a different tone from his first speech; so much so, it was thought he had heard from the Duke of Wellington, for he recommended reconciliation between the King and the Whigs. I suppose there was never before such a scene in Parliament.

Tuesday 15 May

I called on Lord Althorp, when in came the Duke of Richmond, and said: 'Well, I have bad news for you; no shooting this year. Pack up your guns again. I have the intelligence from the Palace, and know it to be true. The Duke of Wellington has been with the King this morning, and given up his commission altogether.'

At a quarter past four I went to the House of Commons. There was much excitement in the streets and near the Houses of Parliament. The Duke's failure was generally known, but nothing was said about Lord Grey.

The House was very full and much expectation alive. Lord Althorp, Graham, Stanley, and Palmerston entered, and took their old seats. Baring then rose, and said that he had to tell the House that the Duke of Wellington's effort to construct a new Ministry had totally failed, and he hoped the new arrangements would be satisfactory.

Lord Althorp stated that Lord Grey had received a message from the King, and proposed adjourning the House till Thursday.

The greatest joy was apparent in the faces of all our friends, and even some opponents seemed rather pleased than otherwise; but we spared our baffled enemies. In the streets there was one universal look, and gesture, and language of delight.

I went to Francis Place; he was overjoyed, and said it was the greatest and most surprising Revolution in History. He told me there would have been a convulsion if the Duke had persevered. The demand for gold was increasing. Birmingham was preparing for resistance; and here, in London, there were symptoms of fighting. Now, he thought, all would be well. I told him not to be so sure of Lord Grey's return.

Charles Greville's Journal

12 May

. . . What is odd enough is that the King was hissed as he left London the other day, and the Duke cheered as he came out of the Palace. There have been some meetings, with resolutions to support the Bill, to express approbation of the Ministers, and to protest against the payment of taxes, and there will probably be a good deal of bustle and bluster here and elsewhere; but I do not believe in real tumults, particularly when the rabble and the unions know that there is a Government which will not stand such things, and that they will not be able to bandy compliments with the Duke as they did with Althorp and John Russell, not but what much dissatisfaction and much disquietude must prevail. The funds have not fallen, which is a sign that there is no alarm in the City. At this early period of the business it is difficult to form any opinion of what will happen; the present Government in opposition will again be formidable, but I am disposed to think things will go on and right themselves; we shall avoid a creation of Peers, but we must have a Reform Bill of some sort, and perhaps a harmless one after all, and if the elements of disorder can be resolved into tranquillity and order again, we must not quarrel with the means that have been employed, nor the quantum of moral injustice that has been perpetrated.

The Tories are very indignant with Peel for not taking office, and if, as it is supposed, he is to support Government and the Bill out of office, and when all is over come in, it is hardly worth while for such a farce to deprive the King and the country of his services in the way that they could be most useful, but he is still smarting under Catholic question reminiscences, while the Duke is more thick-skinned. After he had carried the Catholic question the world was prepared for a good deal of versatility on his part, but it was in mere derision that (after his speech on Reform in 1830) it used to be said that he would very likely be found proposing a Bill of Reform, and here he is coming into office for the expess purpose of carrying on this very Bill against which the other day he entered a protest which must stare him in the face through the whole progress of it, or, if not, to bring in another of the same character, and probably nearly of the same dimensions. Pretexts are, however, not wanting, and the necessity of supporting the King is made paramount to every other consideration. The Duke's worshippers (a numerous class) call this the finest action of his life, though it is difficult to perceive in what the grandeur of it consists, or the magnitude of the sacrifice. However, it is fair to wait a little, and hear from his own lips his exposition of the mode in which he intends to deal with this measure, and how he will reconcile what he has hitherto said with what he is now about to do. . . .

14 May
Nothing more was known yesterday, but everybody was congregated at the clubs, asking, discussing, and wondering. There was a great meeting at Apsley House, when it was supposed everything was settled. The Household went yesterday to St. James's to resign their sticks and badges. . . . It is supposed that this *coup* has been preparing for some time. All the Royal Family, bastards and all, have been incessantly *at* the King, and he has probably had more difficulty in the long run in resisting the constant importunity of his *entourage*, and of his womankind particularly, than the dictates of his Ministers; and between this gradual but powerful impression, and his real opinion and fears, he was not sorry to seize the first good opportunity of shaking off the Whigs. When Lord Anglesey went to take leave of him at Windsor he was struck with the change in his sentiments, and told Lady Anglesey so, who repeated it to my brother. . . .

London, 17 May
The events of the last few days have passed with a rapidity which hardly left time to think upon them – such sudden changes and transitions from rage to triumph on one side, and from foolish exultation to mortification and despair on the other. The first impression was that the Duke of Wellington would succeed in forming a Government, with or without Peel. The first thing he did was to try and prevail upon Peel to be Prime

Minister, but he was inexorable. He then turned to Baring, who, after much hesitation, agreed to be Chancellor of the Exchequer. The work went on, but with difficulty, for neither Peel, Goulburn, nor Croker would take office. They then tried the Speaker, who was mightily tempted to become Secretary of State, but still doubting and fearing, and requiring time to make up his mind. At an interview with the Duke and Lyndhurst at Apsley House he declared his sentiments on the existing state of affairs in a speech of three hours, to the unutterable disgust of Lyndhurst, who returned home, flung himself into a chair, and said that 'he could not endure to have anything to do with such a *damned tiresome old bitch.*' After these three hours of oratory Manners Sutton desired to have till the next morning (Monday) to make up his mind, which he again begged might be extended till the evening. On that evening (Monday) ensued the memorable night in the House of Commons, which everybody agrees was such a scene of violence and excitement as never had been exhibited within those walls. Tavistock told me he had never heard anything at all like it, and to his dying day should not forget it. The House was crammed to suffocation; every violent sentiment and vituperative expression was received with shouts of approbation, yet the violent speakers were listened to with the greatest attention. Tom Duncombe made one of his blustering Radical harangues, full of every sort of impertinence, which was received with immense applause, but which contrasted with an admirable speech, full of dignity, but also of sarcasm and severity, from John Russell – the best he ever made. The conduct of the Duke of Wellington in taking office *to carry the Bill*, which was not denied, but which his friends feebly attempted to justify, was assailed with the most merciless severity, and (what made the greatest impression) was condemned (though in more measured terms) by moderate men and Tories, such as Inglis and Davis Gilbert. Baring, who spoke four times, at last proposed that there should be a compromise, and that the ex-Ministers should resume their seats and carry the Bill. This extraordinary proposition was drawn from him by the state of the House, and the impossibility he at once saw of forming a new Government, and without any previous concert with the Duke, who, however, entirely approved of what he said. After the debate Baring and Sutton went to Apsley House, and related to the Duke what had taken place, the former saying he would face a thousand devils rather than such a House of Commons. From that moment the whole thing was at an end, and the next morning (Tuesday) the Duke repaired to the King, and told him that he could not form an Administration. This communication, for which the debate of the previous night had prepared everybody, was speedily known, and the joy and triumph of the Whigs was complete.

The King desired the Duke and Lyndhurst (for they went together) to advise him what he should do. They advised him to write to Lord Grey (which he did), informing him that the Duke had given up the commission to form a Government, that he had heard of what had fallen from Mr. Baring in the House of Commons the night before on the subject of a compromise, and that he wished Lord Grey to return and resume the

Government upon that principle. Lord Grey sent an answer full of the usual expressions of zeal and respect, but saying that he could give no answer until he had consulted his colleagues. He assembled his Cabinet, and at five o'clock the answer was sent.

Yesterday morning Lord Grey saw the King; but up to last night nothing was finally settled, everything turning upon the terms to be exacted, some of the violent of the party desiring they should avail themselves of this opportunity to make Peers, both to show their power and increase their strength; the more moderate, including Lord Grey himself and many of the old Peer-makers, were for sparing the King's feelings and using their victory with moderation, all, however, agreeing that the only condition on which they could return was the certainty of carrying the Reform Bill unaltered, either by a creation of Peers or by the secession of its opponents. Up to the present moment the matter stands thus: the King at the mercy of the Whigs, just as averse as ever to make Peers, the violent wishing to press him, the moderate wishing to spare him, all parties railing at each other, the Tories broken and discomfited, and meditating no further resistance to the Reform Bill. The Duke is to make his *exposé* to-night.

Peel, who has kept himself out of the scrape, is strongly suspected of being anything but sorry for the dilemma into which the Duke has got himself, and they think that he secretly encouraged him to persevere, with promises of present support and future co-operation, with a shrewd anticipation of the fate that awaited him. I am by no means indisposed to give credit to this, for I well remember the wrath of Peel when the Duke's Government was broken up in 1830, and the various instances of secret dislike and want of real cordiality which have peeped from under a decent appearance of union and friendship. Nothing can be more certain than that he is in high spirits in the midst of it all, and talks with great complacency of its being very well as it is, and that the salvation of character is everything, and this from him, who fancies he has saved his own, and addressed to those who have forfeited theirs, is amusing.

The joy of the King at what he thought was to be his deliverance from the Whigs was unbounded. He lost no time in putting the Duke of Wellington in possession of everything that had taken place between him and them upon the subject of Reform, and with regard to the creation of Peers, admitting that he had consented, but saying he had been subjected to every species of persecution. His ignorance, weakness, and levity put him in a miserable light, and prove him to be one of the silliest old gentlemen in his dominions; but I believe he is mad, for yesterday he gave a great dinner to the Jockey Club, at which (notwithstanding his cares) he seemed in excellent spirits; and after dinner he made a number of speeches, so ridiculous and nonsensical, beyond all belief but to those who heard them, rambling from one subject to another, repeating the same thing over and over again, and altogether such a mass or confusion, trash, and imbecility as made one laugh and blush at the same time.

Lord Holland's[1] diary

May 15. The debate of last night has produced such a sensation in the publick that Tories, waverers, and Court must yield. The Duke of Wellington at ½ past 11 slunk ignominiously away from the enterprize he had so imprudently undertaken, and told the King he was unable to form any Ministry. He could scarcely draw any other conclusion from the general reprobation of all respectable men, Reformers and antireformers, and the loud, universal, and dangerous indignation of the country. In aid of these tremendous monitors I have reason to believe Rothschild informed him that, if he persisted, a demand for Gold in England would encrease to a frightful amount, and the Movement Party in France would precipitate a war. . . .

The King sent a letter to Grey, and grounding his motive exclusively on what passed in Commons and the prospect of passing the bill in consequence thereof with modifications not affecting the principle and without any addition to the peerage for the purpose, offered and solicited Lord Grey to continue. He made no allusion to what Mr Holmes terms, aptly enough, the Interlude of the Duke of Wellington, and manifestly pointed to modifications, arrangements, and compromises with the Anti-reformers as furnishing the means of passing the bill without peers. To this, after deliberation at Lord Grey's, we dispatched a Minute of Cabinet in which we adverted to the failure of the attempt to form a new Ministry, repeated the necessity of having a full security that we should pass the Reform bill unimpaired in its principles and essential provisions, and requested an assurance that HM would enable us to strengthen his Government in the House of Lords. . . . The intelligence of this renewal of communication with Grey checked the active and encreasing violence of the people and suspended the frightful demand of Gold and converted many hundreds of meetings throughout the country in the ensuing days into meetings of joy instead of consternation and despair. The tone however of the letter and the language repeated to us by Court Gossips were far from encouraging, and indicated soreness if not hostility in the King and yet more bitter hatred in the Queen to Lord Grey and his Colleagues. At the levee, where I arrived late, Grey told me that he thought 'the thing would do', and that the King in his audience, though neither cordial nor satisfactory, was better than his letter. I afterwards found that Grey alluded to a letter (the reply to our answer in Cabinet) which he had received this morning, and which was full of irritation, soreness, and reluctance, and indicated as much reluctance to our measure and ourselves as was consistent with any possibility of admitting us to his councils, and more design of getting us in the wrong if a rupture ensued than of desire to prevent one. Even in his conversation the King avowed to Grey that he had always been hostile tho' he had yielded to Reform and that his hatred of it was not abated, and he still persisted in his incredulity of any very general and intense desire for it in the community. To this second letter we framed, after long and earnest deliberation in the Cabinet . . . A Minute, the substance of which was to secure the bill through the

Lords where, as at present composed, there was a Majority against it, there were but two methods of proceeding. The one, to prevail on the existing Majority to disist in their opposition, or the second, to produce a Majority in its favor by the introduction of friends to the measure. The first alternative was not in our power, and the last was the only one which suggested it to our minds unless some other security could be devised. We therefore must either advise the creation of peers or, on any probability being shewn us of passing the bill unaltered, resume the Government and proceed with an understanding that if any obstacle should arise we should be at liberty to surmount it by a creation of peers. . . .

Thursday 16 [17] May
A Cabinet at Lord Grey's to consider of the answer received to our Minute of yesterday. The King in his letter distinctly acknowledged our right to exact some security for passing the bill unmutilated in its principles and essential provisions and as nearly as possible in its present form. . . .

. . . We framed an answer in substance, deferring a final and categorical one till Friday morning, stating in the body of it that the withdrawal of opposition to [the] bill could not depend on us and that . . . if it were not diminished, we remained in the same state as we were on Tuesday the 8th May when we humbly tendered . . . our resignation, unless a creation of peers was resorted to. . . . From Lord Grey's we went to the House of Lords, in full expectation and with no little curiosity, to hear the Duke of Wellington and other of the protestors against the bill as revolutionary, injurious to property, contrary to justice and nearly impracticable, state their reasons for supporting an attempt to form a Ministry to carry this heinous measure and, on the failure of their attempt, absenting themselves from Parliament in order that it might be carried by others. . . . [At the end of the debate] the Duke of Wellington and about 50 or 60 peers rose in a marked way and quitted the house in a body. . . .

The Times *on the demand for gold at the bank, 15 May*

MONEY-MARKET and CITY INTELLIGENCE
Monday Evening
The demand for gold at the Bank is increasing. The counter in the Cashier's office, at which sovereigns are obtained, was beset during the whole day with applicants, chiefly in sums varying from 20l to 100l; besides which, large amounts have been drawn out by the private bankers, for transmission to country correspondents, in anticipation of a general demand for gold under the present excitement which prevails.

One house at the west end of the town procured three parcels of 5,000 sovereigns each on Saturday. A considerable number of small sales of stock was made in the course of the morning, and it was remarked by the brokers that, in a great majority of cases, the produce was taken to the Bank to be converted into gold. It does not appear, however, that the run has yet reached an extent which can justly cause alarm, especially as the

Bank is considered to be well prepared for such an emergency, the high rate of the foreign exchanges being favourable to the importation of the precious metals, which has replenished its coffers and rendered it easy, should it become necessary, to obtain a further supply. . . . According to the best estimate that can be formed, about 1,000,000l in gold may have been drawn out under the influence of the present excitement, which is not the tenth part of what is supposed to be stored up in the Bank. It does not follow, however, that there is no danger of the whole being exhausted, if some step is not taken to allay the popular ferment, and this will, no doubt, be used, or ought to be, in the proper quarter, as an argument for conciliation. This danger is much increased by the private deposits with the Bank, which are now well known to be larger than at any preceding period; and as it is impossible to exercise any control over them, the Directors may find, to their cost, that they ought in propriety to be ranked as part of their circulation.

The funds have been tolerably firm today, and with a tendency to advance, which is owing entirely to its having transpired that up to a late hour today, the Duke of Wellington has been unable to bring over any adherents to the new Administration, and to the belief, consequently, that there is no alternative to the return of the old Ministers to office. . . .

16 May

. . . A steady demand for gold is kept up at the Bank, not materially differing from that of yesterday, by applicants in the Cashier's office, but seldom for more than 100l by each individual. A still more serious demand is, however, threatened on the part of the savings' banks, there having occurred, as it is believed, more or less of a run on all those institutions, in consequence of the existing alarm: a demand from this quarter is not, like that by private persons, obvious to any casual visitor to the Bank, and yet, owing to the very large deposits invested by the savings' banks, may be going on far more extensively. The mode of drawing out is by a week's previous notice, and on the amount wanted being ascertained, an order signed by the trustees is transmitted to the office at the Bank for the management of those institutions, from whence the requisite sum is regularly transmitted. Only the parties concerned can therefore be aware of what is going on. It is known that a notice for withdrawing 16,000l has been given for one week by the Manchester savings' bank, and we have heard that the trustees of the Bloomsbury bank have signed an order for 13,000l, which is probably to be drawn out on Saturday next. These form, probably, not less than 10 per cent of the whole amount deposited in those banks; and, assuming that the others have been run upon in nearly the same proportion, a very large drain would be produced from this cause alone. This is proof, too, how widely the alarm has spread among the lower classes, and that the consequences must be felt still further unless the proper course for restoring confidence is taken. . . .

All depends . . . on the immediate return of the old Ministers to office. Every man of common understanding is convinced that the gold in the Bank will be exhausted in a week if a Tory Ministry is appointed in face of the obstinate determination against it on the part of the people. . . .

Alexander Somerville's[2] Autobiography of a Working Man

At Birmingham, two hundred thousand persons, under the guidance of Thomas Attwood, the eminent banker, the father and the hero of political unions, met on Newhall Hill (where now stands the Town Hall), petitioned against supplies, resolved to pay no king's taxes until the bill passed, and, if need be, to remove bodily the whole two hundred thousand of them, and encamp, with other political unions, on Hampstead or Penenden Heath, to be near parliament. Every day, for months previously, hundreds of people walked into the cavalry barrack yard of Birmingham, to see the Greys. On the Sunday before the meeting on Newhall Hill, there were upwards of five thousand people within the gates, most of them well-dressed artisans, all wearing ribbons of light blue knotted in their breasts, indicating that they were members of the political union. Next Sunday, the barrack gates were closed. No civilians were admitted. We were marched to the riding school, to prayers, in the forenoon, and during the remaining part of the day, or most of it, were employed in rough sharpening our swords on the grindstone. I was one of the 'fatigue' men, who turned the stone to the armourer and his assistants.

It was rumoured that the Birmingham political union was to march for London that night; and that we were to stop it on the road. We had been daily and nightly booted and saddled, with ball cartridge in each man's possession, for three days, ready to mount and turn out at a moment's notice. But until this day we had rough sharpened no swords. The purpose of so roughening their edges, was to make them inflict a ragged wound. Not since before the battle of Waterloo had the swords of the Greys undergone the same process. Old soldiers spoke of it, and told the young ones. Few words were spoken. We had made more noise, and probably looked less solemn, at prayers in the morning than we did now grinding our swords. It was the Lord's day, and we were *working*. The House of Commons had three times passed a bill declaring that fifty-six rotten boroughs should be disfranchised; that the new boroughs of Manchester, Birmingham, Leeds, Greenwich, Sheffield, Sunderland, Devonport, Wolverhampton, Tower Hamlets, Finsbury, Marylebone, Lambeth, Bolton, Bradford, Blackburn, Brighton, Halifax, Macclesfield, Oldham, Stockport, Stoke-upon-Trent, and Stroud, should have each two representatives. On this memorable Sunday, we sharpened our swords to prevent these new boroughs from obtaining any representatives. . . .

The negociations then pending between the King and the antireformers, were unknown to the country, and in their details still are. Most of the transactions beyond the town of Birmingham were unknown to us, though, from general rumour, we knew, unfortunately for our profession, that the country was alarmingly unanimous. When closed within the barracks, booted and saddled, we had no communication with the townspeople night nor day, and knew nothing of their movements. We did not apprehend an immediate collision until the day of the sword sharpening. The danger now seemed imminent. Those of us who had held private and confidential conversations on the subject, had agreed that the best means of preventing a collision with the reform movement and the national will, as expressed by the House of Commons, was to give circulation to the fact that we were not to be depended upon to put down public meetings, or prevent the people of Birmingham from journeying to London, to present their petitions, and support the House of Commons by their presence, if they chose to undertake the journey. We caused letters to be written and sent to various parties in Birmingham and London, to that effect. Some were addressed to the Duke of Wellington, some to the King, some to the War Office to Lord Hill, and some were dropped in the streets. Those letters were necessarily anonymous, but they contained no violent threats. They firmly and respectfully urged that, while the Greys would do their duty if riots and outrages upon property were committed, they would not draw swords or triggers upon a deliberative public meeting, or kill the people of Birmingham for attempting to leave their town with a petition to London. In the letters dropped in Birmingham streets, or sent to parties resident in that town, we implored the people, as they valued success to reform and political friendship with the army, *not* to allow rioting, window-breaking, or any outrage on property; else, if refusing to draw swords on them, in the event of our being brought before a court martial for such disobedience, we would have no justiciation. We would be condemned and shot. 'If you do nothing but make speeches, sign petitions, and go peaceably to present them, though you go in tens of thousands, the Greys will not prevent you.' One of my letters contained that passage, and concluded thus: – 'The King's name is a tower of strength, which they upon the adverse faction, want.' . . .

Happily, the *nine* days of a nation without a government – all classes fervently excited and nearer unanimity than was ever known of the English nation – came to an end. The renewed vote of confidence in the late cabinet by the House of Commons; the petitions of the country to the commons to stop the supplies; the political unions guided by the greatest of them all – the union of Birmingham – resolving not to pay assessed taxes until the bill passed; the rumour industriously spread and conveyed to the highest quarters, and founded on a well-determined resolution of certain soldiers, that the army was not to be relied on, if the constitutional voice of the country was attempted to be suppressed by the unconstitutional use of military power – especially at Birmingham, upon which town the eyes of Britain and of Europe were fixed; all those concurrent causes, of which the last was not the least effective, brought the attempt to establish a government by military power in defiance of the House of Commons to an end. May such attempts be at an end for ever!

[Somerville afterwards wrote a letter to a newspaper to say that the Greys would have acted against any unlawful activity but 'against the liberties of our country we would have never, never, raised an arm.' He confessed authorship to save others from suspicion and was court-martialled and sentenced to a hundred lashes. The severity of the punishment caused a public outcry and there was a Military Court of Inquiry which censured the commanding officer concerned. Somerville who was now something of a celebrity was then allowed to purchase his discharge from the army.]

Le Marchant's diary

Nothing transpired the next day [17 May]. The Whigs were as gloomy as
the Tories. The House had been adjourned till the morrow in order to give
time for negociation. It was a very painful day. The morrow came but
brought no improvement. At 4 o'clock I met Francis Baring, who had just
been told by Lord Durham that things looked as bad as they could. It now
ceased to be a question about the Ministry – they were forgotten – we
thought and talked only of the country. Praed, who was present, asserted
that the King had yielded, and there would be threescore peers in the
Gazette that night.

I was engaged out to dinner but I was so out of spirits that I excused
myself and made a comfortless meal at my club. It only wanted ½ an hour to
5 – the hour when Lord Grey had undertaken to announce the result of the
negociation. Everyone that dropped in forboded evil. At last the clock was
on the stroke of 5 and I hastened to the Lords. Neither Lord Grey nor the
Chancellor were arrived. Lord Althorpe was, and candidly stated to his
friends that he feared it was all over. We deplored that our lot should have
been cast in such evil times, and cursed the blindness of the monarch and
his advisers. Still there was a hope. It was 10 minutes past 5 – no Lord
Grey. Charles Fox then came in and said that he had met Lord G[rey] on
the stairs in the Palace, and Lord G[rey] in passing him had said, 'It is all
right.' We had scarcely heard this when his Lordship and the Chancellor
both arrived. They had been with the King from 25 to 5 till ten minutes
after, and had driven straight to the Lords. They went into the House
immediately, and Lord Grey, having sent Stanley to Lord Althorpe to tell
him what had passed, rose in the most inte[n]sely attentive assembly that
had ever been brought together and announced that the Ministry was
re-established, which was in effect that the Bill was virtually carried. The
King undertook to keep away a sufficient number of peers to leave a
majority in favour of the Bill. There was no other condition. The most
deafening cheers followed. All was now joy and congratulation. The
throne was thronged by members of the other House. They almost wrung
my hand off. Everyone spoke to his neighbour as if some unexpected good
fortune had happened to him. Men's hearts glowed within them and every
selfish consideration was lost in a sense of the public good. Indeed the
crisis had been such that private and public interests were identified. Few
but the most furious partizans of the Duke expected that private property
could long survive a change of the Administration.

In the City the rejoicings were still greater than in the west: not that the
Ministry are favourites with the merchants – Poulett Thompson has
guarded against that – but that commercial men had the sagacity to foresee
the convulsions almost inevitable from the Duke's attainment of power.
Rot[h]schild for some days was constantly spreading false reports of the
restoration of the Ministry. It saved him from ruin for he had entered into
a great speculation for a rise. The City also had grown seriously
apprehensive of a conflict with the Radicals and they knew the Tories were
wholly incapable of that. John Baring (who is in the Opposition) told me

he had no doubt of the moderate Tories ultimately rallying under the banner of the Whigs, as the only remaining hope of security. Some of the aristocracy reluctantly came to the same conclusion. Lord Robert Manners told Bob Smith that when he recovered his seat in Parliament he supposed he should be under the necessity of supporting Lord Grey.

The conduct of the people throughout this awful struggle is the theme of general admiration. Even the moderate Reformers allow it to be one of the best proofs of the advantages of education. The Tories, on the other hand, regret that the people should know their interests, as such knowledge may be incompatible with submission to the present system.

Hobhouse's Recollections

May 17, Thursday. I find disturbances in Westminster, and the panic returning. I went to the House of Commons, and there Ellice told me that the King had written to Lord Grey, stating that the Duke of Wellington, Lord Lyndhurst, the Dukes of Cumberland and Gloucester, and others, would make conciliatory speeches, which would enable the Reform Bill to pass without peers being made.

I heard the Duke of Wellington state his case at the Lords; but so far was he from conciliation, or anything like withdrawing his opposition to the Bill, that every sentence was an attack either on Reform or Lord Grey. He did not say a word about his intended support of the measure, had he been Minister; but he did make use of the expression attributed to him by Baring, about his not deserting the King. Lord Lyndhurst followed him in a still more bitter speech, and did not show the slightest symptoms of concession. I was near Ellice: we both stared, and he said that these men had deceived the King, for he had positively seen the King's letter; and Lord Althorp had announced, in the Commons, that there was 'every probability of the affair coming to a satisfactory result.'

Lord Grey answered in a firm and manly speech, defending the creation of Peers, and stating that he was resolved not to retain office unless he could carry the Bill unmutilated. He spoke too handsomely of the King, and he refuted the Duke of Wellington's charge of leaving the King alone. Lord Mansfield spoke, and indignantly disclaimed the virtue, imputed to him by the *Times* of rejecting the Duke's offer of office. I was satisfied that all was over, and I went to the Commons. I sat down next to Althorp, and told him what had passed. He said: 'Well, so much the better; but it is rather a bore for me to have spoken with so much confidence, though I was quite justified in so doing. Now I shall have my shooting.' 'You may,' I said; 'so shall we. The pitchforks will be here.' 'Not here,' he replied; 'the other House.' I said, 'I don't care for that.'

I found the Members of the House of Commons quite satisfied with the proceedings in their House, and could not persuade them that the Lords would not yield. They had written good news to all parts of the country. . . .

18 May

. . . I came down to the House of Commons at half-past four; found the call going on and every preparation for the Address. Nothing known, except that the Cabinet had agreed upon a minute, and that Lords Grey and Brougham had carried that minute to the King, and were with him at that moment. Althorp, Palmerston, Stanley, Graham, and Grant entered the House; but they knew nothing more. The call went on. Lord Milton came to Ebrington and me, pressing some change in the Address. We advised none, but, at last, Ebrington consented to go out with him to look at the alteration. The call was nearly over, when Tom Duncombe came to the end of the Treasury bench, where I was, and said, 'All was done and settled.' There was a great bustle – many complaints of the Ministers keeping the secret too long. Stanley was called out of the House, but presently returned and said to me, 'All right!' When the call was over Lord Althorp rose, and, in one sentence, told the House 'THAT MINISTERS, HAVING WHAT THEY CONCEIVED A SUFFICIENT GUARANTEE FOR BEING ABLE TO PASS THE REFORM BILL UNIMPAIRED, RETAINED THEIR OFFICES.'

There was great shouting, and some waving of hats, particularly by O'Connell, who, by the way, has behaved very well in this great emergency. . . .

Such for the present, is the conclusion of this memorable interregnum, which has done more, in nine or ten days, to discover the real character of the King, and the people, and the parties in the state, than could otherwise have been found out in as many years. . . .

19 May

I went to Place. He told me that there would, positively, have been a rising if Wellington had recovered power yesterday. Everything was arranged for it; he himself would not have slept at home. . . .

Le Marchant's journal

Tuesday was an exciting day. The opinion was rapidly gathering that a new Administration was impracticable. Peel was understood still to withhold his support. The Chancellor thought he would yield at last, and there is no doubt it would have been the boldest and wisest course if he wished to preserve his party. It is reported and believed that he differed with the Duke on the expediency of an immediate dissolution. The Duke thought it the only mode of establishing the new Government; Peel dreaded civil war. Both, perhaps, were in the right. The latter certainly would have had an uneasy berth at Tamworth. Hill told me that the Union would have sent such a body of their members to that place during the election, that Peel's return would have been impracticable. The accounts from the country now poured in, and were of the most alarming description. Parkes came on a deputation from Birmingham. He told me, that it was with extreme difficulty that the people could be kept from coming to extremities. Hill described the state of public feeling there very forcibly. 'The people,' he said, 'are so excited, that anything at all unusual throws them into confusion. A man blowing a horn is immediately taken for an express, and the arrival of a coach from London at an unusual hour emptied the workshops in an instant. Very little work is done. The workmen walk about, talking of nothing but the Bill.' The account of the vote of the Lords was received as a public calamity. The churches and dissenting chapels tolled their bells the whole night. Well might the General in command be alarmed. He wrote to Lord Hill that he was wholly incapable of resistance in case of an insurrection. His whole force consisted of two troops of the Greys within the town, and two companies of infantry at Dudley. Lord Hill, however, spoke very lightly to Lord Althorp of the danger. At the United Service Club little else was talked of. Strickland showed me a letter from some of his leading constituents at Saddleworth. They told him that people were tired of signing petitions and addresses. They wished to fight it out at once, and the sooner the better. The fight was believed so near at hand, that a manufacturer offered to supply the Birmingham Union with 10,000 muskets at 15s. a-piece. The Unions received an immense increase to their numbers during the week. Bob Smith told me that in his part of Bucks, the respectable classes came to the resolution of not acting as special constables. In Birmingham the magistrates represented to the General in command, that there was not a man in the town who would act.

Lord Lyttelton to Lady Lyttelton

19 May
. . . There is no House of Lords to-day. It has occurred to me that it may not be long ere the *to-day* may be omitted.

22 May
I have good hopes that their numbers on the Opposition side are much reduced, though the deuce a man but Lord Harewood has said upon his legs that he meant to stay away or let the Bill pass unopposed, and I cannot make out that anybody is gone save the Duke of Wellington and Lord Lyndhurst, and *R. Oxford* [Bishop Bagot]. . . .

Hobhouse's Recollections

Monday 21 May
The Lords went into committee on the Reform Bill. The Wellingtonians for the most part did not attend. Lord Grey got on with Schedule D as far as Wolverhampton. Thus the Tories, after describing the Bill as utterly destructive of Church and State and King and property, have given up their opposition to it rather than allow a *creation of Peers*, which could not, by any possibility, produce more mischief than the Bill, and which would

have saved their honour by making them yield only to force (*i.e.* numbers).

22 May

Charles Fox [MP] . . . said to the King, 'By recalling Lord Grey, you have saved the country from civil war.' 'Yes,' said the King, 'for the present'. . . .

23 May

Went to the Levee. The returned Ministers there. The King did not seem very well pleased with his Court, and did not smile upon our leaders. . . .

30 May

I went to the House of Commons, and looked in at the Lords, where the remaining clauses of the Bill were passed with very little opposition, and without any discussion.

Edward Ellice told me that on Monday last the King wrote an angry letter to Lord Grey, complaining of the Irish Reform Bill being hurried on, and of the English Bill passing the Lords without amendments. To this letter Lord Grey, with the unanimous consent of the Cabinet, wrote a very decided answer. The poor King then wrote to say that his first letter had originated in mistake.

There is no doubt, nor concealment now, as to the real inclination, and, indeed, intentions of H.M. to turn out the Government if he can. He is angry at being hissed. . . .

Charles Greville's Journal, *31 May*

Since I came back from Newmarket there has not been much to write about. A calm has succeeded the storm. Last night Schedules A and B were galloped through the Committee, and they finished the business. On Thursday next the Bill will probably be read a third time. In the House of Lords some dozen Tories and Waverers have continued to keep up a little skirmish, and a good deal of violent language has been bandied about, in which the Whigs, being the winners, have shown the best temper. In society the excitement has ceased, but the bitterness remains. The Tories are, however, so utterly defeated, and the victory of their opponents is so complete, that the latter can afford to be moderate and decorous in their tone and manner; and the former are exceedingly sulky, cockering up each other with much self-gratulation and praise, but aware that in the opinion of the mass of mankind they are covered with odium, ridicule, and disgrace. Peel and the Duke are ostensibly great friends, and the ridiculous farce is still kept up of each admiring what he would not do himself, but what the other did.

The Times, *22 May*

DEATH EXTRAORDINARY

Died, at his lodgings at St. James's on Friday, May the 18th, 1832, at a very advanced age, but still in possession of his *faculties*, the Right Hon., Right Rev., and Right Worshipful TORY POWER, A-Squire! Born so long ago as the reign of Charles I, he was given over at the close of that of James II, but rallied under the latter reigns of the House of Hanover, and was kept alive by artificial means until the 3rd. of William IV; when, detected in the act of some disreputable practices, he expired by his own hand. He has left, we lament to say, all those with whom he had dealings, especially those of whom he had been guardian, terribly involved. Selfish and arbitrary in his nature, insatiable in his extravagant propensities, the millions he squandered at the expense of other people seem altogether incredible.

It is prudently determined, we hear, to convey away his remains in the night-time, attended only by some bishops who loved him to the last, (but who decline, nevertheless, contributing to defray the charge of his interment), in order to avoid those marks of public execration which might too probably manifest themselves on so solemn an occasion. The place of deposit is not yet ascertained, but as every parish in Great Britain objects to receive the unhallowed corpse, the spot selected must be extra-parochial, probably the '*cloaca maxima*'. Strange to say, though bankrupt in fortune as well as character, he has left a will carelessly written on the back of some old Acts of Parliament. (Mr. Pitt's Bank-restrictions, and Lord Castlereagh's Six Acts), wherein he devised to Bishop Phillpotts and Lord Lyndhurst, (in trust!) for the joint benefit of the Crown and the Church, all and singular – the produce of the Sinking Fund!!!

The Duke of Wellington to the Earl of Scarbrough,[3] London, 4 June

MY DEAR LORD,

I have received your Lordship's letter of the 3rd. It is not my intention to go to the House of Lords for the third reading of the Reform Bill. I will take care that your Lordship's proxy is not given.

The King's servants recommended to his Majesty to create Peers in order to insure the vote of the House of Lords upon the Reform Bill. His Majesty's ministers resigned because the King refused to attend to their recommendation. His Majesty commissioned me to form another administration for him. I found that I could not form one that was capable of conducting the King's business in the House of Commons; and as I was unable to give his Majesty the assistance which he had a right to require from me, to enable him to resist the advice of his servants to destroy the independence of the House of Peers, I have considered it my duty as a Peer to discontinue my attendance upon the farther discussions of the Reform Bill. Other Peers, without concert with me, have taken the same course. The consequence is that this perilous measure, as all admit it to be, will pass this day.

The independence and the honour of the House of Lords are, I cannot conceal from myself, seriously injured. But as the King would have been reduced to the necessity of creating not less than sixty Peers, contrary to his inclination and wishes, for the purpose of obtaining a vote in favour of this bill, and as the independence of the House of Lords would by this course have been destroyed, while the bill would be voted and a gross indignity would be done to the Sovereign, I cannot but think that upon the whole I have taken the course most consistent with the public interests. I cannot but feel, however, that this course exposes me as usual to the misrepresentations of those who wish to misrepresent every action of my life.

I have troubled your Lordship with this letter, as I wish to justify the confidence which you have reposed in me. It appears that you concur in the view I have taken.

I have the honour to be, &c. &c.,
WELLINGTON

Letters from Thomas Creevey to Miss Ord

26 May
One more day will finish the concern in the Lords, and that this should have been accomplished as it has against a great majority of peers, and without making a single new one, must always remain one of the greatest miracles in English history. The conqueror of Waterloo had great luck on that day; so he had when Marmont made a false move at Salamanca; but at last comes his own false move, which has destroyed himself and his Tory high-flying association for ever, which has passed the Reform Bill without opposition. This has saved the country from confusion, and perhaps the monarch and monarchy from destruction.

2 June
. . . In the House of Lords yesterday Grey, according to his custom, came, and talked with me. It is really too much to see his happiness at its being all over and well over. He dwells upon the marvellous luck of Wellington's false move – upon the eternal difficulties he (Grey) would have been involved in had the Opposition not brought it to a crisis when they did. Their blunder he conceives to have been their belief that he would not resign upon this defeat on an apparent question of form. Thank God! they did not know their man.

5 June
. . . Thank God! I was in at the death of this Conservative plot, and the triumph of our Bill. This is the third great event of my life at which I have been present, and in each of which I have been to a certain extent mixed up – the battle of Waterloo, the battle of Queen Caroline, and the battle of

Earl Grey and the English nation for the Reform Bill. If the Conservative press is aware that the Master-in-chancery who carried this Bill from the Lords to the Commons was our Harry Martin, lineal descendant of Harry Martin the regicide, what a subject it will be for them tomorrow!

Le Marchant's diary

Hopes were entertained to the last that the King would give the royal assent to the Bill in person. The Administration had recommended it, but their recommendation was unfavourably received. The Chancellor then addressed a very urgent letter to the King through Taylor. The latter withheld it on the ground that the King's mind was made up and his feelings strongly excited both against the people and the press for what he conceived to be their unjust treatment of him. The Chancellor however persisted and the letter was delivered and answered very briefly in the negative. Lord Grey expressed himself as [not] very surprised.

Many of the Tories disapproved of the King's fastidiousness and observed that the more popularity he had, the more easily he could dispense with us. They forgot that a weak man once worked up into fury is not easily calmed. They ought to have consoled themselves by the fresh evidence they obtained of the King's aversion to us.

There were very few peers in the House during the ceremony of the Commission of assent. Ministers had been very anxious to avoid the appearance of triumph, so the time had been kept secret. The Duke of Sussex did not enter the body of the House but remained behind the curtain. When the assent was given, he said, loud enough to be heard at some distance, 'Thank God the deed is done at last. I care for nothing now – this is the happiest day of my life.' An old Tory standing behind him, lifted up his hands in horror, and fervently ejaculated, 'O Christ!' The contrast of the 2 countenances was amusing enough.

Courtenay had hardly given the royal assent in the usual words of 'Le Roi le veut' when an anonymous note was handed up to him in these words, 'It surely would have been more appropriate if you had said, "Le canaille le veut".'

Hobhouse's Recollections

31 May
I went to the House of Commons, and sat up till near two in the morning. H.M. will not, they say, go to the House to give the Royal Assent to the Reform Bill. Add to these symptoms I hear, from good authority, Lord Grey himself remarked a change in the King's manner, even to him, before the resignation; and that manner has not altered since the return of Lord Grey to power. Sir James Graham confirmed this, and like the rest is prepared for quitting office. However, the Reform Bill made steady progress in the Lords.

The Tories . . . are prepared for any extremity. They say the Monarchy is at an end. . . .

4 June
Debate on third reading of Reform Bill in the Lords. A little past ten a rumour reached us that the Lords were dividing. I ran away and got before the throne to the rail. Their Lordships were telling, and there was much confusion. Only two Bishops, Grey and Maltby, with us, two against us. Lord Brougham then read the numbers: 106 to 22, and after going shortly over the amendments, said, '*that this Bill do pass,*' and pass it did. . . .

6 June
. . . The King does *not* give the Royal Assent in person to the Great Bill; a very foolish spite, which takes away the grace from what he wishes to be thought or did wish to be thought his own gift. . . .

I went down to the House early to hear the Royal Assent given to the Reform Bill, but was too late. It was just over. A little before four o'clock, the Speaker, attended by Lord John Russell and some thirty or forty Members, went to the Lords. The Commissioners were Lords Grey, Lansdowne, Holland, Wellesley, Durham, and the Lord Chancellor. Only our great Bill received the Royal Assent. The whole proceeding lasted but a short time, and was slurred over as quickly as possible. Not a single Peer was to be seen on the Opposition benches, and not more than nine or ten on the Ministerial side.

A very poor picture was painted, misrepresenting this scene, as I can assert; for I am placed there next to Sir Francis Burdett, whereas I was not in the House.

There were a few people collected about the doors of Parliament; but there was very little excitement. The Ministers were, however, cheered as they left the House.

Thus ends this great national exploit. The deed is done. It is difficult to believe that it is done. I was obliged to leave the House of Commons, being ill; but I see that, when the Boundaries Bill was discussed, Croker took occasion, as might be expected, to allude to Paris running in blood, just as our Reform Bill was receiving the Royal sanction. . . .

Sir Herbert Taylor[4] to Henry Brougham, Windsor Castle, 5 June

My Dear Lord,
I regret that I was not favoured with your Lordship's letter in sufficient time to reply to it by this evening's post, but I hope you will receive this before you attend the King's levee, as I am anxious that you should not speak to him upon a subject which has more than once been brought under his consideration by Lord Grey or by his desire, and upon which I am convinced that his decision had been formed and cannot be shaken.

I have more than once had occasion to hear the King express his sentiments with respect to his going to Parliament to give the royal assent to the Reform Bill, and no later than this morning, in consequence of a question put by one of his Majesty's household, in a letter which I submitted.

His Majesty observed that, in ordinary times, he should have doubted the propriety and necessity of a step for which the precedents are few, if any, but that nothing on earth should induce him to take it in deference to what is called the sense of the people, or in deference to the dictates of the press, its ruler, after the treatment he has experienced from both; that he had endeavoured to discharge of his duty to the best of his judgment, and according to the dictates of his conscience; that he had been misrepresented, calumniated, and insulted; that the insults had not been confined to him – they had been heaped upon his Queen, on all belonging to him; and that the law had been declared not to be strong enough to protect him and them against such insults. Was he to cringe and bow? Was he to kiss the rod held out *in terrorem* by the mob?

He had never attached any value to that popularity which results from the effervescence of the moment – that which is not felt to be due to, and to arise from, a sense of the correct and honourable discharge of duty. But if it had been in his nature and disposition to be misled by applause and acclamations given to his supposed *unqualified* sanction of popular measures, what has recently passed would have undeceived him, and would have discovered to him how valueless is popular favour; how little deserving of the solicitude of those who are responsible to God and to their conscience for their acts. He is told that his giving the royal assent in person to the Reform Bill would be agreeable to the people – to those who, within the last fortnight, had so grossly insulted him; and that, by this step, he would regain the popularity which he is assured he had enjoyed – that he would set himself right again. But he observed, upon this, that he would greatly prefer their continued abuse, to the conviction that he had merited it by degrading himself in courting applause which he has learnt to despise.

I believe that I have correctly stated to your Lordship the King's sentiments expressed to me at various periods, certainly during periods of excitement, and occasionally uttered under irritation of feeling, but nevertheless unchanged; and I freely own that I believe them to have taken such firm possession of his mind, that I should not like to be the man to propose to him to gratify the popular feeling by going to Parliament at this juncture.

Under such circumstances I am certain that you will think that I have correctly availed myself of the discretion which your letter allows me to use in not submitting it to the King. – I have the honour to be, with great regard, my dear Lord, your Lordship's most obedient and faithful servant,

H. Taylor.

T.B. Macaulay to Hannah and Margaret Macaulay, 8 June

. . . The royal assent was given yesterday afternoon to the English Reform-Bill. It was given by Commissioners. The King unfortunately for himself has been induced by that wretched Court faction which surrounds him to give this proof of his impotent enmity to his ministers and his people. If the matter were merely one of party, I should rejoice at the course which he has taken. It has had this effect – that Lord Grey and the Whigs have all the honor of the reform-bill and the King none of it. If we are to have a quarrel with the Court we shall be far stronger and the Court far weaker than if William the Fourth had on this occasion acted in such a way as to make himself popular throughout the country. I fear – I fear – that he has entered on the path of Charles and Louis. He makes great concessions: but he makes them reluctantly and ungraciously. The people receive them without gratitude or affection. What madness! – to give more to his subjects than any King ever gave, and yet to give in such a manner as to get no thanks!. . .

The Times, *8 June*

TO THE EDITOR OF THE TIMES
Sir, – Now that the all-absorbing measure has reached its consummation, I suggest the exertion of your powerful influence to set immediately on foot a penny subscription, for the purpose of erecting a triumphal arch at the western entrance to the metropolis, and answering to the beautiful screen of Hyde-park, to commemorate the event itself, and still further dignify those illustrious men who so courageously fought for and have at length so happily achieved, the people's second bill of British rights.

A statue of William the Reformer surmounting the elevation, supported by the figures of Lords Grey, Brougham, Althorp, and Russell, would be a noble monument of a great and generous peoples' gratitude, to hand down to posterity – to endless time. I am, Sir, your obedient humble servant,
June 5.   J.A.

Thomas Creevey to Miss Ord, 18 [June]

How do you think the Duke of Wellington has been treated on this anniversary of the battle of Waterloo? He went to call on Wetherell at Lincoln's Inn on horseback, and, being recognised, so large a mob assembled there and shewed such very bad temper towards him, that he was obliged to send for the police to protect him home, and he did accordingly return in the centre of a very large body of police and a mob of about 2000 people, hooting him all the way.

Notes

1. Henry Richard Vassall Fox, 3rd Baron Holland (1773–1840), the nephew of C.J. Fox and a Whig politician, held the post of Chancellor of the Duchy of Lancaster in Grey's Cabinet. His political diary was published in 1977.
2. In May 1832, Somerville was stationed with the Scots Greys at Birmingham.
3. Richard Lumley-Saunderson, 6th Earl of Scarbrough (1757–1832) was a strong Tory opponent of the Reform Bill. He died on 17 June 1832.
4. Sir Herbert Taylor (1775–1839) was secretary to King William IV. He played an important role in the Reform Bill crisis as intermediary between Grey and the king.

CHAPTER EIGHT

The Aftermath

What difference, then, did the Reform Act make? When the dust had settled, the political landscape looked much as it had done before. The fears of the Bill's opponents were no more borne out than were the hopes of its Radical supporters in the country. The total size of the electorate had increased by something like 80 per cent, but still only about one in seven adult males in the whole United Kingdom was enfranchised – a fact which was used to justify the continued practice of open and public voting on the grounds that those who exercised the vote should be seen to do so in the interest of the whole of their fellow citizens. Still, if power had shifted away from the aristocracy it had done so only in part, and in partnership with the prosperous middle classes whose allegiance to the system the Reform Bill had secured. They were 'brought into the pale of the constitution' as Gladstone was later to remark of the enfranchisement of the urban working classes in the second half the nineteenth century. These were not wild revolutionaries, but, as Peel's 'Tamworth Manifesto' was to point out in 1834, they were concerned above all with the maintenance of order and social stability rather than with the transference of power to the still uneducated masses. Historians of the post-Reform Act political system have pointed out that in the countryside the voters still deferred to the political wishes of their landlords and social superiors, while the greater freedom of the urban voter was moderated by the continued use of influence and corruption. The experience of candidates like Hobhouse at Westminster showed that electoral practices were little changed and Charles Dickens, reporting the Northamptonshire election of 1835 for the *Morning Chronicle*, found plenty of material on which to found his fictional account of the politics of 'Eatanswill'. Not until the second instalment of Reform in 1867 was something approaching democracy established in the larger towns, and in 1884 in the country districts, and not until the secret ballot in 1872 and the regulation of electoral expenditure in 1883 did the electoral system become something like a modern democratic one.

Yet the crisis of 1830–2 was not lived through in vain. The fact that these later acts were passed with far less threat, or fear, of mass revolution itself testifies to the importance of 1832; Grey and his Cabinet had shown that reform could be achieved through existing institutions and that timely reform even averted revolution. Their courage and persistence enabled nineteenth-century Britain to move peaceably towards the new order, and to provide a model of parliamentary government and representative democracy for other nations to imitate in the twentieth century. What some called 'England's Revolution' was no less real for being gradual, peaceable, and, in the long run, more durable than many carried out by bloodshed.

Lord Ellenborough's diary, 13 June

. . . Yesterday I met my Cheltenham Club. There may have been 60 present, perhaps more. I held moderate language, recommended oblivion & good humour, said even those who voted for the Bill might join us, for we assailed no man's rights, we only meant to defend our own. The 3d Reading of the Bill must draw a line between Reformers & those who desired revolution, or we were lost. The circumstances of the Party are not such as to inspire hilarity, but our meeting was as good as could have been expected. It was not like that at Gloucester.

The feeling of the mob is decidedly worse than it was before the Bill was passed. I was insulted on Friday (the 8th) as I walked in Cheltenham, that is, by cries of 'Reform'–'Burke him'–'Down with the Tories.' There was no attempt at violence, & I did just as I should if nothing had been said. There was a mob of 4 or 500 people before the door of the hotel when I came away from the Club. Some wished me to have my carriage to the back door but I would not. There were 10 policemen who made a lane, & the carriage came up to the door easily. There were some squibs thrown at the carriage, & of course much hooting, but my friends, of whom 20 or 30 remained to see me off, gave a grand cheer & the mob were quiet. I am sure I did good both by showing my friends and my enemies that I feared nothing.

I hope to get up a troop of yeomanry at Cheltenham, but this requires delicate managment, or we shall have *two* troops on the other side, & some fighting. Yeomanry however we must have, or we shall be beaten.

Charles Greville's Journal, *18 June*

Breakfasted on Thursday with Rogers, and yesterday at the Athenaeum with Henry Taylor, and met Mr. Charles Austin, a lawyer, clever man, and Radical. The Bills are jogging on, and there is a comparative calm. The Whigs swear that the Reformed Parliament will be the most aristocratic we have ever seen, and Ellice told me that they cannot hear of a single improper person likely to be elected for any of the new places. [Their choice did not correspond with this statement of their disposition.] The metropolitan districts want rank and talent. The Government and their people have now found out what a fool the King is, and it is very amusing to hear them on the subject. Formerly, when they thought they had him fast, he was very honest and rather wise; now they find him rather shuffling and exceedingly silly. When Normanby went to take leave of him on going to Jamaica, he pronounced a harangue in favour of the slave trade, of which he has always been a great admirer, and expressed sentiments for which his subjects would tear him to pieces if they heard them. It is one of the great evils of the recent convulsion that the King's imbecility has been exposed to the world, and in his person the regal authority has fallen into contempt; his own personal unpopularity is not of much consequence as long as it does not degrade his office; that of George IV never did, so little so that he could always as King cancel the bad impressions which he made in his individual capacity, and he frequently did so. . . .

Robert Lowery[1] on the people's expectations

The excitement on the Reform Bill now agitated all classes of the community, although at first the multitude were more attracted by the contests of the upper classes and by party feeling than an understanding of the principles involved in the Bill; yet it developed thought among the more reflecting, and begat discussion on the principles of government and of national prosperity. It produced thinkers indeed in every class, and more especially the working classes. . . . No part of the country exceeded in fervour the district around Newcastle-upon-Tyne for the Reform Bill. Nor did any association surpass that of the 'Northern Political Union' in talent and influence. Its principal leaders combined philosophic astuteness, literary ability, oratorical powers, and social standing rarely equalled by the leaders of the public in any other district. And with their varied powers they bound the people to them with confidence and admiration. The chief of these was Charles Attwood, brother of Thos. Attwood, of Birmingham, and who possessed a mind of more deep research and wider expansion than his brother. He was engaged as a capitalist in extensive works in the neighbourhood, and had, as a man of science, discovered improvements in the manufacture of glass and soap which he had patented. Thomas Doubleday, a partner in an extensive manufactory, a gentleman of acknowledged literary ability, the author of the 'Philosophy of Populations' also of some essays and tragedies of acknowledged eminence; John Fife, who was afterwards knighted, was one of the most eminent surgeons of the north of England; and Charles Larkin, a surgeon who had been educated for the Catholic priesthood, was an eminent classical scholar, and one of the most commanding orators I have ever heard. Their varied styles of address produced an effective oneness. Attwood would open a meeting with a wide historical survey of the operation of any evil complained of, tracing it in its various forms at different times to our own day, and showing the necessity of its removal. Doubleday would trace the principles sought to be established back to Anglo-Saxon law and usage, and enforce them by the authority of the best writers on political philosophy – and Fife would dissect and lay bare the fallacies of those who opposed the Bill; while Larkin, with his command-ing form and voice, would utter forth, in swelling tones and powerful sentences, a torrent of indignation against those who opposed the measure, which would rouse the passions of the multitude vehemently. Frequently, on particular occasions, a hundred thousand people would come to these meetings, which were held on Newcastle Town Moor, the surrounding villagers marching in rank, with military step, to bands of music. It is well known that the language was often violent, and the opposition was threatened with physical resistance if they should proceed to enforce any laws to stop the unions in agitating for their demands.

The Bill was carried, but popular expectations had been formed not easily realised. The working men thought that the enfranchised middle classes did not do what they might to attempt to realise them, but that they looked more to their own class interests than to those of the

unenfranchised who had helped them to attain the Bill. . . . This produced feelings of disappointment and vexation among the working classes
towards the middle classes, and a current of popular distrust and ill-feeling
set in strongly against them and the Whigs, whose strength they were
thought to compose. . . . The declaration of 'Finality' soon convinced the
masses that, as far as the franchise was concerned, they had got 'nothing
but the Bill', and finding themselves deceived, the people turned to other
modes of improving their condition. . . .

The Times *12 June*

Our friends, the friends of reform and *good government*, have already
received a hint or two from the independent press, that if they wish the
Reform Bill to be of any use to the country, they must exert themselves to
put it into immediate and effective action. It is clear, we presume, to every
man, that a law for the creation of a free constituency must derive all its
value from the energy and wisdom wherewith the new constituents may be
disposed to employ their franchise. No law, however admirable, can
execute itself. No law can operate but through human agents. The best
imaginable statutes for securing the liberty of the subject may be
rendered unavailing by corrupt judges, or stupid and subservient juries;
and the most perfect theoretical precautions that can be devised against
an overbearing prerogative of the crown, or against its acquisition of
undue influence instead of prerogative, may be, and have been, entirely
frustrated by the supine, the sordid, the animal indifference of those
who ought to have guarded conscientiously the public interest from all
encroachments, under whatever form, on the part of the executive
power.

  Our countrymen may be assured, that if they content themselves with
celebrating the triumph of the Reform Bill as a bare historical fact, and
forget it as the introduction to a wide field of urgent and bounden duty,
they will have gained nothing by the bill, or by all the incalculable toil and
exertion which it has cost them, but the shame of discovering, after two or
three years, that the Conservatives have stepped in to ravish from them the
fruit of their labour. If reform and good-government candidates now hang
back, or are not supported by those new constituents who owe their
existence to the public virtue of the preceding electors spurring on the
representatives of the United Kingdom, – if there be no gratitude in the
young possessors of the franchise, to their brethren who eagerly shared
the Constitution with them, and no consistency in the voters under the
old system to prosecute their patriotic work, – if the reform of our
institutions, though framed by liberal statesmen, be left for Tories to
finish, to act upon and pervert, – why then we do allege, that such reform
is but a roll of parchment, ink, and bees' wax, – that the freedom so
obtained is a practical mockery, – that the blind and foolish confidence
derived from such unsubstantial forms, is infinitely more perilous than
our former state of discontent with the corrupt concord which reigned

between the principle and action of the Government, and that the lethargy into which the nation will now have sunk, is a far more fatal symptom than the acute and irritating consciousness which before afflicted it.

Well, then, what is to be done? This. As we know there exists an House of Lords, possessed by a spirit of unrelenting and incurable Toryism, – as we know that, apart from the Reform Bill, which was forced upon many repugnant individuals among its members, the present House of Commons is but slightly attached to Lord Grey's Administration, and may any day in the week be induced to trip it up, on some question unconnected with reform, – under such circumstances Great Britain ought to exhibit, by unambiguous testimony, a determination not to endure for one moment the transfer of power from a Liberal to a Tory Cabinet, before the ensuing Parliament shall have assembled. Whatever may be the case by and by, and however impossible, after a few years more, for any anti-national Government to rule this empire, on principles adverse to those predominating throughout the nation at this time, during the interval which elapses between the birth of the reform law, and its ability to walk alone, that precious offspring of English spirit and intelligence must not be confided to nurses who would have destroyed it, even in the first hour of its conception. First, then, such a spirit must be manifested by the country, as will render the early formation of a Tory Government politically impossible; second, such an organization of the whole constituency throughout the united kingdom ought to be completed, without losing another week, as may secure the return of a large independent and upright majority in the reformed House of Commons, thus rendering the creation of a subsequent Tory Cabinet, if not wholly impracticable, incapable at least of any serious mischief to the state.

We repeat our solicitations, and with deepest earnestness, to our brethren, the electors of Great Britain and Ireland, entreating them to organize, and not to rest until the work be accomplished, election committees in every quarter, for the effectual return to the approaching Parliament of candidates in *the interest of the people*. . . . Let men be sought for . . . who will vote through fire and water for a redress of all practical grievances – men who will take up, not for play, but use, the corn laws, game laws, tithes, perversions of the poor laws, abolition of sinecures, abolition of corrupt pensions, overthrow of monopolies, banking and commercial, abuses of the civil list, defects in the administration of justice, the law of libel, the military law. . . . To these, with sundry other important topics, the attention of candidates ought to be invited and on these their sentiments ascertained. . . .

Rouse, then – rouse ye, countrymen. The question is – Will you have the name only, or the *thing*? Will you have Reform a living principle, pervading – moving – cheering – invigorating the nation? or, shall it be a dead letter, to our mortification, disgrace, and ruin?

Hobhouse's Recollections

20 June
The King was struck on the head with a stone, on Ascot race-ground, by a one-legged ex-pensioner of Greenwich. Both Houses voted addresses to him, and Sir Robert Peel could not resist the temptation to connect the outrage with some intemperate language of the press and speeches in Parliament.

26 June
There was a Review in Hyde Park, which was attended by the King and Queen. The Duke of Wellington was at the head of his regiment. He was cheered by the 'mob of gentlemen,' but coldly received by the crowd. The Queen much hissed.

I afterwards went in full dress to a party at the Duke of Wellington's to meet their Majesties. A hundred or so of the Guards were drawn up in the courtyard, and the whole scene had a very military appearance; it was said that a thousand guests were present. The King made a long speech to the Guards when he gave them their new colours, and said Caesar was the first Grenadier.

This is my first, and probably will be my last, appearance at the Duke's. His pistol-proof blinds are no proof of his wisdom, nor his broken, unmended windows.

27 June
I went to the annual Westminster dinner. Sir Francis Burdett announced this to be the last: Reform having been gained, our occupation was over. . . .

11 July
Went to the great Reform Festival at the Guildhall. Saw and heard the freedom of the city presented to Lord Grey and Lord Althorp. . . . All made Conservative speeches, especially Brougham, who parodied 'the Bill, the whole Bill, etc' into 'the Law, the whole Law, and nothing but the Law'. . . .

16 August
Parliament was prorogued; and Lord Althorp, Lord John Russell, and myself were the only occupants of the Treasury bench who attended the Speaker and some eighty Members to the House of Lords.

There were not many Peers present; and only a few ladies – none of any distinction either for rank or beauty. Lord Grey bore the sword of State, and was the most appropriate personage in the ceremony. . . . The King's speech was, as usual, a poor performance. Reform was mentioned, but without any particular notice. . . .

I saw the King return to the Palace. It was like a funeral procession: scarcely a hat taken off, and positively no cheering. I never saw anything of the kind like it before. What a difference between his prorogation in

April 1831 and this ceremony! I was very sorry and augured no good from this bad reception of royalty.

T.B. Macaulay to Hannah and Margaret Macaulay, 12 July

. . . Yesterday I dined at Guildhall with the Corporation of London. The Common Council voted 6000 £ for the entertainment to the reformers in the two Houses of Parliament. Eight hundred people sate down to the dinner. The Hall, which you must remember, as I have shewn it to you over and over again, was hung with scarlet cloth and most superbly illuminated. I never saw an artificial light at once so brilliant and so soft. It was really like the sun. The lamps ran along the Gothic tracery of the windows and the arches so that the lines of light exactly coincided with the great lines of the architecture. Besides your old friends Gog and Magog a considerable number of figures in armour were ranged round the walls. Banners hung from the roof; – a gorgeous trophy was piled over the Chair of the Lord Mayor. The galleries were occupied by musicians, and there was a splendid display of plate. But the dinner – you will say – what care we for the decorations of the hall? What had you for dinner? The tables, young ladies, were covered with cold things. Every thing was cold except one hundred and sixty tureens of turtle soup, and eighty haunches of venison. Lushington who sate next me dined off cold fowl and ham. But Littleton and I, like Edgar Mortimer and his friend Jackson, agreed cold fowl would be no treat to us, and ate two large dishes of turtle soup apiece. After dinner we had the usual toasts, immense hallooing, stamping, clapping of hands, and thumping of tables. The speeches you will see in the newspapers. I heard scarce [one] word of them owing to the incessant din which was kept up in the hall. The sight was magnificent, and I am glad to have been present. . . .

Hobhouse's Recollections, *18 November*

Three independent electors of Westminster, whose names were unknown to me, called, and asked me to pledge myself to ballot, triennial Parliaments, and abolition of taxes on houses and windows and assessed taxes. I did not hesitate a moment in refusing to give any pledge whatever. I said they were quite right, if they suspected me, to choose somebody else; that I was perfectly indifferent whether I was chosen or not; that if I had not acted in such a way as to beget confidence in fourteen years I never should be able so to do. I did not intend to divide the Reformers; I should soon see how the land lay, and would take measures accordingly; that I should part with the electors on good terms, and look back on our long connection with feelings of pride and satisfaction, without a single regret, and persuaded that the time would come when my view on the subject of pledges would be theirs. . . .

On Saturday, December 8, came on the nomination for the representation of Westminster, at the usual hustings before St. Paul's Church in Covent Garden.

A considerable crowd of friends accompanied Sir Francis and myself. Mr. Hughes, the American Minister, and a son of Casimir Perier were amongst them. We were at first well received, but hissing and hooting soon began; and placards were exhibited, containing caricatures, one of which represented the Secretary-at-War flogging Somerville!! and extracting thirty shillings from his pocket. One man immediately in front dangled a cat-o'-nine-tails at me. Our foreign friends had full opportunity of witnessing the humours of an English contested election.

Le Marchant's diary, Sunday [9 December]

I was present yesterday at the nomination of the candidates for Westminster. The shew of hands in favour of Evans was immense and his partizans were as obstreperous as any demagogue could desire. The sub-collector of Covent Garden market happening to be one of his committee, had filled the galleries to the exclusion of the liberals, and I must confess a more truculent looking set could not easily have been collected. There were, however, in the crowd below a considerable number of Westminster electors decidedly in favour of Hobhouse and Burdett. The fear of their interrupting Evans caused Burdett to be patiently heard. Evans came next. He looked anything but the representative of an English constituency – in short, anything but English. Those who could recollect the jolly goodhumoured convivial countenance of Mr. Fox, or the comely elegance of Burdett, could have drawn comparisons rather odious to their successor on the hustings. Tall and thin, with very sallow complexion, and jet black hair and whiskers, one might almost have mistaken him for an Italian assassin. His speech was dull and but ill adapted to his audience. The applause was moderate. When he had finished, Hobhouse endeavoured to obtain a hearing, but as he had predicted to me just before, the yells and shouts drowned his voice and not a syllable reached beyond the reporters who stood immediately beneath. Hobhouse was less annoyed than I had expected. Fourteen years ago I saw him in the same place, the idol of the same populace, who were then showering the same insults upon his opponent George Lamb. I must confess, however, that Hobhouse was a more generous adversary than Evans showed himself, and conducted himself far more like a gentleman.

In Southwark the Radicals were totally discomfited or rather they were too much divided to form any plan. Their soi disant representative Mr. Murray was faintly cheered and had few hands held up for him, the shew being declared in favour of William Brougham and Humfrey. He withdrew from the contest upon Allen demanding a poll. Allen is a Welshman of good family and an amiable man, but entirely without pretensions to be member for Southwark. He married Romilly's niece and he had the good luck to be Lady Gifford's uncle. One connection brought him political acquaintances and the other a suiclerkship in Chancery. . . .

In Finsbury, Marylebone and Lambeth, the Radicals had the best of it; the Unions sent forth all their members under experienced chiefs, and they were too well organized to be effectually opposed by the divided and scattered forces of the friends of order. No serious tumult happened, and old electioneerers said that there was nothing to indicate a more violent spirit than displayed itself in ordinary elections.

E.J. Littleton's diary, 28 January 1833

. . . Dined with Warrender. . . . Warrender, Sir J. Graham and I sat together till near 2 talking over the state of parties and the aspect of the House. No Government need wish a larger majority than this has of steady friends, but the number of Radical Reformers, men who go all lengths, either from republican opinions, or more generally from poverty or naturally blackguard disposition leading them to make any engagement to the lowest class of the constituency, is very great. It is estimated, including the O'Connellites, at 130. . . . Sir J. Graham told me a prophesy of old Grattan's one day to Tierney made immediately after the Union, and which, pronounced in his usual precise, measured manner, reminded me much of the mind and manner of the man – 'My country owes yours a large debt for centuries of misrule and tyranny. She is about to repay you. Pass a few years and she will pour into the bosom of your Legislature a hundred of the damnedest rascals that ever crossed the Channel.'

Lord Ellenborough's diary, 29 January 1833

This day the first Reformed Parliament met. Cobbett took his seat between Ld. Althorpe & Sir James Graham and declared he should continue to sit there. O'Connell, Hume, &c. sat behind our friends. Cobbett spoke twice. I remember him a dull monotonous speaker. There are different reports – some say his speech was a failure. Others say he will become formidable. He himself says he shall improve, & condense his matter more in four or five weeks. He will answer the Ministers constantly & annoy them very much. He made faces, putting his tongue into his cheek! & some of the Radicals on the other side returned his grimaces! The division was 241 to 31. In the minority 11 Irish, & 3 Englishmen the Ministers considered to be ministerialists. . . .

J.S. Buckingham's account of the opening of the first session of the first reformed Parliament

The intense interest manifested by all classes during the progress of Parliamentary Reform, justifies the belief that a corresponding degree of attention will be paid to its first official labours. The seed only has been sown – the harvest is yet to be reaped: but the husbandman who has been engaged in the labour of the field, though he may be content to wait the reasonable period during which the fertility of the earth, and the rain and the sun of heaven, may be progressively bringing his fruits to perfection, will yet be anxious to see how the early blades look as they shoot above the surface; – whether their first appearance betokens a healthy and vigorous growth, and whether his labours are, by the richness and abundance of the produce, likely to be crowned with ultimate success. . . .

. . . In truth, there must be a new House of Commons, as well as a new code of standing orders. The intelligence of the age demands both. The present building is the mere *adaptation* of what was originally a small chapel, to the use of a legislative assembly. It has not room to contain, comfortably, its actual members. . . . It has no respectable provision for the admission of strangers. It excludes ladies altogether from the pleasure of being witnesses of its proceedings, unless by secreting themselves in a miserably confined spot above the ceiling, called the ventilator. And its rules and orders are one continual tissue of practical falsehoods, as enjoining observances, which the parties who enact or repeat such orders, are themselves among the first to violate. The building is, moreover, seated in the lowest, dampest, most foggy, and most unhealthy part of London. It lies at such an extreme point of the town, that it is a long journey for those who come from the city or the west-end to get at it; and its late hours of business give a crowning finish to a long list of reasons why the present house should be abandoned, a new one erected in some higher and better part of the metropolis, – in the open space now vacant at Charing-cross, or elsewhere, – and its rules, orders, regulations, and hours, reformed altogether. . . .

Among the four hundred members assembled in the House on Tuesday about two o'clock, a large portion seemed to be strangers, and observations such as these were continually heard from the old members who entered – 'Bless me, what a number of new faces!' – 'Why, it will take half the session to become acquainted with all the strangers!' – 'How fresh and rosy the *new* country gentlemen look!' – 'You can tell the unfledged by their awkwardness!' and other similar remarks; and while cordial greetings and hearty shaking of the hand marked the welcome meeting of personal friends or political partizans, the cold and formal introductions that were also passing around, showed that there were many who wished to be more at home than they yet comfortably felt themselves in their new sphere of action.

Soon after two, the breeze that had kept all things in active motion, gradually subsided, and matters seemed to wear a calmer aspect. Most of the members began to seat themselves, and considerable amusement was excited by observing the difficulties under which many felt themselves as to the *first position* they should take up in the House. Mr. Cobbett, not labouring apparently under any such doubt, went straight up to the Treasury-bench, which, by courtesy and usage, is always reserved expressly for the ministers of the Crown, and seated himself immediately beside Lord Althorp, where he remained for a considerable time. His next change of position was to bring himself on the same bench next to his old and very dear friend Sir John Cam Hobhouse. In both of these cases the juxtaposition would have been regarded as at least remarkable, even if unpremeditated, but it became still more so when resulting from a voluntary choice. . . .

On Tuesday, the 5th of February, the Commons assembled for public business at 12 o'clock; and from that hour to 2, the members continued arriving, until the House was literally crammed, and neither sitting room nor standing room could be found for members, who accordingly withdrew, and walked about in the lobby and in the passages until the time for attending in the House of Lords to hear the King deliver his speech in person. The preparations for this were curious. The older and more experienced members, who knew what difficulty there would be in getting into the House of Lords, stationed themselves close to the door of entrance to that building a full hour before the period fixed for its being opened: they were followed by others, who literally lined the passage all the way from the one House to the other, two or three deep – leaving just an avenue for the passage of the Speaker, when he should arrive, to pass along their ranks. The more determined had left even their hats behind them and buttoned their coats in closely, and taken off their gloves, to be prepared for a severe struggle in the crush: and, as the event proved, they acted prudently. About half-past two, the Speaker appeared, and had the greatest difficulty to pass along the avenue described; when, the instant he had passed, a closing-in of the struggling crowd behind him nearly overpowered the Right Honourable Gentleman himself, though he was preceded and followed by officers especially appointed to attend his person: and the crush was so excessive, that the appearance was rather that of a general scuffle or fight than a mere attempt to force an entrance; while the entrance into the House of Lords was so entirely like that of a mob breaking down the barriers of a ring or a race-course, and carried all before them, that even the gravity of the King upon the throne was discomposed; and the panting of the exhausted and breathless Commoners who had thus struggled their way into the House, was the most striking contrast that could be imagined to the stillness and repose which pervaded all the privileged assembly of the Lords. . . .

The scene in the House of Lords on this occasion, to those few who could approach near enough to enjoy a full view of it, of which fortunate number we happened to be, was altogether very brilliant. His Majesty was seated on the throne, attended by the great officers of state. The peers were in their robes, the foreign ministers in their respective dresses of office, the judges in their scarlet gowns, the bishops in their lawn sleeves, and on both sides of the House, on the benches of the peers, extending from the throne to the bar, or barrier which kept the Commons distinct from the Lords, were ranged from 300 to 400 superbly dressed ladies, all plumed with ostrich feathers, many adorned with costly jewels, and from the elegance of their costume, the surpassing beauty of many of their persons, the intelligent expression of their eyes and lips, and the general air and carriage of graceful motion which characterised them, presenting a sight not often to be witnessed even in England, and certainly not to be seen, in any other country of the world with which we are acquainted, to the same extent and perfection as here. What the Turkish ambassador, who was among the strangers present, must have thought of such realization of the favourite *houris* of the faithful, as was here pourtrayed before him, it would be difficult to say; but we conceive his description of this scene of brilliant beauty, when he returns to Constantinople, will be deemed fabulous by many; and if believed at all, will excite in the harems of the seraglio, where it is sure to penetrate, an anxious wish on the part of the sultan's ladies to be admitted to this open display of their beauties now hidden from all admiring eyes, by being immured in the solitude of confinement: and to all it must at least prove this truth, that female loveliness is capable of being greatly heightened, even in its beauty, by intellectual cultivation; and that the dignity of man is never more conspicuous than when woman is made a participator with himself in all the high and refined pleasures which intellectual pursuits afford. . . .

Le Marchant's diary

An old politician being asked what he thought of the new Parliament, said, 'It is full 20 years older than any that has preceeded it. The members will vote less for party motives. They will, however, require to be convinced before they vote. They will also be very severe upon all abuses, and perhaps be more angry with a sinecure than a great financial error.' The House was in sad confusion upon the first night. The members sat where they chose. Cobbett placed himself on the Treasury bench next to Graham.

The King's Speech was most anxiously awaited. The new members thronged to hear it below the Bar, and the interior of the Lords was almost equally crowded with ladies and peers. At length the Speech came. It was [far] from giving general satisfaction. The strong denunciations of wrath against Ireland and the vague promises of relief alarmed the liberals. The first night's debate did not remove their apprehensions. Lord Ormelie's furious attack on O'Connell, though warmly cheered, was not approved of. O'Connell's speech, artful and persuasive in a very high degree, made a deep impression. It required a very skilful answer, and certainly did not receive it from Stanley. His invective upon O'Connell, though pointed and forcible, did more injury to himself than to his opponent. It was not accompanied by a proper confutation of O'Connell's charges, so it looked like invective alone, and the evening ended by O'Connell standing in a much higher position than in the last Parliament. The new members thought he had much right on his side.

Luckily for Ministers O'Connell was not satisfied with this moderate success. He must needs shew his strength, or perhaps shew the Repealers in Ireland that they had not sent so many representatives to the House in vain. One after another these Hibernian orators rose to repeat in lengthy and declamatory harangues their complaints of the wrongs of their country and their accusations against the Ministry. Their coarse manners, fierce deportment and baseless assertions, at length heartily wearied the House, and several members who on the first night would have supported O'Connell, subsequently became his most violent adversaries. It cannot be denied that many of the facts stated in his speech were far from being satisfactorily answered. Still his injudicious tactics produced the same effect as if they had been. Men came to believe him in the wrong partly because they perceived that to be the case with most of his partisans, and partly because the impression made by his speech gradually wore away. Peel and Shaw were the best speeches on the other side. The Tories had reason to be proud of them.

Viscount Morpeth[2] to Viscount Althorp, 26 December 1832

As I have just finished an extensive canvass of the largest constituent body in the empire, and in the progress of it have undergone several courses of interrogation, as well as heard much expression of opinion, it has struck me that it might not be altogether useless if I were to put down upon paper my general impression of the present state of public feeling, as it has come under my notice.

Of Toryism I saw and heard nothing, and in large manufacturing districts it is entirely powerless. Of Radicalism I found infinitely less than I had expected. I am aware that this is in part to be attributed to employment being now tolerably plentiful, and trade healthy, though not brilliant; distress would soon call into play a large floating mass of discontent. Still, I believe the great bulk of the population to be sound and reasonable. Several political unions attempted a demonstration against me, exclusively of my colleague Mr. Strickland, on the grounds of my birth and my not being supposed to carry some liberal opinions so far, but they only proved that they could do absolutely nothing; they embrace but an inconsiderable number of persons, and I think are viewed with jealousy by those who do not belong to them.

The general feeling is very keen in favour of a full measure of Church Reform, but I do not think there is any prevalent wish to destroy the Establishment. I feel sure that it is most essential to the welfare of the Church to take advantage of these dispositions by a large and decided measure of Conservative Reform. Church Rates are the great rock of offence, I should say, more than tithes; but then I speak of a manufacturing district community. The power of the Bishops is not viewed with favour; cheap bread, more corn, a fixed duty of very moderate amount – but these are battles which we manufacturers must fight for ourselves.

We shall win in time. Economy and reduction of taxation speak for themselves. Malt and soap are mentioned most often. I need not say how deep the feeling is respecting Slavery. I think the Radicals care about it least. It strikes me that the non-electors have begun to find that the Ballot would be fatal to their influence over electors, and are consequently cooled about it. The electors in the Cloth-hall, at Leeds, have observed that the suffrage at present descends low enough.

Charles Dickens[3] observes the Northamptonshire election, 1835

. . . You will see or hear by the Chronicle of yesterday, that we had a slight flare here yesterday morning, just stopping short of murder and a riot. Party feeling runs so high, and the contest is likely to be so sharp a one that I look forward to the probability of a scuffle before it is over. As the Tories are the principal party here, *I* am in no very good odour in the town, but I shall not spare them the more on that account in the descriptions of their behaviour I may forward to head quarters. Such a ruthless set of bloody-minded villains, I never set eyes on, in my life. In their carnival moments yesterday after the business of the day was over, they were perfect savages. If a foreigner were brought here on his first visit to an English town, to form his estimate of the national character, I am quite satisfied he would return forthwith to France, and never set foot in England again. The remark will apply in a greater or less degree to all Agricultural places during the pendency of an Election, but beastly as the electors usually are, these men are superlative blackguards. Would you believe that a large body of horsemen, mounted and armed, who galloped on a defenceless crowd yesterday, striking about them in all directions, and protecting a man who cocked a loaded pistol, were *led* by Clergymen, and Magistrates? Or that I saw one of these fellows with my own eyes, unbuckle one of his stirrup leathers, and cut about him in the crowd, with the iron part of it – communicating to the blows all the additional force that swinging it at the end of the leather could give him? Anything more sickening and disgusting, or anything that roused my indignation so much, I never beheld.

. . . The polling begins on Friday and then we shall have an incessant repetition of the sounds and sights of yesterday 'till the Election is over – bells ringing, candidates speaking, drums sounding, a band of *eight trombones* (would you believe it?) blowing – men fighting, swearing drinking, and squabbling – all riotously excited, and all disgracing themselves. . . . [16 December 1835]

. . . The noise and confusion here this morning – which is the first day of polling is so great that my head is actually splitting. There are about forty flags on either side, two tremendous bands, one hundred and fifty constables, and vehicles of every kind, sort, and description. The last mentioned nuisances are constantly driving about and in and out and up [and] down the town, conveying voters to the Poll; and the voters themselves are drinking and guzzling and howling and roaring in every house of Entertainment there is. Our house is so full, and the blue swine, or in other words the conservative electors are such beasts that we have retired into my bed room – a large apartment at the extreme end of a long gallery, with a couple of windows commanding an interesting view of the stable yard. . . . [18 December]

. . . No artifice has been left untried, no influence has been withheld, no chicanery neglected by the Tory party; and the glorious result is, that Mr Maunsell is placed at the head of the poll, by the most ignorant, drunken, and brutal electors in these Kingdoms, who have been treated and fed, and driven up to the poll the whole day, like herds of swine. [from his report in the *Morning Chronicle*, 19 December].

Mr Pickwick observes the 'Eatanswill' election

[Mr. Pickwick and his friends stationed themselves at the Town Arms, head-quarters of one of the candidates, the Hon. Samuel Slumkey.]

The stable-yard exhibited unequivocal symptoms of the glory and strength of the Eatanswill Blues. There was a regular army of blue flags, some with one handle, and some with two, exhibiting appropriate devices in golden characters four feet high, and stout in proportion. There was a grand band of trumpets, bassoons and drums, marshalled four abreast, and earning their money, if ever men did, especially the drum beaters, who were very muscular. There were bodies of constables with blue staves, twenty committee-men with blue scarfs, and a mob of voters with blue cockades. There were electors on horseback, and electors a-foot. There was an open carriage and four, for the honourable Samuel Slumkey; and there were four carriages and pair, for his friends and supporters; and the flags were rustling, and the band was playing, and the constables were swearing, and the twenty committee-men were squabbling, and the mob were shouting, and the horses were backing, and the post-boys perspiring; and every-body, and everything, then and there assembled, was for the special use, behoof, honour, and renown, of the honourable Samuel Slumkey, of Slumkey Hall, one of the candidates for the representation of the Borough of Eatanswill, in the Commons House of Parliament of the United Kingdom.

Loud and long were the cheers, and mighty was the rustling of one of the blue flags, with 'Liberty of the Press' inscribed thereon, when the sandy head of Mr. Pott was discerned in one of the windows, by the mob beneath; and tremendous was the enthusiasm when the honourable Samuel Slumkey himself, in top-boots, and a blue neckerchief, advanced and seized the hand of the said Pott, and melodramatically testified by gestures to the crowd, his ineffaceable obligations to the Eatanswill Gazette.

'Is everything ready?' said the honourable Samuel Slumkey to Mr. Perker.

'Everything, my dear sir,' was the little man's reply.

'Nothing has been omitted, I hope?' said the honourable Samuel Slumkey.

'Nothing has been left undone, my dear sir – nothing whatever. There are twenty washed men at the street door for you to shake hands with; and six children in arms that you're to pat on the head, and inquire the age of; be particular about the children, my dear sir, – it has always a great effect, that sort of thing.'

'I'll take care,' said the honourable Samuel Slumkey.

'And, perhaps, my dear sir –' said the cautious little man, 'perhaps if you *could* – I don't mean to say it's indispensable – but if you *could* manage to kiss one of 'em, it would produce a very great impression on the crowd.'

'Wouldn't it have as good an effect if the proposer or seconder did that?' said the honourable Samuel Slumkey.

'Why, I am afraid it wouldn't,' replied the agent; 'if it were done by yourself, my dear sir, I think it would make you very popular.'

'Very well,' said the honourable Samuel Slumkey, with a resigned air, 'then it must be done. That's all.'

'Arrange the procession,' cried the twenty committee-men.

Amidst the cheers of the assembled throng, the band, and the constables, and the committee-men, and the voters, and the horsemen, and the carriages, took their places – each of the two-horse vehicles being closely packed with as many gentlemen as could manage to stand upright in it; and that assigned to Mr. Perker, containing Mr. Pickwick, Mr. Tupman, Mr. Snodgrass, and about half a dozen of the committee beside.

There was a moment of awful suspense as the procession waited for the honourable Samuel Slumkey to step into his carriage. Suddenly the crowd set up a great cheering.

'He has come out,' said little Mr. Perker, greatly excited; the more so as their position did not enable them to see what was going forward.

Another cheer, much louder.

'He has shaken hands with the men,' cried the little agent.

Another cheer, far more vehement.

'He has patted the babies on the head,' said Mr. Parker, trembling with anxiety.

A roar of applause that rent the air.

'He has kissed one of 'em!' exclaimed the delighted little man.

A second roar.

'He has kissed another,' gasped the excited manager.

A third roar.

'He's kissing 'em all!' screamed the enthusiastic little gentleman. And hailed by the deafening shouts of the multitude, the procession moved on. . . .

During the whole time of the polling, the town was in a perpetual fever of excitement. Everything was conducted on the most liberal and delightful scale. Exciseable articles were remarkably cheap at all the public-houses; and spring vans paraded the streets for the accommodation of voters who were seized with any temporary dizziness in the head – an epidemic which prevailed among the electors, during the contest, to a most alarming extent, and under the influence of which they might frequently be seen lying on the pavements in a state of utter insensibility. A small body of electors remained unpolled on the very last day. They were calculating and reflecting persons, who had not yet been convinced by the arguments of either party, although they had had frequent conferences with each. One hour before the close of the poll, Mr. Perker solicited the honour of a private interview with these intelligent, these noble, these patriotic men. It was granted. His arguments were brief, but satisfactory. They went in a body to the poll; and when they returned, the honourable Samuel Slumkey, of Slumkey Hall, was returned also.

Notes

1. Robert Lowery (1809–63) was a leader of the Chartist movement.
2. George William Frederick Howard (1802–64), Viscount Morpeth (1825–48), 7th Earl of Carlisle 1848, was MP for Yorkshire 1828–32, and for the West Riding 1832–41 and 1848; he was later Viceroy of Ireland.
3. Dickens was reporting the election in December 1835 for the *Morning Chronicle*. He writes to Catherine Hogarth.

LIST OF SOURCES

Unpublished papers

Staffordshire Record Office, the Hatherton papers: the Diary of the 1st Lord Hatherton.

Printed works
(The place of publication is London unless otherwise stated.)

Aspinall, A. (ed.), *Three Early Nineteenth-Century Diaries*, 1952.
The Autobiography and Memoirs of Benjamin Robert Haydon 1786–1846, A.P.D. Penrose (ed.), 1927.
The Correspondence and Diaries of the Late Rt. Hon. John Wilson Croker, vol. II, L.J. Jennings (ed.), 1884.
Correspondence of Sarah Lady Lyttelton 1787–1870, the Hon. Mrs Hugh Wyndham (ed.), 1912.
The Creevey Papers, Sir Herbert Maxwell (ed.), 2 vols., 1903.
The Diary of Frances Lady Shelley 1818–1873, vol. II, R. Edgcumbe (ed.), 1913.
An Eton Boy, being the Letters of James Milnes Gaskell from Eton and Oxford, 1820–1830, C.M. Gaskell (ed.), 1939.
Grant, J., *Random Recollections of the House of Lords*, 2nd edn., 1836.
The Gentleman's Magazine, 1830.
Greville, C.C.F., *A Journal of the Reigns of King George IV and King William IV*, vol. II, Henry Reeve (ed.), 1874.
Hobhouse, J.C., 1st Baron Broughton, *Recollections of a Long Life*, vol. IV, Lady Dorchester (ed.), 1910.
The Holland House Diaries 1831–1840, A.D. Kriegel (ed.), 1977.
Howitt, W., *Eminent Living Political Reformers*, 1840.
The Journal of Mary Frampton, 1779–1846, H.G. Mundy (ed.), 1886.
The Journal of Mrs Arbuthnot 1820–1832, Francis Bamford & the Duke of Wellington (eds.), 1950.
Leconfield, Maud, Lady & Gore, J., *Three Howard Sisters*, 1955.
Le Marchant, Sir Denis, *Memoir of John Charles Viscount Althorp, Third Earl Spencer*, 1876.
The Letters of Charles Dickens, vol. I 1820–1839, M. House & G. Storey (eds.), Oxford, 1965.
Letters of Dorothea, Princess Lieven, During her Residence in London, 1812–1834, L.G. Robinson (ed.), 1902.

The Letters of T.B. Macaulay, vol. II, T. Pinney (ed.), Cambridge, 1974.

The Life and Times of Henry Brougham, written by himself, vol. III, 1871.

The Poor Man's Guardian, no. 22, 19 November 1831.

The Parliamentary Review and Family Magazine, 4 vols., J.S. Buckingham (ed.), 1833–4.

Robert Lowery, Radical and Chartist, B. Harrison & P. Hollis (eds.), 1979.

[Somerville, A.], *The Autobiography of a Working Man, by 'One who has whistled at the plough'*, 1848.

The Times, 1830–2.

Wellington, Duke of (ed.), *Despatches, Correspondence and Memoranda of Field Marshall Arthur, Duke of Wellington 1819–32*, vols. VI–VII, 1877–80.

Wellington, 7th Duke of (ed.), *Wellington and His Friends*, 1965.

Index